DATE DUE

Latin America in the Era of the Cuban Revolution

◆

THOMAS C. WRIGHT

PRAEGER

New York
Westport, Connecticut
London

Library of Congress Cataloging-in-Publication Data

Wright, Thomas C.
  Latin America in the era of the Cuban Revolution / Thomas C.
Wright.
    p.   cm.
  Includes bibliographical references (p.) and index.
  ISBN 0-275-93583-3
  ISBN 0-275-94099-3 (pbk.)
    1. Latin America—Politics and government—1948- 2. Cuba—
History—Revolution, 1959—Influence. 3. Radicalism—Latin
America—History—20th century. 4. Violence—Latin America—
History—20th century. 5. United States—Military policy.
I. Title.
F1414.2.W75 1991
980.03'3–dc20   91-9647

British Library Cataloguing in Publication Data is available.

Library of Congress Catalog Card Number: 91-9647
ISBN: 0-275-93583-3
ISBN: 0-275-94099-3 (pbk.)

First published in 1991

Praeger Publishers, One Madison Avenue, New York, NY 10010
An imprint of Greenwood Publishing Group, Inc.

Printed in the United States of America

The paper used in this book complies with the
Permanent Paper Standard issued by the National
Information Standards Organization (Z39.48–1984).

10 9 8 7 6 5 4 3 2

for Dina

Contents

Acknowledgments

This book owes much to many friends and colleagues. James Kohl, Robert J. Alexander, John Super, Thomas Walker, E. Bradford Burns, Joseph A. Fry, Catherine Zubel, and Daniel Barber read the manuscript and offered valuable suggestions. Dina Titus encouraged and supported the project in many ways. Marion Sumners's help was essential in the early stages, and Jamie Coughtry aided in collecting data. A grant from the Center for Advanced Research, College of Liberal Arts, University of Nevada, Las Vegas, provided time for completion of the writing. My sincere thanks go to all the above. Finally, I am indebted to the students who have taken my course "Revolution and Reaction in Contemporary Latin America" over the years, and who listened to and critiqued the ideas that emerge in the following pages.

Introduction

"January 1, 1959, when Fidel Castro triumphed, began a new era in Latin America." So wrote *New York Times* senior editor Herbert Matthews, a close observer of Fidel Castro's guerrilla war against dictator Fulgencio Batista, in 1961.[1] Echoing Matthews' words, dozens of academic and journalistic studies written in the 1960s proclaimed the Cuban Revolution a major watershed in Latin America's history.

The three decades following Castro's victory have marginalized Cuba from the Latin American mainstream. As a result, the Cuban Revolution today may appear to have been an exotic, aberrant growth on the Latin American body politic. In fact, quite the opposite is true. The Cuban Revolution owes its vast influence in Latin America to the fact that — most evidently in its early years — it embodied the aspirations and captured the imaginations of Latin America's masses as no other political movement had ever done.

Beginning with the Mexican Revolution of 1910, Latin America witnessed the rise of reformist and revolutionary forces dedicated to bettering the material and spiritual condition of the dark peoples, the poor, the illiterate, the exploited — of those who lived their lives on the margins of modern society. Mexico's revolutionary 1917 constitution not only set goals for Mexico but its commitment to political democracy, social justice, and national liberation from foreign economic dominance — in sum, to freedom and human dignity — also set the agenda for twentieth-century Latin American politics. Following the Mexican Revolution, mass movements such as Peru's American Popular Revolutionary Alliance (Alianza Popular Revolucionaria Americana, APRA) and Venezuela's Democratic Action (Acción Democrática, AD) struggled for the creation of new societies with a place for the downtrodden. Leaders such as Nicaragua's Augusto César Sandino and Colombia's Jorge Eliécer Gaitán fought with arms or with their political skills for the same goals. Bolivia experienced Latin America's second social revolution in 1952 when the masses assumed control of the land and the government nationalized the country's basic industry, tin mining.

Despite two revolutions and the unstinting efforts of reformist parties and leaders, Latin America on the whole moved only slowly and tentatively toward the goals of political and social democracy and national liberation. The power and resilience of Latin America's elites, U.S. opposition to change, and engrained attitudes of obedience and resignation among the masses combined repeatedly to thwart the forces of progress. With Castro's revolution in Cuba, however, the waters of revolution poured over the dam, submerging Latin America in political and social ferment that threatened the very foundations of the established order.

Compared with the Mexican and Bolivian Revolutions and the various reformist governments that had held power in Latin America up to 1959, the Cuban Revolution had far greater ramifications for Latin America. There were several reasons for the potency of Castro's revolution outside of Cuba. It provided an explicit blueprint for successful insurrection by reducing the overthrow of governments to a simple matter of faithfully following Che Guevara's handbook on guerrilla warfare. Cuba went far beyond the previous revolutions, carrying out Latin America's most thorough social transformation and becoming the hemisphere's first, and only, country to break completely from U.S. domination. The Cuban Revolution also had a dynamic, charismatic leader who symbolized the revolution and elicited popular sympathy and support throughout the hemisphere. Rejecting territorial limits to his revolution, Castro actively promoted insurrection against established governments and bourgeois power throughout Latin America. Finally, the Cuban Revolution owed much of its influence to timing; as a result of modern communications and Castro's publicity skills, even the marginal, illiterate masses learned about the revolution and its conquests for the common people.

The immense popularity of the early Cuban Revolution — especially in the years of the great transformation from 1959 through 1961 — is easy to understand. During these years Castro constantly made headlines with his social reforms and his measures to throw off what Latin Americans regarded as the yoke of Yankee imperialism. The Bay of Pigs invasion, the improbable victory of a Cuban David against a Yankee Goliath, cemented Castro's hold over the Latin American masses. After that high point, as Castro faced difficult choices, fulfillment of the revolution's promises became increasingly selective: Political democracy was indefinitely postponed, then discarded; individual liberties were subordinated to social justice for the collective; and after the first decade, growing dependence on the Soviet Union compromised the quest for Cuban sovereignty. Yet Cuban influence remained strong for many years, long after failures began to tarnish the revolution's image, because for many Latin Americans the hope and the example that the Cuban Revolution provided in its youth transcended the shortcomings of its later years.

Herbert Matthews attributed Fidel Castro's enormous influence in Latin America to "something new, exciting, dangerous, and infectious [that] has come into the Western Hemisphere with the Cuban Revolution."[2] Today, that something is gone. It is now time for an interpretation of the era of the Cuban Revolution, the period when the forces of change that first burst forth in the Mexican Revolution of 1910 mounted an all-out challenge to the status quo in Latin America — a time when the threat or hope of reform and revolution was never stronger. This era that began with Fidel's triumph in 1959 lasted through three decades until the convergence of several events and trends signalled its extinction in the early 1990s.

In arguing that the Cuban Revolution dictated the broad sweep of Latin American politics for some 30 years, I do not advance a single cause explanation of the political life of a huge and diverse area. Clearly, the mobilizations and the revolutionary movements that swept the hemisphere after 1958 had indigenous roots. They sprang from the poverty and social inequities that characterized Latin America and from the efforts of preexisting political forces advocating reform and revolution. Castro certainly did not create revolutionary ferment from thin air; but by its example, the Cuban Revolution served as a catalyst to the spread and the intensification of social and political conflict to unprecedented levels.

Nor did events in Latin America take place in a vacuum. This could hardly be the case in the age of the global village, with transistor radios penetrating the Andean highlands and television reaching the savannahs of Central America. Latin America felt the influence of the Sino-Soviet split, the Vietnam War, the African independence movements, the U.S. civil rights movement, OPEC pricing policies, ferment within the Roman Catholic church, raw material price fluctuations, the 1968 year of student protest, population growth and urbanization, the eclipse of communism in Eastern Europe, and, of course, the personalities and issues peculiar to each country. All of these internal and external developments and many more influenced the course of Latin American politics after 1958.

Yet the Cuban Revolution was paramount in setting the general terms of political debate in Latin America. The heightening of demands for change, the pan-Latin American scope of the ferment, and the transcendence of the issues — the very nature of economic and political systems was at stake — made the years after 1959 the period of greatest political upheaval in Latin American history. That which distinguishes the 1959–90 period is the paramount influence of the Cuban Revolution — sometimes explicit, often implicit, but never absent.

Rather than taking a country-by-country approach, this study attempts to synthesize the broad trends and phases of the Cuban Revolution's impact on Latin America. The two chapters on Cuba are not intended to provide an exhaustive analysis of the Cuban Revolution; they are selective, in that their purpose is to emphasize those features of Fidel's revolution that made Cuba so influential in Latin America. Three other chapters are country-specific: The military "revolution" in Peru, the Allende government in Chile, and the Sandinista Revolution in Nicaragua are examined in some detail because of their intrinsic interest and because of their importance to the whole of Latin America. The remaining chapters analyze phenomena that affected all or major parts of Latin America: the impact of *fidelismo,* U.S. responses to revolution, rural guerrilla warfare, urban guerrilla warfare, and the new-style institutional military regimes created to fight revolution. The epilogue assesses the gradual decline of Cuban influence from the late 1960s until its eclipse at the beginning of the twentieth century's final decade.

NOTES

1. Herbert L. Matthews, *The Cuban Story* (New York: George Braziller, 1961), 273-74.
2. Ibid., 185.

Latin America in the Era of the Cuban Revolution

1

Fidel Castro's Road to Power, 1952–59

Fidel Castro's successful insurrection against Cuban dictator Fulgencio Batista made Castro and his bearded followers heroes to millions of Latin Americans and inspired scores of attempts to replicate their feat. Especially during the nearly nine years between Fidel's triumph and Che Guevara's death in Bolivia, rural guerrilla warfare was widely embraced as a means of toppling governments throughout Latin America. Fidel's coming to power engendered a mystique about guerrilla warfare, and Che's writings provided both inspiration and practical advice that made rural guerrilla warfare a popular undertaking. Thus the method of insurrection to which Fidel Castro attributed his victory was, in itself, a major reason for the influence of Cuba in Latin American politics after 1958.

Castro's road to power, an unlikely odyssey filled with heroism, suffering, and improbable successes, was not the first time that a popular movement had overthrown an entrenched military dictatorship in Latin America. Such occurrences, in fact, were not uncommon in the region's political history. Yet Fidel's victory was different in that it ushered in the hemisphere's most radical revolution and became a model for emulation by would-be revolutionaries throughout Latin America. This chapter examines the background to the overthrow of Batista and the armed struggle against his dictatorship to illuminate both the subsequent revolution in Cuba and the impact of the Cuban model of insurrection upon the rest of Latin America.

BACKGROUND TO OVERTHROW: THE CONDITION OF CUBA

Most observers of Latin America were shocked that the most radical revolution in the western hemisphere should have taken place in Cuba.

By most of the standard indicators, Cuba was near the upper end of the scale in development and modernization. In per capita gross national product, Cuba in the 1950s ranked fourth in Latin America; its literacy rate was within the top quarter. Cuba ranked third in medical doctors and hospital beds per capita, and it had Latin America's lowest infant mortality rate. Union membership was among the strongest in Latin America — approximately half the labor force — and Cuba ranked second in the proportion of the working population covered by social security. In two indices of consumerism, television sets and radios per capita, Cuba ranked first and second, respectively. While not particularly dynamic, Cuba's economy in the 1950s was relatively strong and was continuing a long trend of diversification. Finally, Cuba's government had the strong and explicit backing of the U.S. government and business sector. By the conventional wisdom that backwardness and poverty breed revolution, then, many Latin American countries seemed more susceptible than Cuba to radical change.

The post-1958 boom in Cuban studies yielded volumes on the question, Why Cuba? Researchers probed Cuban history and reexamined the island's economy, society, and political system to bare the roots of Castro's revolution. The picture that took shape was not a rosy one, but neither did it appear to have presaged a successful guerrilla overthrow and a radical revolution. The elements that made Castro's revolution possible, not inevitable — the conditions that he was able to exploit in building the anti-Batista movement and, once in power, in conducting a sweeping revolution — can be set forth in four broad categories: strong and pervasive anti-U.S. sentiment; the deleterious effects of excessive dependence on sugar culture; fragmentation of Cuban society; and the disrepute in which Cuba's political system and institutions were held.

The endemic anti-Americanism that Fidel Castro was able to draw upon to build support for his anti-Batista crusade and later his revolution had its roots in the historic and continuing U.S. dominance of Cuba. Beginning early in the nineteenth century, while Cuba was still a colony of Spain, expansionists looked to the island as a potential new state. This prospect was especially attractive to southerners, who recognized the potential compatibility of another slave society. While internal U.S. politics worked to check the expansionists, U.S. businessmen invested heavily in Spanish Cuba in the closing decades of the nineteenth century. With a growing geopolitical interest in the Caribbean and substantial investments to protect, the United States watched closely when the second Cuban independence war broke out in 1895. When the sinking of the *Maine* in Havana harbor generated support for intervention, U.S.

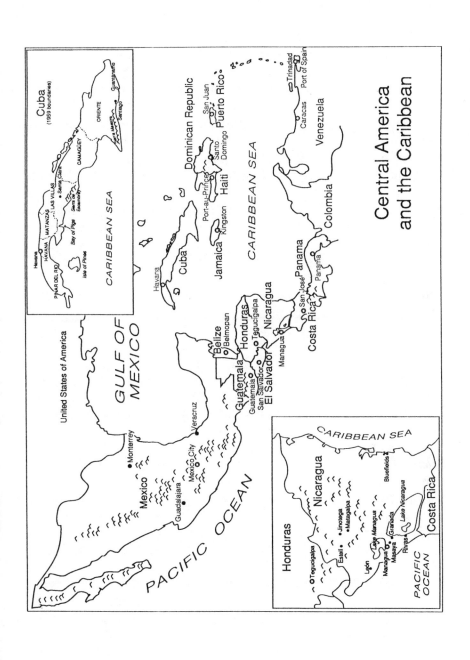

Central America
and the Caribbean

troops entered the fray in 1898 and quickly defeated the Spanish, ensuring the victory of the independence forces.

Cubans quickly learned the truth of what many had feared: Independence from Spain did not mean an independent Cuban nation. Although pledged to granting Cuba independence, the United States, which was entering a phase of expansionism in the Caribbean, could not resist conditioning the withdrawal of its troops on Cuba's adoption of a constitutional provision making the island a protectorate. The Platt Amendment denied Cuba the essence of nationhood — sovereignty — by granting the U.S. government "the right to intervene for the preservation of Cuban independence [and] the maintenance of a government adequate for the protection of life, property, and individual liberty."[1] These and other restrictions written into the 1901 Cuban constitution were a bitter pill for those patriots who had fought two wars for genuine independence. A result of American tutelage during the three-plus decades of the "Platt Amendment Republic," wrote Cuban intellectual Jorge Mañach, was "general civic indolence, a tepid indifference to national dangers."[2]

The United States exercised its right of military intervention by reoccupying the island between 1906 and 1909 and landing troops in 1912 and 1917. Equally debilitating to the development of an independent Cuba were the many instances of overt political intervention supported by the implicit or explicit threat of military action. General Enoch Crowder usurped most of the powers of President Alfredo Zayas (1921–25), choosing his cabinet and ordering fiscal reforms that left U.S. banks in a dominant position. Perhaps the most significant political intervention was that of 1933, when ambassador-at-large Sumner Welles refused diplomatic recognition to the reform-oriented government of Ramón Grau San Martín that was installed following the overthrow of long-term dictator Gerardo Machado. Facing U.S. opposition, the fledgling government was unable to consolidate its power and was quickly replaced by the more conservative and subservient military regime of Fulgencio Batista. Many Cubans look back to 1933 as a critical turning point — a lost opportunity to address Cuba's mounting economic, social, and political problems while moderate solutions were still possible.

U.S. control over Cuba changed complexion but not substance after 1934, when Franklin D. Roosevelt agreed to the abrogation of the Platt Amendment as part of his Good Neighbor Policy toward Latin America. The United States honored its renunciation of military intervention but, as before, U.S. economic and geopolitical interests dictated constant oversight and close political control over the island. By 1927 U.S. direct investment in Cuba had ballooned to over a billion dollars, the largest amount invested in any Latin American country, and U.S. capital dominated the major sectors of the economy, including sugar, transportation, banking, and utilities. U.S. direct investment declined subsequently through the 1940s, reaching the billion dollar level again in the late 1950s. As the U.S. presence shrank, Cubans gained the dominant position in sugar and banking, while the later influx of U.S. capital went into newer sectors such as mining, petroleum, manufacturing, and tourism.

Cuba's dependence on the U.S. market, on the other hand, remained strong. While the proportion of Cuba's sugar going to the United States fell from some 80 percent in the 1920s to less than 55 percent in the 1950s, Cuba still placed approximately two-thirds of all its exports in the traditional U.S. market. In the 1930s sugar imports were put on a quota basis, subject to annual congressional review and approval. This economic control with its accompanying leverage over Cuban politics kept Cuba in a dependent position long after the Platt Amendment disappeared. The pervasive U.S. economic presence combined with the highly visible political levers limiting Cuba's freedom of action continued to engender resentment of U.S. power over the island.

In addition to making Cuba economically subservient to the United States, the heavy reliance on sugar cultivation and export posed both economic and social problems for Cuba. As a primary commodity, sugar was and is subject to the vagaries of climate and the world market. Sugar constituted approximately 85 percent of Cuba's export earnings in the 1950s and over a third of its gross national product; thus, even minor price fluctuations had far-reaching effects on the sugar labor force and on the island's economic stability. Tariff agreements and quotas giving Cuban sugar preferential treatment in the U.S. market, moreover, were based on reciprocity. The favored status of U.S. manufactured goods in the Cuban market stunted industrialization, limiting the possibilities for development.

Reliance on sugar had important social consequences as well. As sugar planting expanded through the 1920s, sugar came to dominate the prime agricultural lands, pushing out peasant farmers and creating a huge rural proletariat, which in the 1950s numbered some 600,000. These landless rural workers outnumbered the poor peasant farmers by more than three to one and constituted nearly a third of the country's labor force. The majority of the rural proletariat worked the cycle imposed by cane cultivation and harvesting, finding regular employment only four or five months per year. Government road maintenance and public works jobs, scheduled during the dead seasons, ameliorated conditions for some but did not substantially alter the poverty and chronic underemployment that prevailed in rural Cuba. The sugar proletariat had demonstrated its potential for radical action during the 1933 uprising when workers seized sugar mills and established soviets in several parts of the island.

Along with the social cleavages typified by the contrast between wealthy sugar planters and their proletariat, two other pronounced divisions impaired the cohesiveness of Cuban society. To sustain the institution of slavery that it had preserved until 1886, Spanish Cuba imported large numbers of Africans through 1850. The result was a racially divided population that, despite steady Spanish immigration over the next century, was still officially 27 percent black or mulatto in the 1950s. The descendants of slaves suffered economic and social discrimination in various forms, including some formal segregation patterned after the U.S. South. Although the racial division was mitigated somewhat by easier social relations than those found in the United States, it occasionally broke into the open as it had in the 1912 "Race War of Oriente."

Another notable fissure in Cuban society was the widely perceived generation gap. Each "generation" of Cuban youth in the twentieth century tended to deprecate the failed efforts of the preceding generation to rectify Cuba's problems. Thus the generation of 1930 blamed that of 1895 for failing to win meaningful independence; Fidel's generation, that of 1953, blamed the 1930 group for the failure to consolidate reform. The wholesale dismissal of the efforts and values of preceding groups of national leaders left young Cubans with no models and traditions, predisposing them to radical and bold approaches to solving Cuba's national problems.

Rounding out the "condition of Cuba" was the widespread disenchantment with Cuba's politicians and its public institutions. From its inception, Cuban government had been too weak and too subject to foreign manipulation to command the respect of its citizens. Added to the anti-national, *vendepatria* (selling out of the homeland) reputation of leaders, parties, and government were the open, massive corruption and the partisan violence that pervaded even the progressive administrations such as the Auténtico Party governments of Ramón Grau San Martín (1944–48) and Carlos Prío Socarrás (1948–52). Nonetheless, many still entertained the hope that better government could be achieved through elections. Thus Fulgencio Batista's 1952 coup and the heightened corruption and violence that characterized his administration shattered most Cubans' remaining illusions and exacerbated their cynicism toward the political system.

U.S. domination of Cuba, subjugation to a vulnerable sugar economy, strong cleavages in the social fabric, and the absence of legitimacy that characterized Cuba's political system gave Fidel Castro and other Batista opponents ample material with which to build a mass following. The poor, the dark, the patriots, the disenchanted — among them, the majority of the Cuban population — were attracted by talk of change and improvements in their lives. Invoking nationalistic slogans and promising economic diversification, social justice, and full implementation of the progressive 1940 constitution, Castro and his counterparts found legions of willing followers and sympathizers. The generalized absence of allegiance to the government and its institutions further facilitated the overthrow of Batista and the instigation of radical change.

THE STRUGGLE AGAINST BATISTA: EARLY STAGES

Fulgencio Batista seized power on March 10, 1952, in a military coup. His action forestalled presidential and congressional elections scheduled for May of that year. Batista was a well-known figure in Cuban politics. As a sergeant, he had led the 1933 revolt that put the reformist government of Grau San Martín in power; four months later, responding to strong U.S. pressure, he engineered the overthrow of Grau. As leader of the military, Batista had exercised considerable influence over the governments of the 1930s and had served a presidential term from 1940 to 1944. Although his administration proved more progressive than most observers expected, Batista never escaped his identity as the U.S. instrument for thwarting reform in 1933–34. His lack of personal popularity was compounded by his method of taking power in 1952 — for despite heavy military influence in politics, Cuba had been governed under civilian institutions during most of its republican life. The proximity of the scheduled elections may have added to Batista's problems, as parties and individual politicians poised for contesting office were not easily reconciled to the denial of anticipated victories.

As a result, Batista's government was widely resented and resisted from its inception. Students and members of the progressive Ortodoxo Party were particularly active in the opposition. Underground papers and a clandestine radio had been established by June 1952, while Ortodoxos and their allies organized in underground cells. From its first weeks, then, the Batista regime faced street demonstrations and hostile propaganda. It responded with repressive measures including press censorship, closing of universities, arbitrary arrest, and selective assassination

— all of which engendered more opposition. In the face of this active and widespread resistance, Batista was unable to consolidate his administration and conduct the business of state with any degree of normalcy.

One of the early leaders of the opposition was Fidel Castro, a lawyer in his mid-twenties who had been an Ortodoxo candidate for a congressional seat in the aborted election. Castro was the son of a moderately wealthy sugar planter in Oriente province. He attended Jesuit schools, obtained a law degree from the University of Havana, and had extensive experience in university politics. Castro was one of the most active Ortodoxos, organizing cells and publishing an underground paper called *El Acusador.*

Castro achieved prominence as a result of his attack on the Moncada Barracks on July 26, 1953. The date of the Moncada assault gave the name to Castro's own movement, and this formative event continues to be central in the lore of the Cuban Revolution. Fidel's plan involved a group of 165 followers, predominantly young men, attacking the second largest army barracks in the country, located in Santiago in eastern Cuba and staffed by 1,000 troops. The maximalist notion, typical of Castro's approach to taking power and carrying out revolution, was that a successful attack would produce such shock waves as to mobilize the populace and bring down the regime.

Predictably, Castro's approach failed, leaving half his followers dead and most of the remainder captured. Typical also of Fidel was the bungling of some basic preparations. He wrote later in a candid admission: "Due to a most unfortunate error, half of our forces, and the better armed half at that, went astray at the entrance to the city and were not on hand to help us at the decisive moment."[3] Defending himself in a military court martial, Fidel presented a historical analysis of Cuba's ills and argued eloquently the duty of patriotic Cubans to take up arms against Batista. These arguments failed to persuade the military judges, who sentenced Castro to 15 years on the Isle of Pines. However, Fidel's arguments soon appeared as a pamphlet, *History Will Absolve Me,* which circulated clandestinely and disseminated Castro's name and message throughout the republic.[4]

The story of Fidel Castro might have ended with his imprisonment had it not been for a general amnesty declared by Batista in May 1955 in an attempt to court the support of moderates. Castro immediately left Cuba for Mexico, where he used his indefatigable energy to coordinate the new 26th of July Movement (Movimiento 26 de Julio, M-26-7) in Cuba, publicize himself and his cause, and organize another assault on Batista. In Mexico he met the young Argentine medical doctor, Ernesto

"Che" Guevara, and recruited a few dozen Cubans to join the crusade. Again, Castro's chosen method was to win by shock — to accomplish a seemingly impossible feat, expose the regime's weakness, and provoke a generalized uprising against Batista. The target, even less plausible than the Moncada Barracks, was the entire city of Santiago, Cuba's second largest. This time Fidel planned for the eventuality of defeat. He engaged Colonel Alberto Bayo, a republican veteran of the Spanish Civil War, to instruct his men in military skills and tactics that might enable survivors to continue the fight in the Sierra Maestra outside of Santiago. This precaution would serve Fidel well.

During Castro's imprisonment and Mexican exile, the struggle against Batista proceeded on a number of fronts. Through the efforts of Fidel and his lieutenants, the M-26-7 organized nationwide, absorbing much of the Ortodoxo Party membership and developing cells in cities and countryside. The more moderate Auténtico Party pursued a variety of approaches to ousting Batista. The two former presidents split over strategy: Grau favored participation in the 1954 election that Batista held; after Grau's failure, Prío's insurrectional line prevailed and Auténticos tried military conspiracies, an exile invasion, and guerrilla warfare. The Revolutionary Directorate (Directorio Revolucionario, DR), formed by the University of Havana student federation in late 1955, carried out propaganda, street demonstrations, strikes, urban uprisings, and guerrilla war. At least three major attempts against Batista failed in 1955 and 1956: a strike of 500,000 sugar workers; a military conspiracy led by Colonel Ramón Barquín, which was discovered prematurely; and a Moncada-style assault on the Goicuría Barracks. *Life* magazine published pictures of soldiers shooting surrendered attackers of the Goicuría Barracks, damaging the international reputation of Batista's government. The DR assassinated Batista's chief of military intelligence and other officers in November 1956, and sporadic cane burnings began in rural zones. Before embarking on the second phase of his fight against Batista, Fidel developed relations with the major anti-Batista forces and signed the Mexico City Pact of September 1956 with the DR, agreeing to coordinate efforts, reject all compromise with Batista, and establish a post-Batista government based on a 19-point program.

FROM THE SIERRA MAESTRA TO HAVANA, DECEMBER 1956–JANUARY 1959

While in Mexico, Fidel announced that he would return to liberate Cuba before the end of 1956. The secret plan, developed in coordination with M-26-7 operatives in Cuba, was to capture Santiago by a combination of marine assault from Mexico and a simultaneous uprising of supporters in the city on November 30. As in the Moncada case, the attack on Santiago was plagued by mistakes and miscalculations. The launch *Granma* departed from the Mexican port of Tuxpan on November 25 in a storm, an inauspicious start that Che Guevara recorded:

> We began a frenzied search for the anti-seasickness pills, which we did not find. We sang the Cuban national anthem and the "Hymn of the 26th of July" for perhaps five minutes and then the entire boat took on an aspect both ridiculous and tragic: men with anguished faces holding their stomachs, some with their heads in buckets, others lying in the strangest positions, immobile.[5]

Arriving two days late, Castro's 82 men landed in the wrong spot and after three days of wandering were surprised by army units. Had they arrived on the appointed day, their presence might have secured the victory of the urban insurgents who took control of Santiago for a few hours. Fifteen of Castro's followers from the *Granma* were soon able to regroup and make their way into the Sierra Maestra; the rest were dispersed, captured, or killed.[6]

In the aftermath of his second defeat, the ever-ebullient Fidel, with his brother Raúl, Che, and the others, had to choose between abandoning the fight and falling back to a strategy that was clearly not the preferred one. Out of desperation rather than choice, then, was born the rural guerrilla war. The story of the Sierra Maestra is one of heroism, courage, and fanatical dedication to a cause and a method of struggle. The *barbudos,* or bearded ones, emerge from the accounts of their ordeal as larger-than-life characters. Fraught with incredible hardships, laced with tragedy and near-catastrophe, punctuated by dramatic turning points, and set against overwhelming odds, the odyssey of Fidel's seizure of power is a romantic episode that spawned legends and lent itself to the creation of powerful myths.

Castro's idea of victory was not only the defeat and overthrow of Batista. As leader of M-26-7, he headed one of several rival groups that wanted to cap the struggle by installing themselves in power and developing post-Batista Cuba on their own terms. The main opposition groups were constantly organizing and agitating, sometimes alone and sometimes in concert. M-26-7, having been built on the broad base of the Ortodoxo Party, was the largest opposition group. The DR was a group with revolutionary credentials to match Fidel's and initially the strongest resistance force in Havana; other student-based groups were also active. Organized labor was a powerful force, but owing to an accommodation with Batista, it was not consistently in the opposition until late in the struggle. The Popular Socialist Party (Partido Socialista Popular, PSP, the Cuban communists) not only refrained from action but denounced Castro for his "bourgeois adventurism." The Auténticos were a collection of establishment politicians seeking to recapture what they had lost in 1952. Their strengths were their international prestige, access to money, and a broad following within the Cuban middle class. Other opposition to Batista came from within the armed forces, both army and navy, which sought to save military prestige by disassociating themselves from the dictator.

As Fidel recognized, the United States was the final arbiter of Cuban politics: Regardless of the relative strengths of the contenders, if the United States decided to back a group or coalition as replacement for Batista, Washington was likely to have its way. With an array of safe contenders from whom to choose, Washington would certainly not tap the unpredictable Castro to be its pawn in Cuba. Thus Castro's challenge was not only to fight more effectively than his rivals but also to outmaneuver them so as to avoid the replacement of Batista by a popular moderate or conservative acceptable to the United States and the general population of Cuba. Such a development would effectively end Fidel's chances of taking power.

During 1957, three major overthrow attempts were launched, the success of any of which would have preempted the Sierra Maestra guerrilla fighters. On March 13, DR carried out a bold strike on the presidential palace in an attempt to assassinate Batista. The attackers fought their way to the third floor, where Batista was located, and barely fell short of their objective. The DR paid dearly for its failure; its founder, José Antonio Echevarría, was killed in the attack and the police quickly wiped out most of the remaining leadership. A second major action was a spontaneous uprising sparked by the police assassination of popular M-26-7 leader Frank País in Santiago on July 30. This August general strike spread throughout the country, supported by all anti-Batista groups and the populace at large, but fizzled after a week or two. On September 5, a naval revolt broke out in Cienfuegos; it collapsed in part because a coordinated uprising in Havana was called off.

In response to these 1957 uprisings, Batista increased the repression on the urban underground and purged the military. His success against the resistance was not achieved without cost, however: The repression and accompanying suspension of individual liberties alienated broader segments of the population, giving the moderates a growing voice in the opposition. The Auténticos stepped up their activities, the church called for mediation of the conflict, and the country's major economic interest associations called for Batista's resignation. The United States itself began seeking alternatives to Batista and early in 1958 embargoed arms for his army as a means of pressuring him to cooperate.

During 1957 and the first months of 1958, the cities continued to be the main theatre of the war between Batista and the opposition. This circumstance offered Castro the great advantage of being virtually neglected while the government's security forces concentrated on beating back the urban-centered uprising. Batista's initial public response to Castro was to claim that he had been killed along with the other invaders from Mexico and to deny the existence of armed rebels in the mountains. His military response was to try to isolate Castro in the Sierra Maestra where presumably he could do no harm and to prevent reinforcements of men and supplies from reaching the guerrillas. Batista's commanders strengthened military outposts on the perimeter of the Sierra Maestra, sent additional patrols into the mountains, and carried out sporadic aerial bombing, but did not mount large-scale offensive operations against the rebels.

Thus left in relative peace, Castro's *foco,* or guerrilla band, evolved in 17 months from the humblest of beginnings with 15 defeated men seeking refuge in the mountains into a force capable of turning back the best offensive that Batista could send against it. In the first days after the disastrous landing, the ragtag band aspired to little more than day-to-day survival. Che described the early period in the Sierra Maestra as follows: "In that period it was very difficult to enlarge our army; a few men came, but others left; the physical conditions of the struggle were very hard, but the spiritual conditions were even more so, and we lived with the feeling of being continually under siege."[7] The immediate needs were sustenance and safety from army units. Both were obtained through the passive or active cooperation of the scattered peasantry of the Sierra Maestra, some of whom had been recruited in advance by M-26-7 operatives from Santiago. This peasant support, combined with the army's strategy of cordoning off the entire mountainous zone to contain the guerrillas, gave Castro's group the ability to scout the terrain and establish ever-expanding networks of trusted peasants. Free from concerted government pressure, the guerrillas were gradually able to establish a "liberated zone" — an area in which they could operate with relative security from army attack — in the Sierra Maestra.

The guerrilla band was still tiny and virtually untested when *New York Times* senior editor Herbert Matthews discovered and introduced it to the world in February 1957. Desperately seeking the publicity that Batista's censorship denied him, Castro arranged for Matthews to cross army lines into the *sierra* and be taken to the rebel camp for an extensive interview and a look at the guerrilla operation. Fidel knew how to take advantage of such a providential opportunity. Although having only 18 men at the time, by his later admission, he told Matthews that his troops operated in "groups of ten to forty" and claimed that rebel victories had lowered army morale. Deeply impressed, the veteran correspondent wrote that Castro "has mastery of the Sierra Maestra" and opined that "General Batista cannot possibly hope to suppress the Castro revolt."[8] Matthews' story appeared in the *Times* on February 24. Owing to a temporary lifting of press censorship, even Cubans were able to read about Castro for the first time.

The Matthews interview put the lie to Batista's claim that Fidel and his followers had been wiped out. The publicity helped recruiting, and the force grew substantially. At the time of its second military victory, an attack on a 53-man garrison at El Uvero on May 28, 1957, the guerrilla band boasted approximately 100 men. El Uvero, according to Che, was "the victory which marked our coming of age."[9]

The strategy at this stage was not to conquer and hold additional territory, but to engage the enemy in carefully prepared ambushes at the perimeter of the liberated zone, inflict casualties, and retreat to safety before reinforcements or air power could arrive. It was critical in this stage for the guerrillas to choose the engagements, avoiding confrontations with superior forces that could defeat them. The goals of this phase were to cause increasing numbers of troops to be committed to the perimeter of the Sierra Maestra and to score enough small victories to establish military credibility and demoralize the army. Following several months of successful small-scale offensive operations, Fidel took a major step in March 1958 by sending a column under the command of his brother Raúl to establish a second front in the mountains of northern Oriente province.

During the first year and a half of Fidel's campaign in the mountains, while the struggle to overthrow Batista was centered in the cities, Batista's success against the urban underground, labor, students, and the military conspirators severely weakened Castro's main rivals among the active fighting groups. In order to pursue insurrection in a less dangerous setting, the DR, the Auténticos, the Ortodoxos, and an independent group set up guerrilla operations in the Escambray Mountains of central Cuba beginning in mid-1957. But rather than eliminating the implicit struggle for supremacy in the anti-Batista movement, the decline of Castro's rivals seemed to intensify it. Just as the field cleared, Fidel became locked in a power struggle within his own M-26-7. The cleavage was between Fidel and the National Directorate, the formal governing body of M-26-7 that had been set up during Fidel's exile to run and expand the movement. This division soon came to be known by those involved as the *sierra* versus the *llanos,* or plains; it involved Fidel and his tightly knit group of guerrillas versus the movement's formal leadership based in the cities, primarily Santiago and Havana. Thus during the last year and a half of the campaign against Batista, Fidel seems to have spent as much time and energy fighting his own allies within the movement as he did fighting the army.

The internecine struggle is important because it casts light on the role of the rural guerrilla within the anti-Batista movement as well as on Fidel Castro. The major accounts of the 1957–58 period are written from one vantage point or the other. Che's *Reminiscences of the Cuban Revolutionary War* quite naturally reflects the attitudes of Castro and the barbudos. Carlos Franqui's *Diary of the Cuban Revolution,* published much later, offers the perspective of the urban M-26-7 underground.[10] Despite differing interpretations, both sides agree on the issues that drove a deep wedge between the majority urban and the small guerrilla wings of the movement.

At one level, the differences involved the strategy and tactics of the fight against Batista. Although M-26-7 had begun in the cities and although guerrilla warfare was clearly a fallback position for Fidel, Castro began to feel after a few months in the sierra that the foco was the correct approach, and he began to deprecate the efforts of his collaborators in the llanos. Fidel's attitude of guerrilla superiority was not without merit. Increasingly, urban efforts at propaganda, agitation, strikes, and sabotage appeared insufficient to dislodge the dictator. The city groups suffered a succession of defeats, losing their underground leader with the assassination of Frank País in July 1957; other important leaders, including Armando Hart, Carlos Franqui, and Javier Pazos, were constantly harassed by police and thus limited in their ability to function. Once on the defensive, the underground delivered far less in arms and money to the sierra than Fidel deemed adequate — a charge contested by the urban leaders. The greatest failure of the M-26-7 urban leadership was the thwarted April 1958 Havana general strike, which Fidel had hoped would be the fatal blow to Batista.

Contrasted with the disappointing performance of the urban cadres, the record of the guerrillas appeared strong. They had gone in a year from defeat to having a secure liberated zone, some offensive capability, and by February 1958 the ability to broadcast to the country over Radio Rebelde. The foco thus appeared more successful than the campaign in the llano, especially if one overlooked the fact that Batista focused on pounding the urban underground while leaving the Sierra Maestra to the barbudos, convinced that they could do little harm away from the population centers.

At another level, the sierra-llano rift can be seen as a power struggle for control of M-26-7 and for position in post-Batista Cuba. No one who has followed Fidel Castro's career can doubt that he has always wanted to be the man in charge, whether of a country or a cocktail party. On the other side, many leaders of the urban M-26-7 had worked diligently and loyally for years, risking their lives daily while Fidel failed in his major overthrow attempts and opted for what appeared to be a relatively safe method of struggle. As their uprisings failed and their comrades died, the urban leadership may have found Castro's airs — his glorification of the guerrilla, his appropriation of the mantle of maximum national hero José Martí, his tendency to ignore the official movement governing board when making decisions — annoying.

By the beginning of 1958, these small misunderstandings blossomed into a behind-the-scenes power struggle. Fidel, Raúl, and Che indicated in internal correspondence their disdain for and growing distrust of the llano. Fidel wrote M-26-7 leaders in Santiago in January 1958: "I am at the point of asking the Movement not to bother about us any more and to abandon us to our fate and leave us on our own once and for all. I'm tired of having my feelings misinterpreted. I'm not meanly ambitious. All the honors and responsibilities don't mean a damn to me."[11] Following the failure of the Havana general strike, which disrupted the M-26-7 underground and further discredited urban leaders, Fidel wrote: "No one will ever be able to make me trust the organization again."[12] He further complained that "the Movement has failed utterly in the job of supplying us," blaming "egotism, . . . incompetence, negligence, and even the disloyalty of some comrades."[13] An October 1958 report from Franqui to the M-26-7 Executive Committee revealed the feelings of the urban leadership: "I believe very strongly in the role of the leader of our Revolution. But I believe that his collaborators cannot be a group of extras who provide only the appearance of democracy, a chorus who praise his successes."[14]

While the internal power struggle within the resistance heated up, Batista finally turned his army loose on the guerrillas. Having been forced by the Matthews interview and corroborating evidence to admit the guerrilla presence, Batista had adopted the public posture that Castro's group was too insignificant to warrant a commitment of troops to root it out of the mountains. However, repeatedly stung by guerrilla ambushes and Fidel's inflated claims of rebel victory and strengthened by his defeat of the Havana general strike, Batista decided to deal with the guerrillas head-on. With considerable fanfare and the appearance of complete confidence, the army in May 1958 launched what it announced would be a quick campaign to exterminate Castro's guerrillas. Unable to get its tanks, half-tracks, mortars, and even jeeps into the mountainous terrain, however, the army could only wait with its firepower on Castro's perimeter or send foot patrols into the Sierra Maestra in search of the rebels. This strategy played directly into Fidel's hands. His troops merely taunted the massed army and then, controlling the terrain, freely ambushed the columns dispatched to find and finish them. In August, after three months of frustration and substantial losses of men and equipment, Batista's commanders called off the campaign in August and returned to the strategy of sealing off the guerrillas. Having won his first major battle, Castro enjoyed a surge in prestige and power.

The failure of the offensive against Castro revealed that the 40,000-man Cuban army was far less capable than it appeared to be. Having fought no wars, its officers and soldiers were inexperienced in combat. Like other armies schooled in conventional warfare, it was frustrated by the innovative guerrilla approach. As the pillars of Batista's support, army commanders were chosen primarily for their loyalty, secondarily for their military abilities. Corruption was also rampant within the army, and Castro found it easy to bribe officers to permit people and supplies to slip through army lines into the sierra.

By the latter months of 1958, it was clear that the Batista regime was unraveling. The failure of the offensive against Castro revealed glaring weaknesses, causing anticipation of an imminent collapse. The PSP, a long-time ally of the dictator, had turned against him in February 1958 when it sensed serious erosion of his position. The mounting urban repression with which Batista defended himself produced a growing alienation of previously neutral and even pro-Batista middle and upper classes. In response to these developments the moderate opposition and the United States, seeking alternatives to Castro, urged Batista to resign in time for a caretaker government to conduct national elections. Rather than resigning, Batista conducted his own elections for congress and a president on November 3. With the exception of loyal pro-Batista groups, most eligible voters boycotted, making the elections a farce and denying all legitimacy to the hand-picked government slated to succeed the dictator in February 1959. Rather than arresting the collapse of the regime, the sham elections hastened it.

The end came for Batista shortly after Castro, buoyed by the defeat of Batista's summer offensive, expanded his military operations to Central Cuba. At the end of August, Fidel dispatched a column of 150 men under Che Guevara from the Sierra Maestra to the mountains of Las Villas province. Its objectives were to cut communications between Havana and Santiago, take control of the DR and other guerrillas already operating in the Escambray Mountains, and strike a decisive blow that would bring down the regime. A second column under Camilo Cienfuegos, headed originally to Pinar del Río in the island's far west, also arrived in Las Villas after a seven-week march through army-held territory. When the final offensive was launched in early November, Castro's total guerrilla forces had reached roughly 1,000 troops.

After capturing numerous villages and cutting the central highway and railroad, Che's guerrillas attacked Santa Clara, Cuba's fourth largest city with a population of some 80,000, on December 29. The city fell after heavy fighting on January 1, 1959. News of the imminent fall of Santa Clara prompted Batista to abandon a New Year's Eve party at his palace and take a waiting plane to the Dominican Republic and the fraternal embrace of dictator Rafael Trujillo. After a triumphant motorized march through the heartland of Cuba, Fidel and his guerrillas from the Sierra Maestra, their ranks swollen by last minute converts, rolled into Havana on January 8 to a heroes' welcome. Total guerrilla strength at the fall of Batista did not exceed 3,000.

MYTHOGENESIS, OR THE MYTH
OF THE HEROIC GUERRILLA

Even before Castro's seizure of power the myth of the heroic guerrilla had begun to gain currency. The myth of the heroic guerrilla is the founding myth of the new Cuba; just as any new nation embellishes the heroic deeds and character traits of its founders in the process of forging national identity and institutional legitimacy, a society created by revolution creates its own founding myth by exaggerating the faults of the *ancien régime* and embellishing the feats and qualities of its revolutionary leaders. The founding myth of the Cuban Revolution, like other founding myths, is a selective recounting of history. It tells the story of the victory from the viewpoint of the victors.

Having struggled and suffered for 25 months in the Sierra Maestra against overwhelming odds and at great personal sacrifice, and having developed an attitude of superiority vis-à-vis the urban resistance for its repeated failures to dislodge Batista, Fidel and his cadre of guerrilla fighters quite understandably attributed to themselves the victory and the beginning of a new Cuba. In believing and in broadcasting that message, they were not wrong nor were they lying. However, they overlooked and, perhaps inadvertently, discredited the work and sacrifice of thousands of members of the urban resistance, including the great bulk of M-26-7. Some of these men and women had been in the front lines of resistance for four and a half years before Fidel's dozen went to the Sierra Maestra to launch a new front in the war. Fidel acknowledged this distortion in a 1968 article, written during a period of reassessment following the death of Che Guevara in his attempt to replicate the Cuban model in Bolivia:

> Almost all attention, almost all recognition, almost all the admiration, and almost all the history of the Revolution [have] centered on the guerrilla movement in the mountains. . . . This fact tended to play down the role of those who fought in the cities, the role of those who fought in the clandestine movement, and the extraordinary heroism of young persons who died fighting under very difficult conditions.[15]

The myth of the heroic guerrilla also omits the work of the urban resistance in tying down Batista's forces in the cities during all of 1957 and the first four months of 1958. Without the repeated demonstrations, uprisings, strikes, assassination attempts, and acts of sabotage carried out by DR, M-26-7, students, parties, organized labor, and military dissidents, Batista almost certainly would not have neglected Castro, allowing his forces to grow and strengthen themselves without significant military pressure until the army finally launched its belated offensive in May 1958. The myth also downplays the role of the urban cadres of M-26-7 in supplying weapons and recruits to the Sierra Maestra and fails to credit the same group with proselytizing among the peasantry of the area prior to Castro's arrival — a role of considerable importance in view of the universal peasant distrust of outsiders.

The myth of the heroic guerrilla, firmly anchored in the history of the guerrilla war, grew up as the result of several circumstances. Most fundamental were the undeniable heroism and the epic quality of the guerrilla phase of the struggle against Batista. When the charisma and commanding presence of Fidel and the colorful and engaging personality of Che Guevara are added, the figure of the guerrilla fighter assumes a larger-than-life quality. From the appearance of Herbert Matthews' story in February 1957, the international press found the guerrillas more appealing and newsworthy than the student protests, general strikes, and military revolts that were the standard stuff of Latin American politics. Fidel's highly developed sense for publicity further helped to focus news coverage on the guerrillas. After the victory, Fidel institutionalized the guerrilla struggle in the new regime by installing Sierra Maestra veterans in most important positions, thus making guerrilla khakis, boots, and beards the official dress as well as the symbol of the revolution.

The guerrillas also attained their preeminence in the founding myth by default. In the power struggle over the succession to Batista, Fidel had swept aside numerous leaders of the urban resistance; in the authoritarian climate that Castro quickly imposed after taking power, there was no room for questioning the official version of the war. Thus the great majority of those involved in the anti-Batista movement had no one to tell their story until much later, after the heroic guerrilla was firmly established. Finally, Che Guevara's *Guerrilla Warfare* and other writings gave the Cuban guerrilla war something of the status of a holy crusade, completing the formulation of the myth of the heroic guerrilla.

The founding myth of the heroic guerrilla was an important asset to Fidel Castro in legitimizing the revolution and in maintaining popular support during times of external threat and economic hardship. One of the myth's functions was to link the revolution to Cuban history, reassuring Cubans that however radical or unorthodox Fidel and his policies appeared, they were rooted in the national experience. Both his method — guerrilla warfare — and his goal — national independence — placed Castro squarely in the tradition of José Martí, Antonio Maceo, and Máximo Gómez, who had fought guerrilla wars for independence from Spain. The suffering, sacrifice, perseverance, and indomitable will of the guerrilla also served as models for the behavior of citizens struggling to throw off Yankee imperialism and build a new Cuba at times when massive amounts of volunteer labor were needed and material rewards were scarce. In his speeches, Fidel frequently exhorted the people to sacrifice in the spirit of the Sierra Maestra, and a generation of children was indoctrinated in the values of self-abnegation and struggle characteristic of the heroic guerrilla. In these and other ways, the myth of the heroic guerrilla became an explicit and central part of the political culture of Castro's Cuba.

The myth of the heroic guerrilla also became a major Cuban export. For those Latin Americans already committed to revolution, the example of Cuba's successful guerrilla war provided hope and a model. For the many more who had not been committed to radical politics before, the romantic version of the Cuban revolutionary war and its heroic guerrillas was a siren song that lured them to action. After Che Guevara published *Guerrilla Warfare* in 1960, Latin Americans had available a handbook on how to emulate Castro's victory. Unfortunately for the many who died trying to follow the Cuban example, the myth of the heroic guerrilla was a very selective recounting of Fidel Castro's road to power.

NOTES

1. Jaime Suchlicki, *Cuba from Columbus to Castro* (New York: Charles Scribner's Sons, 1974), 96–97.
2. Quoted in ibid., 105.
3. Fidel Castro, *History Will Absolve Me* (Bungay, U. K.: Richard Clay [The Chaucer Press], 1968), 40.
4. Ibid.
5. Che Guevara, *Reminiscences of the Cuban Revolutionary War,* tr. by Victoria Ortiz (New York: Grove Press, 1968), 40.
6. The biblical number 12 is often used in accounts of the origins of Fidel's guerrilla band, but reliable observers counted 15 men at the outset of the Sierra Maestra campaign.
7. Guevara, *Reminiscences,* 81.
8. Matthews, *The Cuban Story,* 29–38.
9. Guevara, *Reminiscences,* 117.
10. Carlos Franqui, *Diary of the Cuban Revolution,* tr. by Georgette Felix et al. (New York: Viking Press, 1980).
11. Castro to Santiago leaders, 13 January 1958, ibid., 279.
12. Castro to Celia Sánchez, 16 April 1958, ibid., 300.
13. Castro to Mario Llerena and Raúl Chibás, 25 April 1958, ibid., 310.
14. Franqui to Castro and M-26-7 National Executive, October 1958, ibid., 431.
15. Quoted in Edward González, *Cuba under Castro: The Limits of Charisma* (Boston: Houghton Mifflin, 1974), 92.

2

Cuba:
Making the Revolution

Within months of coming to power, Fidel Castro demonstrated his commitment to creating a new Cuba. Within two years, Castro had laid the foundations for a thorough revolution in Cuba's social, economic, and political structures and in 1968 completed the transition to socialism with the "revolutionary offensive" against the last vestiges of capitalism on the island. In Cuba's foreign affairs the shape of revolution was clear by 1962 when, after breaking with and being attacked by the United States, Fidel cemented his alliance with the Soviet Union. The speed and thoroughness of the transformation of Cuba — both unprecedented in Latin America — provided example and inspiration to the masses of Latin America and the political left and instilled fear in the elites, the political right, and the U.S. government.

Although Castro soon embraced socialism as the model for Cuba's new economy and society, it is important to note that it was in the first two years of his government — prior to his declaration of socialism — that Fidel instituted the most dramatic revolutionary changes. He was guided in part by the well-known program that M-26-7 had been proclaiming for several years before the triumph. Its ten points included: national sovereignty; economic independence; work for all; social justice; education; political democracy; civil authority; religious freedom; public morality; and constructive friendship with all countries. Evident in the M-26-7 program was the intention of addressing the historic "condition of Cuba" — U.S. dominance, lopsided reliance on sugar with its attendant social and economic problems, social fragmentation and injustice, and a discredited political system.

Castro was also guided during his early years in office by his own maximalist proclivities. From the 1953 assault on the Moncada Barracks, Fidel had exhibited a tendency to attack the greatest challenges in order to have the maximum impact. The period of seasoning in the Sierra Maestra demonstrated the persistence and dedication of Fidel and his followers. These experiences and characteristics, which one scholar has called the "Moncada Barracks mentality" and the "Sierra Maestra complex," quickly came to the fore in Castro's Cuba as Fidel set out to rectify, preferably overnight, the "condition of Cuba."[1]

Finally, Castro had an unusual opportunity in his early years to tackle Cuba's problems head-on. While the political system was already in disrepute before Batista's coup, under the dictator the last semblance of legitimate authority disappeared. Thus the flight of Batista left a power vacuum that no individual, group, or institution associated with the old regime could pretend to fill. Even the Auténticos and other moderates who claimed a role in the new government as a result of their opposition to Batista lacked influence alongside Fidel, whose enormous popularity and control over the rebel army made him the uncontested *caudillo*, or supreme leader. In this situation, there were no restraints on Castro's appetite for change. In fact, with his support based on the poor, the working and some of the middle classes, and on youth, and with the elites effectively out of the political equation, momentum for radical innovation grew quickly after the victory.

A MARXIST REVOLUTION

Many participants, observers, and scholars have addressed the intriguing question of Fidel's turn to Marxism and the motivations for his establishment of socialism and the alliance with the Soviet Union. Rather than searching for Castro's motives, our purpose is to discover the reasons for the ascendancy of the Cuban Revolution as the driving force in Latin American politics for over a quarter century. Nonetheless, a brief review of the process of establishing communist party rule and of the competing interpretations of Fidel's conversion to Marxism-Leninism elucidates a central aspect of the Cuban Revolution — one that inevitably affected the revolution's influence in Latin America and Washington's reaction to the threat of insurrection in the hemisphere.

During the fight against Batista the Cuban Communist Party (PSP) remained on the sidelines, denouncing Castro's unorthodox methods of insurrection, until the outcome was apparent. Despite the resulting antagonisms, Castro established a working relationship with the PSP and its leader, Carlos Rafael Rodríguez, in the months following the victory. During the next two years, Castro's relations with the PSP became closer. On April 15, 1961, Fidel publicly affirmed the socialist character of the revolution, calling it a "socialist revolution carried out under the very noses of the Yankees."[2] The new governing alliance was formalized three months later with the merger of M-26-7, PSP, and DR into the Integrated Revolutionary Organizations (Organizaciones Revolucionarias Integradas, ORI). After some months of public hints of his own Marxist sentiments, Fidel declared in a long speech on December 2, 1961: "I am a Marxist-Leninist and I shall be a Marxist-Leninist until the last day of my life."[3] The founding of the Communist Party of Cuba (Partido Comunista de Cuba, PCC) in 1965 completed the fidelista-communist merger.

The establishment of communist party rule in Cuba followed a course unique in the annals of communist accessions. Rather than the PSP's capturing the revolution, Fidel took over the PSP for his own ends. Fidel was either titular or de facto head of each succeeding organization and his trusted veterans of the Sierra Maestra rather than PSP cadres dominated the important positions in the party and the government. This relationship between long-time communists and those whose first loyalty was to Fidel remained stable over the years. Since the establishment of a formal communist state in 1976, Castro has held the positions of head of state and head of party without interruption, and with his brother Raúl and other Sierra Maestra veterans continues to dominate the political and military leadership.

An early hypothesis explaining the communist path of the Cuban Revolution was that Castro had been a communist throughout the anti-Batista struggle; he had hidden his true colors — to avoid alienating many Cubans and inviting U.S. intervention — until he was firmly entrenched in power. This conspiracy theory, understandably popular with the many Cubans who felt betrayed by Castro, gained little credence among scholars and dispassionate observers.

Most analysts of the Cuban Revolution assume that Fidel is a converted Marxist; the debate focused on whether Castro embraced Marxism of his own volition or whether the United States forced him into Marxism and the Soviet alliance. Some concluded that U.S. opposition to Fidel's reforms and continuance in power drove Fidel to seek an alliance with the Soviet Union — the only power capable of protecting his revolution from the U.S. military threat. In order to achieve Soviet support in the dangerous game of confronting the United States in its own backyard, the argument went, Castro had to demonstrate his firm ideological and practical commitment to Marxism. Thus, as the climate of relations with the United States worsened after mid-1959, Castro, guided by his brother Raúl, Che Guevara, and others of his Sierra Maestra cadre, incrementally laid the basis for a socialist economy and brought the PSP into the governing apparatus. Within three years, Castro had become sufficiently trustworthy for the Soviets to risk the provocative step of installing nuclear missiles to protect the revolution from the United States. Fidel Castro, Che Guevara, and other participants and observers, while acknowledging the effects of pressure from the United States, have argued that the decisions that laid the basis for a socialist economy and a communist party government were Castro's free choice. Enjoying immense personal prestige and power in the months following his triumph, Fidel was in a position to take the revolution in any direction he might choose. In explaining his move toward communism, he alleges a gradual conversion, basically completed by 1959, to a Marxist-Leninist world view and a conviction that Cuba's and Latin America's problems could not be resolved within the framework of capitalism: "I have had a very interesting and very effective schooling. That is simply . . . the process which, from my first questionings until the present moment, made me into a Marxist revolutionary."[4]

Fidel's alignment with the PSP was also a pragmatic decision designed to consolidate his power. Even before the victory, Fidel's bitter feud with the urban M-26-7 had weakened his faith in the organization that he had created. With Batista's fall, the common enemy uniting the heterogeneous movement was gone. The PSP offered ideological sophistication, a highly centralized organization, and a historic although currently weakened hold on major blocs of the labor movement. After concluding that a Marxist approach was necessary, Fidel turned to the communists to tutor his inner circle, to add structure to his huge but amorphous popular following, and to aid in establishing socialism. The PSP alliance would also enhance Castro's claim to Marxist legitimacy and hence to Soviet aid.

Opposing the nascent accommodation with the PSP was a strongly anticommunist group within M-26-7; encouraging it were Raúl, Che, and other influential collaborators. The issue became open when a few of the anticommunists publicly denounced Castro's increasingly pro-PSP orientation. In a swift and decisive reaction, Fidel attacked the anti-communists as antirevolutionary and virtually antipatriotic and purged several of their spokesmen between June and December 1959. Among them were air force commander Pedro Díaz Lanz and Major Huber Matos, who became Cuba's most celebrated political prisoner until his release in 1979.

Whatever the exact circumstances of Fidel's critical decisions regarding Marxism, working with the PSP, and the alliance with Moscow, it is beyond dispute that he reneged on his promises to hold elections. He turned his back on western democracy, calling it "the dictatorship of the capitalists."[5] Fidel was undoubtedly correct in claiming the incompatibility of western democracy with social revolution; given the corrupting power of money in elections and the restraints on action inherent in constitutional democracies, the far-reaching changes in Cuba's economy and society to which Fidel was committed would have been watered down or thwarted completely. In attacking capitalism, Fidel was attacking the sustenance of his opposition. Yet the establishment of a communist state, even though it was clearly Fidel's own brand of communist state, disillusioned some of Castro's early supporters in Latin America as it did many in Cuba. It also confirmed the views of those conservatives in Latin America and Washington who argued that reform must be resisted because of its unpredictable course and potentially dangerous consequences.

THE DOMESTIC REVOLUTION

By the end of 1960, both the domestic revolution and the realignment of Cuba's international relations were well advanced. While influenced by the M-26-7 program in its broad outlines, by the Marxists within Fidel's inner circle, and by Fidel's somewhat blurry vision of a new Cuba, the dual revolution proceeded without any strict guidelines or preexisting blueprint for achieving specified ends through prescribed means. Rather, the far-reaching changes were often guided by impulse and improvisation, reflecting the maximalism of the Moncada Barracks approach and the reliance on will, sacrifice, and dedication that characterized the Sierra Maestra experience.

For the first four and a half months after the overthrow, however, Fidel's formal posture was one of moderation. Castro and the other principal opposition forces had agreed in advance on Manuel Urrutia, a respected judge, to be president. Urrutia chose a moderate cabinet, balanced between anti-Batista bourgeois figures and Castro collaborators. Castro retained the title of commander-in-chief of the Rebel Armed Forces and, with that, his veto power over the formal government. Relations with the United States were correct if not cordial: The United States recognized the Urrutia government a week after Batista's flight and sent a new ambassador, Philip Bonsal, who was free from taint by association with the former regime. Castro visited the United States in April, invited by the Newspaper Editors Association to address its convention. His 15-day visit became a successful goodwill tour in which enthusiastic audiences cheered his moderate pronouncements wherever he appeared.

Beneath the facade of moderation, there were early signs of Castro's commitment to breaking with the past. In mid-February Fidel assumed the post of prime minister, replacing the moderate José Miró Cardona and formalizing his direct control of the government. The trial, imprisonment, and execution of numerous Batista officials and collaborators were further signs of Fidel's seriousness of purpose. The well-publicized summary trials, resulting in over 550 executions, confirmed Fidel's pledge from the Sierra Maestra to punish those most responsible for the repression, torture, and assassinations of the opposition to Batista. Given the normal procedure of exiling the operatives of deposed Latin American regimes, however, the executions raised significant concerns among the Cuban elites and the U.S. government. In March, Castro implemented three populist measures that hinted at the shape of the revolution to come: He took over the management of the U.S.-owned telephone company and cut its rates; he decreed the forced sale of vacant urban lots to end land speculation and reduce prices; and he slashed urban rents by 50 percent. Castro also called off the elections he had been promising throughout the struggle against Batista, saying "Revolution first, elections later."[6]

Concern turned to hostility when Castro unveiled the centerpiece of his emerging plan for transforming Cuba. Announced at a televised ceremony in the Sierra Maestra, the agrarian reform law of May 17, 1959, launched the redistributive phase of the revolution by mandating the expropriation of large agricultural properties. The declaration of agrarian reform began the revolutionary transformation of Cuba's economy and, as a consequence, of Cuban society. The social revolution unfolded as a result of the state's incremental appropriation of businesses and property, which eventually made nearly every Cuban worker a state employee subject to wages and benefits set by a government committed to creating an egalitarian society.

The agrarian reform law realized a long-standing aspiration of many Cubans. The 1940 constitution had banned *latifundia* (very large rural holdings) but left definition and implementation for future legislation that, given the power of U.S. and Cuban sugar interests, was not enacted until Castro's initiative. The law established the maximum legal holding at 30 *caballerías* (403 hectares or 995 acres), with exceptions for unusually efficient units of up to 1,342 hectares. It also abolished renting and sharecropping and prohibited foreign ownership of agricultural land. The land taken, much of it owned by large U.S. sugar and cattle companies, passed into different types of holdings. Nearly 100,000 renters and sharecroppers of expropriated land received 27 hectares and had the right to purchase 40 hectares more where the land was available; unutilized land became state property; and large sugar and cattle holdings worked by wage labor became cooperatives or state enterprises rather than being broken into inefficient small parcels. Compensation was to be awarded to expropriated owners in 20-year government bonds bearing 4.5 percent interest, with prices to be based on assessed value as reflected in the tax rolls. In practice, then, compensation would be well below pre-1959 market value — leading the U.S. government on June 11 to demand "prompt, adequate, and effective compensation" for its citizens.[7]

By 1961, implementation of the agrarian law and other government actions had created a mixed agricultural economy in which small and medium private holdings of 67 hectares or less constituted approximately 39 percent of Cuba's total agricultural surface, large private holdings of over 67 hectares 19 percent, and cooperatives and state farms 42 percent. In only two years, Fidel's agrarian reform had progressed remarkably, but with the official adoption of socialism further action became necessary. Thus by 1962 the cooperatives were converted to state farms, with the approval of the affected workers, and a second agrarian reform law of October 1963 limited private holdings to 67 hectares. Some 10,000 properties exceeding that size were expropriated and their land was incorporated into the state farm sector, which by 1965 encompassed approximately 60 percent of Cuba's agricultural surface and continued to grow through purchase and selected expropriations to reach 68 percent in 1971 and 79 percent in 1977.

The continued existence of a large private farm sector — some 250,000 holdings averaging 13 hectares and occupying nearly 40 percent of total agricultural surface in 1965 — was an anomaly in the context of Cuba's socialist economy. Castro addressed this problem through the mechanism of the National Association of Small Farmers (Asociación Nacional de Agricultores Pequeños, ANAP), which organized a large majority of the smallholders into production cooperatives. This, combined with close regulation of all aspects of small farms, including the obligatory sale of produce at fixed prices to the state and the prohibition against selling land except to the state, blurred the distinction between peasant farmers and workers on state farms. This transformation of agriculture put the most valuable sector of the Cuban economy and approximately half of the country's economically active population under state control.

Complementing the agrarian reform program, nationalization of the Cuban economy proceeded on several other fronts. A major impetus to the growth of the state sector was the confiscation of all properties of enemies of the regime and of exiles. Within weeks of coming to power,

Castro created the Ministry for the Recovery of Stolen Property (Ministerio de Recuperación de Bienes Malversados) with sweeping powers to seize the assets of Batista and his collaborators, "counter-revolutionaries," and, after 1960, of all exiles. During most of his first 15 years in power, Castro maintained a policy of fairly easy emigration that removed real and potential enemies as well as promoting the transfer of major economic assets to the state. Initially composed primarily of Batista collaborators and supporters, the flow of exiles swelled with Cubans' deepening realization of Castro's revolutionary intentions. While all socioeconomic groups were represented among the emigrants, the upper and middle classes predominated in the exodus, which reached some 600,000, or nearly a tenth of Cuba's 1958 population, by 1974. As a result, the state inherited a significant share of the Cuban-owned businesses, real estate, and rural land through the phenomenon of voluntary exile.

Another major blow to private property in Cuba came between August and October 1960 in the midst of a flurry of actions and counteractions pitting Havana against Washington. In response to the cancellation of the Cuban sugar quota in the U.S. market, Castro decreed the expropriation of all U.S.-owned property in Cuba without compensation. Agricultural land had already been affected by the agrarian reform law and the oil refineries had been nationalized, but the extent of U.S. investment was such — over a billion dollars — that the expropriations between August and October transferred to the Cuban state major portions of the public utilities, banking, transportation, communications, sugar refining, insurance, industrial, mining, and tourism sectors and made it the employer of hundreds of thousands of additional workers.

The onslaught against U.S. holdings was a signal for the accelerated expropriation of the remaining Cuban- and foreign-owned enterprises. By 1964 the only remaining significant private activities outside of agriculture were retail business and services. The final thrust of the drive to eliminate private business was the "revolutionary offensive" of 1968. In one blow the nearly 56,000 remaining private businesses throughout the country were expropriated: Restaurants, laundries, mechanic shops, and beauty parlors overnight became part of the state-owned economy. After the elimination of small business, the only remaining vestiges of the capitalist economy were the small farmers, whose economic rights were severely limited.

After the revolutionary offensive, every working Cuban was subject to state-set wages or other income. In 1968 the scale ran from 96 pesos per month for a cane cutter to 900 pesos per month for a supreme court judge. Despite this wide discrepancy indicating considerable privilege, all unskilled and most skilled workers earned between 96 and 250 pesos monthly, with most salaries above that level reserved for government functionaries. The minimum retirement pension was 60 pesos per month. On one hand, this wage scale reveals pragmatic concessions to important government functionaries, professionals, and skilled labor — the groups most likely to want to emigrate — as a means of keeping them in Cuba. On the other hand, the great compaction of wage differences between 1958 and 1968 clearly reveals Castro's commitment to the M-26-7 program's goal of social justice.

More revolutionary than the leveling trend of wages were two other elements of government policy. First, full-time, year-round work was guaranteed for all Cubans. To underscore the significance of work for all, even at the wage of a cane cutter, one only needs to compare the new order with the 1950s when Cuba had approximately 10 percent year-round unemployment and 25 percent of the labor force worked less than half the year. For the poor masses of Cubans, 96 pesos per month year round was a monumental gain. The second policy that raised living standards for the less well-paid was the provision of free social services. In the early years after the victory, Castro redirected much of the national budget toward establishing cradle-to-grave social welfare: education, health care, rent, transportation, housing, retirement benefits, and vacations.

Establishment of the socialist variant of the welfare state must be seen in the context of the major economic problems of the 1960s, which set back Cuba's development, caused aggravating shortages of food and other essentials as well as consumer goods, and ultimately made the island even more dependent on foreign countries than before. Fidel's Moncada Barracks approach to economic development simply did not work. His impatience to end Cuba's excessive dependence on sugar motivated a major cutback in cane planting after 1959, but a concurrent program of crash industrialization and agricultural diversification did not take up the slack as sugar revenues dwindled.

As minister of industry between 1961 and 1965, Che Guevara experimented with moral incentives and various kinds of planning and market strategies, honestly attempting to revolutionize the norms of work and production in pursuit of communism and the "New Cuban Man." However, his goals were thwarted by the hard realities of imbedded attitudes, infrastructural weaknesses, heavy defense expenditures, and a damaging U.S. economic blockade. Reacting to the failed plans of the early 1960s, in 1963 Fidel reversed his approach to sugar, extending plantings and setting the implausible goal of a 10 million ton harvest in 1970 — nearly twice the average harvest of the 1950s. Having made the 10 million tons the national priority of the late 1960s, Fidel directed all available investment capital and labor to sugar, weakening the recently established industrial and agricultural enterprises. By the 1970s the period of greatest experimentation was over and modest economic growth resumed.

The economic failures of the 1960s prevented the full development of social services for all Cubans, especially those in remote rural areas. Nonetheless, with full-time, year-round employment available at fixed wages and a host of free social services developed as fully as austere conditions permitted, a large share of Cuba's population, possibly a majority, was materially much better off after a few years of revolution than it had been under the old order. Despite the imperfections of the system and the glaring shortages that required the establishment of rationing in 1962, life improved markedly in terms of health, nutrition, housing, educational opportunity, and economic security. The redistribution of resources threatened the wealthy and the better-off middle classes, of course; the majority of the upper class and substantial numbers of the middle class chose exile over loss of status and, for many, a greatly reduced standard of living. Those who stayed, even those among the more highly paid groups, were leveled. This picture of changes in living standards in revolutionary Cuba sums up the social revolution: It took from the rich and the comfortable and gave to the poor and needy. Even though the Cuban economy failed to develop as projected, the revolution was an austere success. It was this redistribution of societal goods, not the statistics on economic performance, that made the Cuban Revolution so appealing to millions of Latin Americans.

THE REVOLUTION IN FOREIGN AFFAIRS

The domestic revolution and the revolution in international relations were closely intertwined. Such a close connection between domestic and foreign policy was nothing new: Throughout Cuba's republican history, U.S. dominance closely circumscribed Cuban governments' freedom of action in domestic policy. So long as Cuba's economic health depended on favorable U.S. sugar tariffs and quotas, no government could afford to antagonize Washington with policies seriously detrimental to U.S. business interests in Cuba. This meant that any legislation granting labor benefits, raising taxes, regulating utility rates, or in any way affecting the profits or security of the ubiquitous American companies had to be moderate or, as in several cases, had to remain on the books without enforcement. As demonstrated in 1933, reformist governments were not welcome.

Adding to this historical constraint on reform in Cuba was the Cold War mentality that increasingly shaped U.S. foreign policy after World War II. In the era of the perceived communist threat, Washington viewed reform movements in Latin America with suspicion or hostility and in several cases opposed them with military force. The CIA-orchestrated 1954 overthrow of the progressive Arbenz government in Guatemala was an instructive example of U.S. reaction to a reformist government considered too close to the communists.

Despite the connections between the revolutions in domestic and foreign affairs, one should not conclude that one drove the other. Castro took power convinced that Cuba needed both a social revolution and a release from its historic subservience to the United States, and he quickly set out to achieve both. The timing of domestic events inevitably affected the timing of developments in international relations, and vice versa; but Castro's commitment to creating a new Cuba clearly involved both arenas.

The agrarian reform law was the first substantive issue to drive a wedge between Cuba and the United States, but its impact was heightened by the already tense climate of relations resulting from provocations by both sides. In addition to the mass executions of Batista officials and Fidel's open domination of the government, Castro's enormous popularity in Latin America also made Washington nervous. Castro aided exile invasions of Panama, Nicaragua, and Haiti, but denied it; however, he acknowledged responsibility for a thwarted invasion of the Dominican Republic in June 1959 and promised more efforts to export his revolution. Reports of Fidel's cooperation with the PSP gave U.S. officials additional grounds for concern.

Meanwhile Washington contributed to the provocations. From early 1959 Cuban exiles, at first primarily Batista supporters and officials, conducted air and sea raids from Florida unhindered by U.S. authorities. During his April visit, Fidel was continually harassed by questions about his possible communist inclinations — questions that were surely legitimate but that reminded Fidel of the United States' pretensions to veto power in Cuban politics. U.S. officials, among them Vice-President Richard Nixon, openly urged the Eisenhower administration to take a strong stand against Castro. In December, Secretary of State Christian Herter publicly hinted of possible cuts in Cuba's sugar quota, thus invoking the long-established levers of control over Cuba. What

Washington did not realize, however, was that its use of economic leverage and military threats, rather than bullying Fidel into submission, only reaffirmed what he knew had to be changed in Cuba's economy and its foreign relations.

The first concrete step in Cuba's realignment in international relations came when Soviet Deputy Prime Minister Anastas Mikoyan visited Cuba in February 1960 to sign a large-scale trade and loan agreement with Castro. Tensions with Washington escalated in early March when the French ship *La Coubre,* delivering arms from Belgium, blew up in Havana harbor killing 75 dock workers and wounding 200; Fidel accused the United States of sabotage. On March 17 President Eisenhower approved a CIA plan to train and equip an army of Cuban exiles for guerrilla action on the island or an invasion patterned after the CIA-orchestrated invasion of Guatemala. The CIA plan, intended as a clandestine operation, promptly became an open secret when recruitment of exiles began.

Between April and October 1960, skirmishing gave way to all-out economic warfare. When the first shipment of Soviet-supplied oil arrived in April, the American-owned refineries, with the backing of the U.S. government, refused to process the crude. After a standoff, Castro expropriated the refineries between June 29 and July 2. On July 6 Eisenhower, invoking powers granted by a law passed just a few days earlier, cancelled the Cuban sugar quota for the remainder of 1960 — some 700,000 tons. In response to that measure, Castro completed the expropriation of all U.S. holdings on the island. This bold action locked in the collision course that was already set.

At the time of the expropriations, the United States was experiencing its periodic campaign paralysis. While the Nixon-Kennedy campaign focused heavily on Cuba, the Eisenhower administration refrained from military action but increased diplomatic pressures against Castro. In August Eisenhower attempted unsuccessfully to have the Organization of American States (OAS) condemn Cuba. On January 2, 1961, alleging that the U.S. embassy in Havana was full of CIA operatives, Castro asked the Eisenhower administration to reduce the size of its embassy staff to the number that Cuba had in Washington. In response, Eisenhower broke diplomatic relations the following day. The incoming Kennedy administration promptly extended the economic pressure on Castro by setting the 1961 sugar quota at zero.

From the break in diplomatic relations it was only a short step to war. Although he had campaigned on getting tough with Castro, Kennedy hesitated after being informed of the CIA's training of exiles in

Guatemala. By April, two new factors pushed him toward action. The use of Guatemalan territory for training the exile army was becoming a volatile issue in Guatemala; thus despite its strong anti-Castro sentiment, the government of Miguel Ydígoras Fuentes began pressing Washington to remove the irritant. Concurrently, U.S. intelligence learned that Cuban pilots training in Czechoslovakia to fly Soviet MiGs were scheduled to return shortly to Cuba, combat-ready and with their new planes. The necessity of dealing with an expanded and modernized air force would mean more overt U.S. involvement than Kennedy wanted. Thus after extensive debate among his advisors and escalating pressure from some, on April 5 Kennedy decided to strike; five days later, the invasion force moved to its embarkation point in Nicaragua.

The Bay of Pigs operation had primary and secondary objectives. The first, reminiscent of Fidel's own Moncada Barracks approach, was to set off a general uprising against Castro that would result in his rapid overthrow. This objective rested on assumptions of Castro's lack of popular support and of a much stronger opposition than existed. The secondary goal, to be sought if the first failed, was to capture and hold sufficient territory to allow the landing of a Cuban government-in-exile that would then call for U.S. aid in a civil war against Castro. The operation was designed to appear as a purely Cuban exile affair, with no U.S. involvement.

The CIA plan failed in both objectives. Estimates of the strength of the opposition to Castro, apparently projected from exile attitudes, from the existence of a sizeable guerrilla force in the Sierra de Escambray, and from the activities of several small resistance groups, were greatly exaggerated. Moreover, having expected U.S. military action for several months, Castro was prepared for the invasion. He had created a 200,000-man militia to back the army. In September 1960 he had called for the creation of Committees for the Defense of the Revolution (CDRs) to exercise "revolutionary collective vigilance"; these mass organizations had grown rapidly and spread throughout the island by the time of the invasion.[8] Finally, upon learning of the imminence of the invasion he arrested over 100,000 people of questionable loyalty to forestall collaboration with the invaders. Thus the hoped-for popular rising against Castro did not even start.

The secondary objective also failed, owing to miscalculations and the constraints on U.S. involvement imposed by the official line that the invasion was a Cuban exercise. The greatest miscalculation was that 1,400 men could succeed against Castro's army and militia. Nonetheless, as a prelude to invasion, planes with Cuban markings bombed air fields on April 15 to take out the tiny air force. Cuban spokesmen immediately denounced the bombing in the United Nations as a U.S. action, which the Kennedy administration denied. But fearing more adverse publicity and a strong international reaction, Kennedy cancelled a second raid, scheduled for the following morning, despite the failure of the first bombing to eliminate all of Castro's air power. Thus when Brigade 2506 hit Girón beach at the Bay of Pigs on April 17, it was met not only by troops but by planes, which sank two supply ships of the exile flotilla and pinned down the landing party in swamps. Over 1,100 of the invaders surrendered by April 20, to be held captive for 20 months until ransomed by U.S. shipments of food and medicines. In addition to humiliating the United States, the Bay of Pigs fiasco strengthened Fidel's support and control in Cuba, heightened his popularity in Latin America, and accelerated Cuba's realignment with the Soviet Union.

The revolution in Cuba's international relations was complete by late 1962, when the United States and the Soviet Union came to the brink of nuclear war over the placement of Soviet nuclear missiles in Cuba earlier that year. From the perspective of global nuclear strategy, Cuba offered the Soviets their first opportunity to deploy short-range missiles capable of striking the United States and offsetting the U.S. advantage of missile sites in Europe. For Castro, they represented protection against further U.S. aggression. Upon learning of the missiles' deployment, Kennedy placed a naval blockade around Cuba to intercept a Soviet convoy bringing additional missiles to the island. The world watched tensely as the Soviet fleet steamed toward the blockade until, at the last minute, the ships turned back. Premier Khrushchev subsequently agreed to remove the missiles already installed; in return, the United States pledged not to invade Cuba. The Soviet-Cuban alliance was firm.

The years from 1962 through 1968 were years of testing the alliance. Always an ardent nationalist, Fidel was not content for Cuba to fall from the eagle's talons into an equally dominant bear's hug. Thus for the next six years, Fidel and his regime gave various signals that despite owing its survival to Soviet intervention and a growing reliance on Soviet economic aid, Cuba enjoyed independence in foreign policy.

The major independent line was Castro's active support of revolution in Latin America — a policy that countered the traditional Soviet approach of working gradually to build communist parties and allies for revolution at some future time. In addition to exhorting revolutionaries to act, Fidel offered material aid, training, and financing to insurrectionary groups throughout Latin America. In 1966 he hosted the Tricontinental Congress, a conference of revolutionary governments and organizations from Latin America, Africa, and Asia whose purpose was to accelerate revolution throughout the Third World. The following year Castro established the Latin American Solidarity Organization (Organización Latino Americana de Solidaridad, OLAS), a bureau of Latin American revolutionary parties and guerrilla groups provocatively designed as a parallel organization to the Washington-dominated OAS. The scope of his activities suggests that Castro may have been attempting to make Havana the seat of a third camp in international communism, along with Moscow and Beijing.

While Fidel overtly pushed the overthrow of governments, the Soviet Union attempted to maintain correct relations and to broaden its formal diplomatic contacts in Latin America so as to foster good working conditions for local communist parties. The resultant friction between Havana and Moscow surfaced in several conflicts, most notably Castro's 1962 purge of a PCC "microfaction" led by PSP veteran Aníbal Escalante and a second purge of the reinstated Escalante clique in 1968 on charges of fostering Soviet interests against those of Cuba. The testing period effectively ended in 1968, however, when Castro, to the dismay of many of his supporters, endorsed the Soviet intervention that ended Alexander Dubcek's "Prague Spring" in Czechoslovakia. To many observers, this gesture of subservience to Moscow signalled Castro's reluctant abandonment of the quest for an independent foreign policy.

Cuba strengthened its ties to Moscow during the 1970s. It joined the Soviet-led trade organization COMECON in 1972, cementing the island's role as sugar purveyor to the East Bloc. Soviet aid became increasingly important to sustaining Cuba's economy. While Fidel had his own reasons for involvement in Africa — Cuba's historic and ethnic ties to Africa, the opportunity to pursue revolution in a promising setting, and the aggrandizement of Cuba's international power — the dispatch of 50,000 Cuban troops to Angola, Ethiopia, and other African countries in the mid-1970s was widely interpreted as Cuba's playing the role of Soviet surrogate. Overall, as the 1970s wore on Cuba exhibited more of the traits of a Soviet client state.

Despite the ultimate failure of his aspirations for a truly independent Cuban foreign policy, Castro had achieved more by the end of the missile crisis than any Cuban or other Latin American could have imagined possible. A militarily weak island republic 90 miles from Key West, historically dominated by the United States, had rejected its master and won the confrontation with it. In fulfilling the anti-imperialist aspirations of the Latin American left, Castro set an example that enflamed nationalist sentiment throughout the hemisphere. For many years the fact that Cuba had failed to achieve full sovereignty was far less important to Latin American progressives than the fact that Castro had broken the ties of subservience to Washington and Wall Street — ties stronger in the Cuban case than they were in any other Latin American country.

THE STYLE OF THE REVOLUTION

The popularity of the Cuban Revolution in Latin America was based primarily on the concrete accomplishments of the first few years: throwing off the yoke of U.S. dominance and instituting drastic changes in Cuba's economy and society for the benefit of the masses. But dramatic as these developments were, they alone do not explain the enthusiasm that Castro's revolution generated in Latin America. The other ingredient that made the Cuban Revolution such an intoxicating brew was the style of the revolution — the charisma of its leader, the visible and enthusiastic support of the majority of Cubans for Castro, the David and Goliath character of Fidel's challenge to the United States, and the élan of the revolution's programs and policies. This flair contributed not only to the revolution's initial impact in Latin America but also to sustaining its popularity long after the early accomplishments began to be overshadowed by the loss of independence to the Soviet Union, the lackluster economic record, and the prolongation of Castro's personal dictatorship.

Castro's credentials as a charismatic leader are well established. Even after 30-plus years in power, he is a spellbinding orator and a dominant presence in any setting. During his early years in office he repeatedly demonstrated his remarkable ability to inspire crowds with emotional, extemporaneous four- or five-hour speeches rallying support for volunteer harvest labor or calling for vigilance against Yankee aggression. His exhortations to more sacrifice and the deferment of rewards were the sustenance that kept the revolution going during the period of worst economic hardships in the 1960s. Fidel's ascetic style, his proclivity for personal contacts with ordinary Cubans, his physical size and athletic prowess, the martial figure that he projected with khakis, boots, beard, and cigar — all of these traits complemented Fidel's intelligence, perseverance, flair for publicity, and extraordinary powers of persuasion to make him one of the twentieth century's most fascinating and effective political leaders.

The David and Goliath quality of Castro's challenge to Washington was another element that cemented Fidel's power at home and gained sympathy and support for the revolution throughout Latin America.

Through his defiance of the United States, which often amounted to taunting, open provocation, his refusal to back down under escalating U.S. pressure, the nationalization of U.S. assets, and finally the defeat of the Washington-sponsored Bay of Pigs invasion, Castro acquired the international stature of a second Bolívar — a new liberator of Latin America. His successful challenge of the hegemonic power of the hemisphere struck a sympathetic chord throughout Latin America, where almost every country had a primary symbol of U.S. imperialism — United Fruit Company in Central America, International Petroleum Company in Peru, Anaconda and Kenecott Copper in Chile, the canal in Panama, and so on — against which nationalist politicians railed but rarely acted. Fidel's actions against the United States, then, combined with his flamboyant and provocative style of pulling Uncle Sam's beard, gave vicarious satisfaction to the millions who possessed even a modestly nationalistic outlook.

Another characteristic that made the Cuban Revolution so influential in Latin America was the active support that Castro's government enjoyed within Cuba. The massive turnouts for Fidel's speeches and the obvious enthusiasm of the crowds for the revolution and its policies were but a partial barometer of popular support. More impressive was the widespread participation of millions of Cubans in the tasks of the revolution such as volunteer labor, the literacy campaign, and the CDRs, which continued to grow after the Bay of Pigs invasion until some 2 million, or half the island's adult population, were enrolled by 1964; as late as 1985, some 5 million Cubans were CDR members. After the invasion crisis the CDRs became more routinized and diversified in their functions, assuming the roles of neighborhood civic association, organizer of volunteer labor, overseer of the rationing system, and dispenser of justice in petty matters while continuing their original mission of exercising vigilance and enforcing conformity.

In addition to the ongoing work of the CDRs, volunteer labor was solicited as needs arose. Castro declared 1961 the "year of education" and launched a drive to eradicate illiteracy in Cuba. Some 271,000 volunteers, mainly students, spent all or part of nine months in every corner of the island instructing the illiterate 24 percent of the adult population in the fundamentals of reading and writing. Their efforts reportedly reduced the illiteracy rate to under 4 percent, a respectable rate even for developed countries. With the disruption that accompanied the nationalization of agriculture and later with the rapid expansion of cane, great amounts of volunteer labor were needed for harvest. Construction of the Havana Green Belt also depended on volunteer labor.

Observers have raised questions about volunteer labor in revolutionary Cuba. Did individuals volunteer out of love of the revolution, or were they motivated by minor privileges or self-promotion? Was extra labor really volunteered or subtly coerced? Regardless of the answers, the fact is that in the 1960s millions of Cubans participated in their government's work. This is the picture that reached Latin America where the poor and the disenfranchised — a majority in most countries — saw government as the oppressor at the service of vested interests. They could hardly avoid being favorably impressed by their perceptions of a government that, by contrast to their own, enjoyed the active support and benefitted from the volunteered sweat of its citizens.

Castro's impatience, his Moncada Barracks approach to getting things done, carried over to the revolution and contributed to the style that made the Cuban Revolution appealing to the Latin American masses. While Fidel's impatience for economic development, especially evident in the failed crash industrialization program, was a dysfunctional approach to economic management, other aspects of his élan were well received. The speed of the agrarian reform, the boldness of the literacy campaign, and the brashness of the nationalization of U.S. investments gave the revolution its momentum and sent out the message that nothing was impossible if the political will and the support of the masses were in place. Despite the prevailing sense of urgency in the Latin American capitals and Washington, the pace of change in Cuba contrasted with the endless technical studies, budget reviews, and political compromises needed for the elected governments that predominated in the early 1960s to move from rhetoric to action. The contrast favored Cuba.

Fidel was well aware of the value of style in selling his revolution abroad. Throughout the struggle against Batista he had repeatedly demonstrated his mastery of public relations skills, and once in power his use of television, symbols, and his own charismatic powers helped him to portray the revolution in the most positive light. Castro announced his major policy moves in symbolic settings and in dramatic speeches. Newspaper, magazine, and book publishing became servants of the state and of Castro's publicity needs — much of their production aimed for export. Radio Havana set up a special section to broadcast throughout Latin America, not only in Spanish and Portuguese but also in the Indian languages spoken by significant numbers, such as Quechua and Aymará. No opportunity was lost to bring student, labor, and other groups to Cuba to show off the socialist paradise in the tropics.

In sum, the impact of the Cuban Revolution, while based on the substance of change in Cuba, was greatly enhanced by the style that characterized the Castro regime during the 1960s and beyond. There is no doubt that the same concrete accomplishments, carried out by faceless bureaucrats under the direction of a gray leader ascendant owing to his expertise in intraparty maneuvering, would have excited the masses of Latin America considerably less than Castro's revolution did. It was evident at every turn that Fidel and the revolution were inseparable.

NOTES

1. Edward González, *Cuba Under Castro: The Limits of Charisma* (Boston: Houghton Mifflin, 1974).

2. Martin Kenner and James Petras, eds., *Fidel Castro Speaks* (New York: Grove Press, 1969), 74.

3. Quoted in Thomas L. Karnes, ed., *Readings in the Latin American Policy of the United States* (Tucson: University of Arizona Press, 1972), 280.

4. Lee Lockwood, *Castro's Cuba, Cuba's Fidel* (New York: Vintage Books, 1969), 160.

5. Ibid., 147.

6. Jorge I. Domínguez, *Cuba: Order and Revolution* (Cambridge, Mass.: Harvard University Press, 1978), 144.

7. Hugh Thomas, *Cuba: The Pursuit of Freedom* (New York: Harper and Row, 1971), 1223.

8. Richard R. Fagen, *The Transformation of Political Culture in Cuba* (Stanford, Calif.: Stanford University Press, 1969), 169.

3

Fidelismo and the Radicalization of Latin American Politics

Fidel Castro's improbable victory over Batista sent a tremor throughout Latin America at the beginning of 1959. During the next three years, each bold stroke in the social transformation of Cuba and each clash with the United States set off an aftershock. The example of Castro's actions combined with his and Che Guevara's strident calls for revolution in the hemisphere had an immediate and profound effect on Latin American politics. This potent force was *fidelismo*.

Reduced to essentials, fidelismo was simply the attitude that revolution should be pursued immediately. The most visible symptom of fidelismo was a dramatic growth of demands for change. In virtually every country, the intensity of political activity increased after Castro's victory as new actors, new social issues, and more aggressive challenges to the existing order came to the fore.

The connection between the Cuban Revolution and the political ferment in Latin America was explicit. Fidel Castro and the Cuban Revolution dominated discussion and debate in the press, on the streets, in the universities; the slogan *"Cuba sí, Yanqui no"* became ubiquitous on the walls of Latin America. The term *"fidelista"* and its synonym *"castrista"* entered the political lexicon as new movements appeared and existing ones embraced the new faith in revolutionary action.

Governments blamed Castro for the political agitation affecting their countries. They were often correct in alleging Cuban interference in their internal affairs, for Castro mounted invasions, trained guerrillas, sent propaganda and money to fidelista groups, and occasionally dispatched arms and even personnel to support guerrilla activities. Nor was he reticent in calling for revolution, as in his 26th of July speech of 1960, when he threatened to "convert the Cordillera of the Andes to the Sierra Maestra of the Hemisphere."[1] Yet the expulsion of Cuban diplomats, the severing of diplomatic relations, the banning of travel to Cuba, and other measures designed to restrict contact with the island generally failed to dampen the high levels of political mobilization. The example of Cuba, translated into fidelismo, was the driving force of political destabilization throughout Latin America. As Che Guevara observed: "Each time that an impudent people cries out for liberation, Cuba is accused; and it is true in a sense that Cuba is guilty, because Cuba has shown the way. . . . This Cuban example is bad, a very bad example."[2]

INITIAL IMPACT OF THE CUBAN REVOLUTION

The Cuban Revolution occurred at a time of civilian ascendancy in Latin American governments. The mid- to late 1950s, labeled by an observer as "the twilight of the tyrants," witnessed the demise of Perón in Argentina (1955), Peru's Odría (1956), Colombia's Rojas Pinilla (1957), and Pérez Jiménez of Venezuela (1958).[3] With the exception of Castro's own emerging personalist regime, only five dictators remained after the fall of Batista, all in small, poor countries. Four of these regimes were long-term personal or family dictatorships: those of the Somoza family in Nicaragua; François "Papa Doc" Duvalier in Haiti; Rafael Trujillo in the Dominican Republic; and Alfredo Stroessner in Paraguay. The fifth was a military-dominated regime in El Salvador. Despite these exceptions to the democratic trend, the proportion of Latin America's population living under elected governments had never been higher than in 1959.

Owing to the predominance of civilian governments, Latin America was particularly vulnerable to destabilization by the impact of the Cuban Revolution. With the exception of Chile, Uruguay, and Mexico, Latin American countries were subject to periodic coups and periods of military government. Bolivia, for example, averaged nearly two overthrow attempts per year in its first century of republican history, a pattern that persisted into the 1950s; Venezuela had experienced a total of three years of civilian government in the twentieth century and only a few more since its independence in 1821; and the first transition from one elected government to another in Guatemala's history did not occur until January 1991. While Bolivia, Venezuela, and Guatemala are among the extremes, civilian political institutions in most countries had shallow roots and thus were ill prepared to withstand the tempest unleashed by the Cuban Revolution. At the same time, the armed forces in those countries were accustomed to intervening when crises created disorder and weakened the civilians' ability to govern. Thus when fidelismo swept over Latin America, most of the civilian regimes were endangered by the surge in

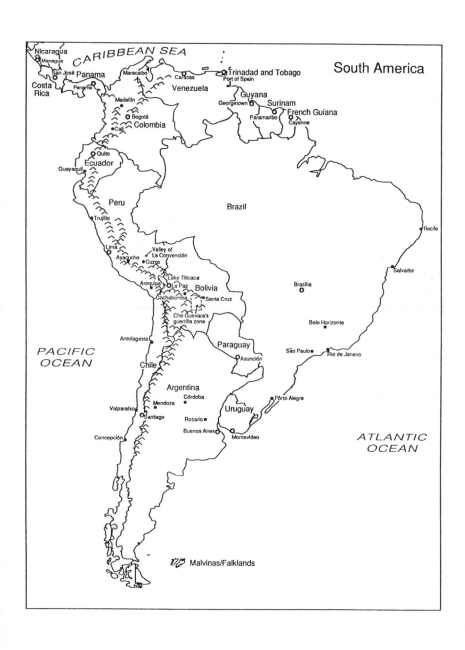

South America

demands for reform, the political awakening of previously inert groups, and the attempts to overthrow them by the Cuban guerrilla method.

Most of the individual components of the political turmoil so evident after 1958 were not new: Student demonstrations, revolutionary propaganda, strikes, coup attempts, and exile invasions were part and parcel of the Latin American political scene. But the intensification of political conflict in the early 1960s propelled many governments toward collapse. Thus in several countries, the political ferment generated by fidelismo led to preemptive military coups to remove civilian governments considered too sympathetic toward or too ineffectual against fidelista forces.

One of those governments was that of Ecuadorean President Carlos Arosemena, overthrown in July 1963 on charges of communist sympathies after the formation of Castroite groups, strikes, land invasions, and guerrilla outbreaks created a climate of unaccustomed turmoil. The military junta that overthrew Arosemena banned the communist party and vowed to wipe out "pro-Castro terrorist bands."[4] In Guatemala, the Castro era opened with persistent rumors of Cuban-sponsored exile invasions, which led President Eisenhower to dispatch navy ships to patrol Central American waters in November 1960. Meanwhile, frequent pro-Castro rallies, guerrilla activity, and intermittent government impositions of states of siege underscored popular support for Cuban-style revolution. Finally, the impeccably-credentialed right wing Guatemalan president, General Miguel Ydígoras Fuentes, was overthrown in May 1963 by more conservative officers in reaction to the ever-mounting pressure from fidelistas and their supporters. Similar circumstances led to military coups in Honduras and the Dominican Republic in 1963.

Despite the magnitude of the challenge, the majority of civilian governments weathered the storm of the early 1960s. Governments with the strongest institutional bases, and hence the greatest ability to resolve the conflicts created or exacerbated by the Cuban Revolution, were among the least affected. In traditionally democratic Uruguay, pro- and anti-Castro demonstrations were common, a new fidelista party bearing the acronym FIDEL was formed, labor and students grew more militant, and the government cracked down on what it called communist propaganda from Cuba. Nonetheless, the government's survival was not threatened until late in the 1960s when the Tupamaro guerrillas took up arms. In Chile, another bastion of constitutional democracy, the strongly established political system was able to absorb the initial impact of the Cuban Revolution with relatively little instability. However, the example of the Cuban Revolution — especially land reform — contributed to a leftward movement of the Chilean electorate that brought a reformist government to power in 1964 and culminated with the election of Marxist Salvador Allende in 1970.

Mexico, where the broad-based Institutional Revolutionary Party (Partido Revolucionario Institucional, PRI) had governed for 30 years as heir to the great revolution of 1910, was only mildly affected by the Cuban Revolution. Mexico's rejection of Washington's Cuba policy — Mexico was the only OAS member that did not break relations with Havana — spared the government some of the wrath directed toward those governments that supported U.S. proposals for sanctions against Castro. Nonetheless, President Adolfo López Mateos cracked down on demonstrators following a general increase in student and other leftist activity, especially after the Bay of Pigs invasion. Noteworthy developments in the early years after Castro's victory included the founding of the fidelista National Liberation Movement (Movimiento de Liberación Nacional, MLN) and the establishment of a new national peasant movement to compete with the PRI-affiliated organization. Significant guerrilla activity did not appear in Mexico until the early 1970s.

The other civilian governments experienced varying degrees of instability in the early 1960s. In Peru, land invasions, establishment of numerous pro-Castro groups and newspapers, bank robberies to finance revolution, formation of a revolutionary peasant movement, and several outbreaks of guerrilla warfare punctuated the years after Castro came to power. Latin America's oldest and most influential mass-based reform party, Peru's American Popular Revolutionary Alliance (Alianza Popular Revolucionaria Americana, APRA), lost its left wing in a schism over how to respond to the Cuban Revolution. The 1962 military coup that overthrew the conservative civilian government of Manuel Prado was partially motivated by the radicalization of Peruvian politics after 1958.

In Colombia, fidelismo had a radicalizing effect on struggles already underway. Colombia had been rent by violence, primarily rural activity usually described as banditry, especially since the Bogotazo of 1948 in which popular reformist presidential candidate Jorge Eliécer Gaitán was assassinated. The years following Castro's victory witnessed an increase in both urban and rural violence: Rural violence alone was estimated to be costing over 200 lives monthly in 1962. The formation of fidelista-style fronts was largely an attempt to channel the endemic violence into explicitly revolutionary movements.

The democratic left Democratic Action (Acción Democrática, AD) government of Rómulo Betancourt came to power in Venezuela just six weeks after Castro's victory. What began as a political friendship between Betancourt and Castro soon became a bitter rivalry as the two approaches to change became competitive — Venezuela's with U.S. moral and financial backing. Thus despite a solid record of achievement in reform, including an ambitious agrarian reform program, Betancourt's government not only struggled against Venezuela's long history of dictatorships but also against a fidelista campaign of guerrilla warfare, urban sabotage, strikes, coup attempts, and constant agitation. Although he survived and turned the government over to an elected successor in 1963, Betancourt relied heavily on the use of martial law to make reform prevail over revolution in Venezuela.

Fidelismo played a role in compounding an already tense political climate in Argentina. Following the military removal of Juan Perón in 1955, the powerful *peronista* unions and party apparatus continually battled the military and the succeeding moderate government of Arturo Frondizi to recover their lost political rights. So deep and bitter was the pro- and anti-Perón division in Argentina — a fissure that continues today — and so fierce the battle that the influence of fidelismo was subsumed within that struggle. Nonetheless, influenced by the Cuban Revolution, the Peronist resistance embraced rural guerrilla warfare as one of its strategies and launched two rural focos — the 1959 Uturunco movement in Tucumán and the 1963–64 foco of the People's Guerrilla Army (Ejército Guerrillero del Pueblo, EGP). In 1962, weakened by the Peronist–anti-Peronist struggle exacerbated by the impact of fidelismo, the Frondizi government fell to a military coup.

Along with the usual pro-Castro demonstrations and the founding of fidelista action groups, a guerrilla movement broke out in Panama in April 1959. An invasion force of Panamanian exiles from Cuba landed in the same month after the United States, apprised of the plot, had sent patrol boats and military supplies to the Panamanian government. Castro denied having sanctioned the attack. Given the thorough U.S. dominance of Panama as a result of the canal's presence, much of the ferment touched off by the Cuban Revolution was directed toward the United States rather than at the Panamanian government itself. In November 1959 the worst anti-American riots in years rocked the country as Panamanians demanded sovereignty over the canal zone, and nationalist sentiment continued to grow through the 1960s and 1970s.

In Bolivia, where peasants had received land in the 1952 revolution, fidelismo had relatively little impact. It spawned mini-factions, accentuated party competition, and encouraged the left and the tin miners' union to more aggressive positions. Costa Rica, which had fought a civil war in 1948 and thereafter attained a good measure of political stability, likewise experienced little of the turmoil that beset other countries.

Latin America's dictatorships did not escape the impact of fidelismo. Encouraged by the overthrow of Batista, opponents of the dictatorships redoubled their efforts to topple the regimes in Nicaragua, the Dominican Republic, Haiti, Paraguay, and El Salvador. Buttressed by the proscription of serious opposition, a low level of party and union activity, censorship of news and books, and possessing well-oiled machinery of repression, these governments were usually able to snuff out internal dissent with relative ease. The exception was El Salvador, where progressive officers overthrew the conservative regime of José María Lemus in October 1960. The new government, however, was unable to consolidate its power and was replaced after four months by a stridently anti-Castro military-dominated regime.

Unable to mount effective movements inside their countries, opponents of the other four dictatorships had to rely primarily on invasions from abroad that Cuba encouraged and, in at least one case, directly controlled. In all instances the exile invasions were defeated before they could ignite a popular uprising or carve out liberated zones from which to wage guerrilla war. Nonetheless, the number of invasions and minor uprisings — six against Stroessner in 1960 alone — kept these dictatorial regimes in a state of alert for several years. The dictators proved resilient: Apart from Lemus, only Trujillo fell during the early years of the Cuban Revolution, the victim of an assassination in 1961. The Somoza regime lasted until 1979, the Duvaliers until 1986, and the Stroessner dictatorship finally ended in 1989. These were the regimes that Che Guevara, in *Guerrilla Warfare,* assured the world would be the next to fall after Batista.

Taken as a whole, Latin America in the first few years after Castro's victory experienced political turmoil of a level associated only with major crises. Prior to the Cuban Revolution there had been two other waves of political unrest that affected most Latin American countries: that caused by the economic dislocations of World War I, and that set off by the impact of the Great Depression. The level and intensity of the political mobilization following the Cuban Revolution were greater than those of the first two cases, and the impact of fidelismo was more widespread throughout Latin America. Moreover, the stakes were higher in 1959: the very economic and social foundations of Latin America were at issue. The titles of journalistic and academic studies of Latin America in the 1960s reflected the prevailing view of a continent in the throes of revolution: *Latin America: Evolution or Explosion?; Latin America: The Eleventh Hour;* and *Latin America: World in Revolution.*[5]

RISE OF THE AGRARIAN REFORM ISSUE

One of the most far-reaching effects of the Cuban Revolution was to make agrarian reform a pressing political issue in most of Latin America. The example of Cuba's agrarian reform program was the main but not the only factor influencing the Latin American countries to debate, legislate, and in several instances to implement agrarian reform in the 1960s. Castro consistently portrayed his revolution as an agrarian revolution, not only in its results but in its origins. Minimizing the roles and contributions of the urban resistance and the sugar proletariat in the overthrow of Batista, the official version of the struggle elevated the peasants of the Sierra Maestra to a level second only to that of the guerrillas themselves. Fidel certainly had needed and received peasant support, and late in the campaign, in October 1958, he had decreed the agrarian reform law of the Sierra Maestra to reward the peasants and consolidate their loyalty. Peasant support was thus linked to the success of the Cuban model of rural guerrilla warfare, and such peasant support, as in Cuba, could be won by promises of land. Che Guevara explicitly advised guerrillas to exploit "the age-old hunger of the peasant for the land on which he works or wishes to work" by raising "the banner of agrarian reform."[6] Thus the very existence of Latin America's traditional systems of land tenure, which denied ownership and decent living standards to the vast majority of the rural population, came to be seen as a liability, a condition that the fidelistas would exploit.

Agrarian reform, designed to achieve a more equitable distribution of land, improve living conditions for the rural masses, and promote economic development, thus came to be an issue that could not be ignored after 1958. The extreme left promised radical agrarian reform in order to mobilize peasant support for revolution. Reformist parties pushed land redistribution as a means of attacking the power of the large landowners and the national oligarchies as well as a step toward social justice and economic development. Acknowledging the potency of the issue, many conservative parties and interest groups embraced token to moderate agrarian reform as a means of preempting the revolutionaries and reformers. The United States also embraced agrarian reform as a means of countering Cuban influence and made it a centerpiece of the Alliance for Progress.

Agrarian reform was not new to Latin America in 1959. The Mexican Revolution of 1910 had launched an agrarian reform program that continues today. Chile and Colombia had established modest programs of land subdivision in the 1920s and 1930s. The Arbenz administration in

Guatemala initiated agrarian reform in the early 1950s; its expropriation of United Fruit Company land was a major cause of U.S. intervention to overthrow the government. Bolivia experienced a thorough land redistribution in the wake of its 1952 revolution. Economists in the United Nations' Economic Commission for Latin America (ECLA) had been preaching throughout the 1950s that agrarian reform was an essential prerequisite to the region's economic development. But it was the Cuban Revolution, by linking revolution to land hunger, that brought a new sense of urgency to the agrarian reform issue throughout Latin America.

Latin America's 1960 population of 208 million was 56 percent rural, defined as living in the countryside or in towns of approximately 2,000 or fewer. Some 52 percent of the entire Latin American population worked in agriculture. The agricultural population was unevenly spread through the region. In Argentina, the country with the most productive agricultural sector, only 20 percent of the labor force worked in agriculture, in Uruguay 21 percent, and in Chile 30 percent. At the opposite extreme, the labor forces of Haiti, Honduras, and Guatemala were 83, 70, and 67 percent agricultural, respectively.

In general, land tenure in Latin America was skewed into patterns in which a relatively small number of large holdings, or *latifundios*, co-existed with large numbers of tiny plots, or *minifundios*. Representative examples in the mid-1960s include Chile, where the largest 7 percent of the farms occupied 81 percent of the land while the smallest 37 percent of the properties accounted for only 0.2 percent of agricultural surface; Brazil, where 60 percent of the land was held by 5 percent of the owners while 23 percent owned only 0.5 percent of the land; and Guatemala, where 0.1 percent of the owners held 41 percent of the agricultural surface alongside the 88 percent who owned 14 percent of the land. These figures describe a land tenure system characterized by large landowners' dominance of the best lands, with smallholders capable of subsistence production or less holding inferior lands; the U.S. or Western European-type family farm was notable by its scarcity in most countries. Land tenure figures of course do not indicate the great numbers of landless who worked year-round or seasonally on the large holdings or squatted on the public domain. The main exceptions to the rule of extremes in land tenure patterns were Mexico and Bolivia, where revolutions led to the destruction of the traditionally dominant haciendas in many regions, and Costa Rica, which had evolved a reasonably balanced land tenure pattern through its peculiar historical processes.

Working and living conditions for the landless masses varied greatly among countries and among regions within countries. In settings of modern commercial agriculture, such as Argentina, Uruguay, the Peruvian coast, or the banana districts of Central America's Caribbean coast, wage labor prevailed and some of the work force was unionized; while actual wages and living conditions were usually low compared to those of urban workers, some of the more onerous and degrading working conditions were absent. By contrast, in highland Ecuador and Peru the systems of *huasipungueaje* and *pongueaje* were still entrenched: There, resident workers on backward haciendas not only owed most of their working time to the *patrón* in exchange for minimal grazing or cropping rights, but also had personal service obligations in the owner's rural or city houses and no rights of tenure or appeal. These Indian workers, moreover, were often held in virtual slavery through debt peonage. In Guatemala, where racial and linguistic differences shaped landowner-peasant relations as in the Andes, conditions for the Indian peasants were not much better. In Chile the traditional system of *inquilinaje*, while not as brutal as rural labor in the Indian countries, had been tightened in the late nineteenth and twentieth centuries to become much more exploitive.

Landless rural laborers, excluding those employed in the modern sector, were the most thoroughly marginalized of the Latin American populations. For the great majority of landless workers and for many subsistence or sub-subsistence smallholders who depended on large landowners for seasonal work and credit, political participation was either nonexistent or meaningless. Literacy and property requirements, and the simple absence of voter registrars in rural districts disenfranchised great numbers. Where a large conservative vote was important in presidential elections to offset the growing weight of the cities, landowners registered their workers and dependents and dictated their votes. The other potential avenue to political participation was union membership; however, rural unions in most of Latin America were illegal, landowner-dominated (white), or simply repressed by landowners and cooperative local authorities.

The continued political marginalization of the rural masses was crucial to the status quo in national politics as well as to landowners' uncontested control of land and labor. If given a free vote as a result of union pressures or of attaining economic independence from the patrón through land acquisition, the rural masses would undermine landowners' dispro-portionate power in national politics. If the Andean departments of Peru, the Northeast states of Brazil, or the Central Valley provinces of Chile did not elect conservative landowners or their surrogates to the national congress, where they traditionally enjoyed a veto power or at least the ability to dilute offensive legislation through coalition politics and trade-offs, the more progressive representatives of the cities and export enclaves would prevail, undoubtedly sacrificing landowners' interests.

Thus the situation was a closed circle: Lack of access to land and unions kept the rural poor disenfranchised; lack of effective political participation kept them landless, poor, and at the mercy of the landowners. The influence of the Cuban Revolution inspired fidelistas and reformers as well as some among the rural masses to try to break this deadlock; it threatened landowners not only with the loss of their land but also with the loss of their traditional political power based on exclusion. The latter would cause the diminution or even the collapse of conservative electoral power at the national level, threatening vested interests of all economic sectors.

Even while agrarian reform was debated in academic tracts, the press, and national congresses, many Latin American peasants took matters into their own hands in the 1960s and beyond. There was ample precedent for the mobilization of the rural poor after the Cuban Revolution. The second half of the nineteenth century was a period of endemic peasant rebellion, especially in the Indian countries of Latin America where landowners used new legislation and the power of the national state to wrest from the Indians their communal lands. Recovery of village lands was the driving force of the peasant movement led by Emiliano Zapata in the Mexican Revolution. In Chile rural strikes, attempts to unionize, and calls for land division appeared sporadically but persistently from 1919 onward. El Salvador experienced a massive peasant uprising against landowners in 1932, which the authorities put down with thousands of deaths; this episode is known simply as "La Matanza" (the slaughter). The Bolivian peasant uprising of 1952 followed nearly two centuries of Indian rebellions in pursuit of land and justice. Overall, no country had escaped some degree of peasant unrest expressed in land invasions, strikes, unionization efforts, or rebellion against landowners and the authorities.

However, the political awakening of rural Latin America after Castro's victory differed from the agrarian unrest that preceded it in degree and in kind. While earlier outbreaks had been primarily regional and normally local in scope, the agrarian agitation after 1958 was widely spread through Latin America. Many of the earlier agrarian movements had been politically unsophisticated: sometimes messianic, sometimes primitive *jacqueries*, sometimes localized risings based on specific narrow grievances. The situation was different by the 1960s. The advent of the cheap transistor radio put illiterate peasants in touch with the outside world for the first time and let them know about Cuba's agrarian reform. The Cuban Revolution, moreover, spurred both Marxists and reformers to proselytize among workers and smallholders, promising agrarian reform and unionization. As a result, the peasant movements of the 1960s were sometimes national in scope and were often led by non-peasants versed in the political arts.

In several cases, peasant movements became major forces in national politics. Brazil, where peasant leagues gained wide membership, will be examined separately. In Peru the peasant movement in the remote valley of La Convención became a major factor because of the example it provided for the country's millions of landless Indians. A series of strikes began in 1960 under the leadership of Hugo Blanco, a Trotskyist from nearby Cuzco, and by 1962 the region's approximately 150 peasant unions launched a series of land invasions under their own agrarian reform decree. The military government sent in troops to quell the thousands of mobilized Indians and subsequently declared the valley an agrarian reform zone in an attempt to preempt Blanco and other organizers. Despite these measures, the continuing rise of peasant militancy in Peru produced a wave of land invasions involving some 300,000 people that swept the Andean regions following the 1963 election of President Fernando Belaúnde Terry, who had campaigned on a platform of moderate agrarian reform.

The mobilization of Chilean rural workers after Castro's victory was a major factor in a dramatic leftward shift of national politics. While rural organization was not entirely new to Chile, the impact of fidelismo unleashed not only a heightened demand for land among the peasants but a fierce competition between fidelistas and the non-Marxist left to capture the large but heretofore landowner-controlled rural vote. Beginning in the early 1960s, rural Chile erupted in demonstrations for land, violence, land occupations, and the formation of labor unions in defiance of restrictive statutes. Progress in freeing the peasantry from landowner electoral control was graphically demonstrated in elections beginning in 1961. The success of the left in destroying the traditional power base of the right opened the way for the elections of Christian Democrat Eduardo Frei in 1964 and Socialist Salvador Allende in 1970.

Elsewhere the combination of rural awakening and proselytization by urban cadres contributed to the climate of agitation and instability sweeping Latin America after 1958. Yet the extent of peasant mobilization should not be exaggerated. Despite their grievances, their heightened political awareness, and the currency of the agrarian reform issue in national politics, many Latin American peasants were held back by conservative attitudes of deference and resignation that had been ingrained over the centuries. The continuance in most countries of the intimidating traditional alliance of landowner and state, with its effective powers of repression, also deterred peasants from action. Conservative attitudes, fear of reprisals, and the peasants' innate distrust of outsiders often fostered resistance to leftist organizers who ventured out from the city. And to their dismay, the guerrilla fighters who took to the hills expecting support from the downtrodden peasants were usually disappointed. Thus while peasant movements achieved substantial power in some countries, the spectre of bloody peasant revolution did not materialize.

FIDELISMO AND THE LATIN AMERICAN LEFT

At the time of the Cuban Revolution, the left in Latin America was divided among Marxist and reformist parties, unions, student federations, and professional organizations. Marxist groups included the Moscow-oriented communist parties, subject to the control of the Communist Party of the Soviet Union, which were found under various names in every country; socialist parties without binding international connections; and small Trotskyist parties and factions. The non-Marxist left included personalist parties, especially Argentina's peronistas; secular reformist parties, of which Peru's APRA, Venezuela's AD, and Mexico's PRI were prototypes; and in some countries a Christian left, the largest of which were the Chilean Christian Democratic Party (Partido Demócrata Cristiano, PDC) and Venezuela's Independent Elections Committee (Comité Pro Elecciones Independiente, COPEI). APRA, PRI, and the peronistas by 1959 were more left in rhetoric than in deed; nonetheless, they were historically reformist and retained mass followings among the poor and the working classes of their countries.

While parties, unions, and other organizations of the left were found everywhere, their strength was roughly proportionate to a country's level of development. A sizeable industrial work force and a significant middle class were prerequisites to the rise of active and influential left parties. Thus the larger countries of South America generally had more powerful Marxist and moderate left groups than were found in the less developed countries of Central America and the Caribbean.

The Cuban Revolution had an immediate positive effect on the Latin American left. The groundswell of demands for change and the radicalization of Latin America's politically participant population invigorated the left, increasing its electoral appeal and its ability to mobilize the populace for demonstrations, strikes, and other direct action. Parties and groups identifying with the Cuban Revolution stood to gain simply by waving the banner of fidelismo. Those of the non-fidelista left gained by embracing the social reforms and the anti-Yankee stance of the Cuban Revolution while rejecting its communist features.

The left did not merely wait to harvest the additional votes, membership, and support that might accrue from the radicalization of labor, intellectuals, youth, and other elements of the population who already participated in politics; it set out actively to develop followings among the politically marginalized population — especially the peasants. As noted above, the impact of fidelismo precipitated competition in rural Chile between Marxists and Christian Democrats, resulting in the unionization of thousands of the rural poor and the delivery of their votes to the left. In Brazil's Northeast, Christians and fidelistas recruited among the politically marginal peasantry, and left cadres penetrated the once-forbidden countryside of several other countries with unprecedented tenacity.

The left also cultivated the growing masses of urban poor. By the 1960s, rural to urban migration had created huge rings of slums around Latin America's large cities: Lima's *barriadas*, Santiago's *callampas*, Buenos Aires' *villas miseria*, Rio de Janeiro's *favelas*, whose residents generally belonged to a lumpen proletariat lacking regular work, access to utilities and social services, and even security of tenure for their hovels. These new city dwellers were not as marginal to politics as their rural cousins; they were sometimes courted by paternalistic politicals such as Perón, Odría, and Rojas Pinilla who traded handouts for votes. After the Cuban Revolution heightened the appetite of the unorganized urban poor for change and improvement, Marxist and reformist cadres turned more intensely to proselytizing them through establishing neighborhood organizations, staging protests for the extension of utilities and services to the slums, and directing self-help projects.

Even while boosting the left, the Cuban Revolution also dealt some setbacks to the Marxists and, to a lesser extent, to the moderates. For the Marxists, and particularly for the communist parties, Castro's spectacular moves were a challenge to their entrenched modus operandi and to their very conceptions of revolution. Since their founding, the mainline, Moscow-affiliated communist parties throughout Latin America generally followed the lead of the Soviet Communist Party in matters of strategy. With a brief hiatus, the Moscow line after 1935 was to set aside the armed struggle in favor of legal means and cooperation with progressive nonproletarian parties. Comintern policy was to build communist strength over the long run through labor union activity and coalition politics in order to have a vanguard party in place when the "objective conditions" of sufficient economic and political maturity had been reached. Because they were handy scapegoats and thus easy targets for government crackdowns, the communists often collaborated with dictators such as Batista in exchange for the legal status that allowed them to pursue organizational activities. Following Castro's victory, enthusiastic expressions of support for the Cuban Revolution by the communists would likely bring repression and the loss of their highly valued legality.

The mood in Latin America after 1958 was clearly one of impatience with the status quo, of which the orthodox communist parties were a part. Fearing the loss of the party's vanguard status as a host of new groupings appeared on the left, some communist militants pushed for a more fidelista approach. However, the party apparatus tended to be dominated by older bureaucrats, loyal to Moscow, who valued security and hewed to the gradualist strategy that deferred insurrection indefinitely. The dilemma grew worse for the communist parties after Fidel took his unorthodox revolution into the communist camp, for his views then enjoyed the patina of communist legitimacy even when they directly contradicted the word from Moscow. And the word from Cuba was straightforward and unmistakable: "The duty of every revolutionary is to make the revolution."[7]

Despite these pressures, only four communist parties adopted the insurrectionary line, and then for only a few years. The Venezuelan Communist Party, the most active of these, formally embraced the armed struggle in 1962; it reasserted the primacy of the legal struggle in 1965. In virtually every country, dissidents left the communist parties, founded fidelista groups, and either supported or actively participated in guerrilla warfare and other approaches to overthrowing their governments. One of these dissidents, Carlos Marighela, summarized the fidelistas' brief against the established communist parties by criticizing the Brazilian party's "incapacity to lead . . . inside the big industrial firms in the country; also its lack of contact with the peasants. All its activities consist in organizing meetings and publishing policies and information. No action is planned; the struggle has been abandoned."[8] Once split, the Marxists rarely achieved unity on any issue or strategy; rather, the constant squabbling, ideological hair-splitting, and debate over strategy and tactics kept the left divided. The Sino-Soviet split of 1964 further weakened the Marxists as pro-Chinese factions split from the Moscow-oriented parties in some ten Latin American countries. The case of Peru demonstrates the extreme of Marxist fragmentation: By 1964 there were Trotskyists; Moscow-oriented communists; Chinese-oriented communists; the Movement of the Revolutionary Left (Movimiento de Izquierda Revolucionaria, MIR), formed by APRA dissidents; and several independent groups all claiming to have the correct approach to revolution and denouncing the errors of the others' ways.

The non-Marxist left parties suffered similar fragmentation under the impact of fidelismo as their left wings lost patience with electoral politics. Even where the democratic left held power, as in Venezuela and Chile, frustration at the slow pace of reform, contrasted with the pace of change in Cuba drove some out of the parties and into advocacy of immediate revolution: The MIR broke away from Venezuela's AD in 1960, taking with it most of the AD youth movement and a substantial bloc of congressmen; and the Chilean Christian Democratic Party lost its left wing in 1969 with the founding of the Movement for Unitary Popular Action (Movimiento de Acción Popular Unitaria, MAPU), which formed part of the Allende government in 1970. These defections did not weaken the democratic left to the extent that the Marxist groups were hurt by fragmentation; nonetheless, the cluttering of the political landscape with quarreling mini-parties set back the chances for cooperation in the electoral as well as the guerrilla arena — and cooperation was crucial to the success of either reform or revolution.

FIDELISMO AND THE BRAZILIAN CRISIS, 1959–1964

The collapse of Brazil's civilian government and institutions provides a useful case study of the impact of fidelismo on Latin American political systems. When it happened in 1964, the military coup was not blamed on Castro's influence or the impact of the Cuban Revolution but on the threat of a communist takeover. The semantics, however, should not obscure the fact that the Brazilian Communist Party was not a threat to the government; rather, as elsewhere around Latin America, it was the stimulus of fidelismo upon existing, exploitable social, economic, and political conditions that brought on the Brazilian crisis.

In the five-plus years between Castro's victory and the military coup, Brazil exhibited the typical signs of fidelismo. The incidence of strikes grew sharply, stimulated by inflation as well as by fidelista activism. Several new fidelista political organizations appeared, including an action-oriented spin-off of the Brazilian Communist Party, and preexisting groups, such as student federations and labor unions, became radicalized. In emulation of Cuba's effort, four competing literacy campaigns were underway by 1963; they pursued the dual purposes of attacking a sociocultural ill afflicting half of Brazil's adult population and of extending the franchise to the poor by qualifying them to meet the literacy requirement for voting. Land invasions grew more widespread during this period, some apparently spontaneous and others organized by the *ligas camponesas* or peasant leagues.

The peasant leagues of the Northeast were perhaps the single most threatening element in the popular mobilization affecting Brazil. Begun in 1955, the leagues initially manifested the messianic traits common to rural movements in the poor Northeast and made modest demands, such as decent burials. By 1960, under the leadership of Francisco Julião, the peasant leagues had adopted a more radical stance, demanding land reform and sponsoring strikes, land invasions, and resistance to squatter evictions. This politicization was fueled in part by a combination of drought in the Northeast and declining real income for workers on the sugar plantations. It was also driven by the influence of the Cuban Revolution. Julião and 100 peasants visited Cuba in May 1961; after returning, Julião organized a peasant congress whose slogan was "We want land by law or by force."[9] In response to the unprecedented rural mobilization, landowners armed themselves and set up or strengthened their private security forces.

What was particularly threatening about the peasant leagues and the rural awakening was the very obvious dependence of Brazil's political system on the exclusion of the rural masses. Owing to the literacy requirement, the relatively developed southern states of Rio de Janeiro, São Paulo, Paraná, and Rio Grande do Sul commanded a majority of the country's qualified voters and thus could elect the president. Neutralizing the president, who was likely to be moderate or progressive, was a congress that reflected Brazil's federal structure. The senate consisted of three members per state, giving a great preponderance and a veto power to the eighteen rural and poor states over the four urban industrial states of the south. Thus as in Chile the prospect of agrarian reform threatened not only landowners but also urban vested interests and the large share of the middle class that identified with upper class values and political attitudes. Also frightening was the prospect of a simple electoral reform: granting the vote to illiterates.

The political crisis in Brazil went further than in other countries because in contrast to most of his counterparts, President João Goulart aligned himself with the mobilized forces in Brazil. Goulart had been elected vice-president in 1960 and had assumed the presidency in August 1961 upon the surprise resignation of President Jânio Quadros after less than seven months in office. Because of Goulart's pro-labor stance and association with the late dictator Getúlio Vargas, a large faction within the military opposed his accession. A compromise allowed him to take office, but with somewhat reduced powers. By a five-to-one margin, a January 1963 plebiscite restored to him the full constitutional presidential powers.

During the period of his diminished authority, Goulart began to manifest his sympathy for reform. He attended the 1961 peasant congress and in his May Day speech of 1962 called for a thorough agrarian reform. After the plebiscite, he sponsored an agrarian reform bill that was easily defeated in Congress; a bill to enfranchise illiterates met the same predictable fate. However, Congress did pass a 1963 law legalizing rural unions and setting minimum wages. Bogged down with many restrictions and delaying obstacles, the law was intended as window dressing; however, its effect was to further stimulate the rural mobilization sweeping Brazil.

The standoff between president and congress on agrarian reform and enfranchisement of illiterates ordinarily would have killed both issues, but Brazil was not experiencing normal times and Goulart was not an ordinary president. Whether motivated by conviction or opportunism — the debate continues — Goulart opted to push ahead with his reforms, relying on the state of rural and urban mobilization to intimidate Congress and keep the military in its barracks. At a huge rally on March 13, 1964, he issued decrees authorizing a mild version of his agrarian reform bill and nationalizing the oil refineries and announced his intention of introducing legislation for a more radical agrarian reform and the enfranchisement of illiterates and enlisted military men. This action threw down the gauntlet, for if Goulart could set fundamental national policy by decree, the gates were open to full-scale agrarian reform and enfranchisement of illiterates; in other words, the gates were open to revolution. During Goulart's final months, U.S. personnel on the scene thought "in terms of Brazil as another Cuba."[10]

Goulart capped off his challenge to the Brazilian establishment by granting a pardon to 2,000 enlisted sailors and marines who had received military punishment for holding a political meeting. This override of military discipline, which the officer corps saw as an open invitation to sedition, raised worries about military insurrection and the possibility of a fate similar to that of Cuba's professional army after its defeat and dismemberment by Castro. Having alienated conservative and moderate civilians and the military establishment, Goulart had little chance to survive in office. The coup came on March 31, 1964.

The case of Brazil during the high tide of fidelismo in Latin America is unique. Whereas the turmoil unleashed by fidelismo was usually met with a combination of token reforms and heightened repression, in Brazil the president himself attempted to meet the demands of the mobilized poor and simultaneously to mold them into a broad base of support. Goulart miscalculated in both attempts: Brazil's civilian and military establishments would not tolerate a fidelista-style revolution led from above; and despite their state of mobilization, the urban and rural masses were no match for the armed forces, and they knew it. Thus when Goulart called for popular resistance to the coup, his call went unheeded.

The nature of the military-dominated government that replaced Goulart reflected how seriously the conservatives and the officer corps perceived the revolutionary threat in Brazil. The military soon determined that civilians of any political hue could not be trusted to govern until the conditions that had fostered radicalization had been eliminated. This ambitious task brought severe repression and economic hardship for Brazil's masses for many years. The impact of the Cuban Revolution on Brazil thus gave birth to the first of the new antirevolutionary military regimes that would come to the fore in the 1970s.

NOTES

1. Hugh Thomas, *Cuba: The Pursuit of Freedom* (New York: Harper & Row, 1971), 1293.

2. Che Guevara, *Guerrilla Warfare*, intro. and case studies by Brian Loveman and Thomas M. Davies, Jr. (Lincoln: University of Nebraska Press, 1985), 169.

3. Tad Szulc, *Twilight of the Tyrants* (New York: Henry Holt, 1959).

4. *Current History* 45, no. 265 (Sept. 1963), 186.

5. Mildred Adams, ed., *Latin America: Evolution or Explosion?* (New York: Dodd, Mead, 1963); Gary MacEoin, *Latin America: The Eleventh Hour* (New York: P. J. Kennedy, 1962); and Carleton Beals, *Latin America: World in Revolution* (New York: Abelard-Schuman, 1963).

6. Guevara, *Guerrilla Warfare*, 78–79.

7. Fidel Castro, "The Second Declaration of Havana," 4 Feb. 1962, in Martin Kemmer and James Petras, eds., *Fidel Castro Speaks* (New York: Grove Press, 1969), 115.

8. Carlos Marighela, *For the Liberation of Brazil*, tr. by John Butt and Rosemary Sheed (Harmondsworth, Eng.: Penguin Books, 1971), 183.

9. E. Bradford Burns, *A History of Brazil*, 2d ed. (New York: Columbia University Press, 1980), 498.

10. Morris H. Morley, *Imperial State and Revolution: The United States and Cuba, 1952-1986* (London: Cambridge University Press, 1987), 171.

4

U.S. Responses to Revolution

The revolution in Cuba was a serious blow to U.S. economic and strategic interests in Latin America. Fidel's revolution violated two canons of Washington's Latin American policy. First, in expropriating American property Fidel challenged the doctrine of no expropriation without full and immediate compensation that had been a cardinal rule since the beginning of U.S. economic expansion in the 1890s. Second, Castro crossed the line of acceptable behavior by embracing communism and aligning Cuba with the Soviet Union in defiance of the U.S. position, previously ratified by the OAS, that communism was incompatible with the institutions and way of life of the Western Hemisphere. In short, by establishing a socialist economy and an alliance with the Soviet Union, Castro for the first time opened a breach in U.S. hegemony over the Western Hemisphere.

As humiliating and daunting as the Cuban Revolution was to the United States, a far greater potential threat was the spread of Cuban-style revolution throughout Latin America. While the United States could survive the economic and strategic loss of a single island, it feared the exportation of the Cuban model of revolution to other countries. The rise of fidelismo throughout Latin America made it clear that the United States faced the urgent task of developing new strategies for dealing with a completely unprecedented situation — a hemisphere that appeared to be on the verge of revolution.

ELIMINATION OF REVOLUTION
AT THE SOURCE

For the first 28 months after Fidel came to power, the primary U.S. approach to Castro was to quell the revolution in Cuba itself, thereby not only eliminating revolution at its source, but also in the process preventing its spread. This strategy ran the gamut from pressuring Castro toward moderation — a difficult challenge — to attempting to eliminate him through military intervention, insurrection, and assassination.

U.S. efforts to influence Fidel toward moderation basically consisted of the use of escalating economic leverage over the very dependent and vulnerable Cuban economy. In the early months after Fidel's triumph, however, the Eisenhower administration declined to use direct economic persuasion. Whether out of apprehension, lack of concern, or simply waiting for Castro to ask, Eisenhower did not offer Castro aid for rebuilding the island's economy from the war-inflicted damage. For his part, Castro chose not to request aid during his April 1959 visit to the United States in order to protect his nationalist image. In the words of National Bank of Cuba President Felipe Pazos, who accompanied Castro on the trip, "I heard him expressing fears of being invited to the White House and of being photographed with the President of the United States as one more Latin American leader 'sold out' to imperialism."[1] Fidel seemed to believe that the Eisenhower administration would offer aid without his requesting it, thereby strengthening the Cuban bargaining position.

The United States did respond to Fidel's nationalistic economic measures, beginning with the May 1959 agrarian reform law, by threatening or implementing economic sanctions to slow or halt the leftward movement of the revolution. The main U.S. weapon was the sugar quota, which Eisenhower suspended in July 1960. In taking this and other measures, the Eisenhower administration, failing to gauge the full extent of Castro's commitment to ridding Cuba of U.S. economic dominance, was employing the standard tools for a conventional situation. Castro, however, was not intimidated. Every American step elicited a progressively more radical countermeasure, as when Fidel responded to the American oil refineries' refusal to refine Soviet crude by confiscating the facilities.

By late 1960, with all U.S. investments nationalized and the sugar quota cancelled, Washington escalated the economic pressure on Cuba by applying a trade embargo. On October 19 the Eisenhower administration prohibited all exports to Cuba except medicines and nonsubsidized foodstuffs; these exceptions were soon eliminated. In the aftermath of the Bay of Pigs failure, the Kennedy administration extended the embargo to prohibit all imports from Cuba and of Cuban origin and increased the pressure on NATO allies to deny Castro essential materials and markets. The embargo was designed simultaneously to cause such economic hardship as to provoke an uprising against Castro and to serve as a warning to other Latin American governments about the consequences of straying from the fold.

U.S. economic sanctions were a primary cause of the economic problems that plagued Cuba in the 1960s. Closing the U.S. sugar market was not particularly successful, as Cuba had already begun exporting to the Soviet Union and subsequently expanded its markets there and in Eastern Europe. But the general trade embargo caused serious dislocations: Given the preponderance of American equipment throughout the Cuban economic infrastructure, the withholding of spare parts alone was a major blow, requiring replacement of complete plants in some cases. The reorientation of Cuban trade raised transportation costs substantially, and U.S. pressure gradually brought most of the European allies to cut back or suspend their dealings with Castro. A notable exception, illustrating the color blindness of money, was the significant growth of trade between Castro's Cuba and Franco's Spain. U.S. pressure on the Latin American countries to suspend trade was largely symbolic, given that only a small fraction of Cuba's trade was with Latin America. Overall, while the U.S. embargo inflicted substantial economic damage, it was a complete failure in its primary purpose of causing popular discontent leading to an insurrection against Castro.

U.S. direct actions to eliminate Castro were no more successful. The Eisenhower, Kennedy, and Johnson administrations resorted to CIA- and mafia-executed assassination plots against Castro, employing poison pens, poisoned cigars, and a plan to substitute a lethally contaminated diving suit for the one Fidel normally wore on his frequent skin diving excursions. Seeking to provoke an uprising against Castro, the United States trained, armed, and sustained exile raiding parties, underground opposition, sabotage units, and for a time guerrilla operations in the Sierra de Escambray and Oriente province. It also beamed anti-Castro propaganda to the island via radio. Following the Bay of Pigs, Washington launched "Operation Mongoose" to coordinate and intensify the internal subversion activities. One of the more bizarre Mongoose plots involved alerting Cubans to the impending second coming of Christ. On the day of Christ's announced return, a U.S. submarine would surface and set off fireworks along the coast, prompting a rebellion against the anti-Christ, Castro. One CIA agent called this "elimination by illumination."[2] By 1964, however, the United States abandoned its efforts to incite uprisings in the face of convincing evidence of Castro's popularity, his tight control over potential dissidents, and the difficulty of sustaining resistance groups without the physical presence of an embassy.

DIPLOMATIC ISOLATION OF CUBA

In concert with its attempts to eliminate Castro, the United States also sought to limit Cuba's ability to influence Latin America by terminating formal contacts between the island and the rest of the hemisphere. This approach to containment was designed to eliminate the opportunities for promoting revolutionary activity provided by normal diplomatic relations, such as placing political operatives in embassies and using diplomatic pouches to transport money, propaganda, and even arms for fidelista groups. Castro's ability to show off the accomplishments of the revolution and offer indoctrination and guerrilla training also depended on the freedom of Latin Americans to travel to the island. Thus in pressuring the hemispheric countries to break diplomatic relations with Cuba, the United States was attempting to limit Castro's possibilities of creating and supporting revolutionary movements in those countries.

From the beginning of its effort to impose collective diplomatic sanctions on Cuba, the United States relied on a Cold War corollary of the Monroe Doctrine. The 1954 Declaration of Caracas was a statement of anticommunist principles that the Eisenhower administration rammed through the OAS as justification for the overthrow of the Arbenz government in Guatemala: "The domination or control of the political institutions of any American state by the international communist movement . . . would constitute a threat to the sovereignty and political independence of the American states, endangering the peace of America."[3] Although adopted reluctantly, this argument had been easier for the United States to sell in the Latin American political climate of the mid-1950s than it was in the era of predominantly elected governments in the early 1960s. The few remaining dictatorships, of course, embraced the Caracas doctrine, as did some of the more conservative constitutional governments. But in its first formal test of Latin American sentiment, an August 1960 OAS foreign ministers' meeting, the United States was unable to persuade the gathering to condemn Cuba; it got only a mild statement on totalitarianism and nonintervention — the latter potentially applying to the United States as well as Cuba.

While the dictatorships and a number of the more conservative governments voluntarily broke relations with Cuba, the ultimate success of the U.S. drive for hemispheric diplomatic isolation of Castro depended on a significant change in the attitudes of the more liberal Latin American governments. Those governments initially tended to view Castro as a bilateral problem between the United States and Cuba in which the OAS should not take sides. Over the next four years, however, the impact of fidelismo on their own countries combined with relentless U.S. pressure drive the majority of OAS members — eventually, all but four — to agree that Cuba was a menace that must be controlled. These countries broke their own relations with Cuba and then came around to voting with the United States to require all OAS member states to implement collective sanctions.

The first step was the expulsion of Cuba from the OAS. Meeting in Punta del Este, Uruguay, in January 1962, the OAS foreign ministers agreed to the expulsion, with Mexico opposing the move and Brazil, Argentina, Chile, Bolivia, and Ecuador abstaining. The United States had wanted stronger measures, but could not even get the support of the largest and most powerful of the Latin American countries for the mild step of expulsion from the principal hemispheric organization. By July 1964, however, the required two-thirds of member states were ready to back the United States in its quest to isolate Cuba. By this time the elected governments of Argentina, Ecuador, and Brazil had been replaced by military regimes; only Mexico, Chile, Bolivia, and Uruguay voted against Washington, while Argentina abstained. The sanctions agreed upon, which all OAS members were required to implement, included the suspension of diplomatic relations, trade, air and maritime transportation, and travel to and from Cuba. All member states complied except Mexico, which followed its established nationalistic course of rejecting Washington's lead in foreign policy. With the exception of Mexico, the OAS sanctions remained firm until the Chilean government of Salvador Allende reestablished relations with Cuba in 1970.

The diplomatic isolation of Cuba was successful in reducing Castro's ability to aid Latin American revolutionaries. Cuba lost the conveniences of a physical presence in other countries and of diplomatic immunity, while the prohibition of travel to Cuba discouraged all but the most committed from risking the trip; those who did often faced the expense of traveling through Eastern Europe to reach Cuba. While the disruption of contact between Cuba and the rest of Latin America succeeded in impeding Castro's intervention in those countries, it did little to reduce the most important influence that the Cuban Revolution exercised in the hemisphere: the power of its example.

THE MILITARY RESPONSE

Concurrently with its efforts to eliminate Castro and to reduce his ability to support fidelista forces in Latin America, the United States readied a military response to revolutionary threats in the hemisphere as part of a general reordering of Washington's global military strategy. In the early post–World War II years the United States had relied on its nuclear arsenal and the doctrine of massive retaliation, combined with military and economic aid to friendly governments, to contain revolutionary movements in underdeveloped parts of the world. The strategy of massive retaliation was premised on the assumption that Moscow controlled all dangerous political movements throughout the world and, under threat of nuclear strikes against the Soviet Union, would rein them in upon demand. By the latter years of the Eisenhower administration, critics of U.S. military posture had begun to point out that while the country's nuclear strategy might work against the Soviet Union, it had no deterrent effect on the unconventional wars of national liberation that had broken out in the colonial world of Africa and Southeast Asia and on the type of guerrilla war that Castro had employed in Cuba.

Faced with threatening situations in Southeast Asia and Latin America and with potential dangers throughout the Third World, the Kennedy administration shortly after taking office turned its attention to developing strategies for dealing with unconventional warfare. A major component of the Kennedy doctrine of "flexible response" was counterinsurgency. The president took a keen personal interest in the topic. He read Mao Zedong and Che Guevara on guerrilla warfare, ordered the creation of special courses on counterinsurgency for diplomatic and military officers posted in Third World countries, and set up a "Special Group for Counterinsurgency" to formulate policy.

U.S. military policy toward Latin America after World War II, formalized in the Rio de Janeiro Treaty of 1947, had been based on the concept of collective hemispheric security against external aggression by the Soviet Union. Given the remoteness of Latin America from anticipated theaters of war and the obvious impossibility of outfitting 20 republics' armed forces for nuclear war, Latin America was of minor importance to the U.S. global military strategy. Thus U.S. military assistance consisted primarily of maintaining small missions in each country, training Latin American officers in techniques of conventional warfare at the service schools in the United States and Panama, and providing equipment — much of it obsolete. By law, the equipment sent to the Latin American militaries could serve only external defense purposes unless the White House determined that internal security considerations warranted an exception.

In response to the alleged communist threat to Guatemala under the Arbenz administration (1950–54), the United States had begun to reconsider its military strategy in Latin America. The 1954 Declaration of

Caracas, which equated internal subversion with international communist penetration, began to blur the line between internal security and external defense. When the Cuban Revolution raised the prospect of guerrilla warfare and general insurgency in the hemisphere, the United States quickly forgot the Soviet military threat to Latin America. In the words of Kennedy's secretary of defense, Robert McNamara, "Our objective is ... to guard against external covert intrusion and internal subversion designed to create dissidence and insurrection."[4] Public Law 87-135 of September 1961 translated the Kennedy administration's thinking into legislation directing U.S. military aid toward fighting the spread of revolution.

Although the United States moved rapidly to develop its own counterinsurgency capabilities, featuring the army's Special Forces or Green Berets and parallel corps in the navy and air force, the guiding premise of Washington's counterinsurgency concept for the hemisphere was that each country should be prepared to deal with subversion within its borders. Thus the Military Assistance Program for Latin America emphasized training and equipping the hemisphere's armed forces for their newly important internal security role. Preparation of the Latin American militaries involved both new strategies and hardware; innovation in both accelerated as U.S. involvement in Vietnam deepened. Army troops had to be taught to emulate the guerrillas' ability to live in and off of the jungle, to set traps and ambushes, and to use all types of personal combat in addition to weapons. Sophisticated lightweight weapons and communications equipment were developed to enhance the troops' mobility on the ground, while, as in Vietnam, helicopters were to provide rapid deployment to the guerrilla zones and supplemental fire power. One of the most useful new technologies for Latin America was infrared aerial photography, which could detect even a small band of guerrillas in areas too rugged or remote for effective reconnaissance by normal methods. The counterinsurgency units developed in Latin America, like the Green Berets who trained them, were instilled with a strong sense of mission and an esprit de corps appropriate to an elite group within the armed forces.

Civic action, used extensively in Vietnam, was the preventive aspect of the military response. Civic action was designed to secure the loyalty of the peasantry — on whom the insurgents depended for support — to the government. Citing the U. S. Army Corps of Engineers as an example of military involvement in projects for civilian benefit, the United States promoted the use of troops to build or improve roads, schools, clinics, water systems, and other public works in those remote areas of the country where government services were least developed and fidelistas most likely to select sites for guerrilla operations. Civic Action Mobile Training Teams consisting of specialists in engineering, agriculture, education, and public health were dispatched in 1961 and had done training in most Latin American countries by 1965. While civic action was widely employed, some officers, feeling that manual labor demeaned military honor, resisted the imported concept. Critics pointed out that no correlation could be established between civic action programs and living standards or degree of loyalty to government; others noted that in some countries civic action tended to focus disproportionately on road building to facilitate military access to potential insurgency zones. In any case, as in Vietnam, civic action was a cornerstone of U.S. counterinsurgency efforts in Latin America.

Complementing the training and equipping of the Latin American militaries for counterinsurgency was a parallel program for the police. This approach to internal security recognized the primary role of police in day-to-day enforcement of order, the importance of effective crowd control and riot prevention, and the potentially greater role the police could play in gathering intelligence on subversive groups. Training and equipping police was also far more economical than providing the expensive hardware needed for military counterinsurgency. Accordingly, President Kennedy expanded the small program of assistance to foreign police and placed it in the Agency for International Development's (AID) Office of Public Safety (OPS). OPS trained police in most hemispheric countries and at the Inter-American Police Academy in the Panama Canal Zone and the International Police Academy in Washington. The advent of urban guerrilla warfare in the late 1960s highlighted the importance of police counterinsurgency training, but instruction in interrogation techniques, widely denounced as torture, also gave the left a useful propaganda weapon.

Latin American officers received regular and counterinsurgency training in the Panama Canal Zone and at over 100 service schools in the United States, while officers and enlisted men alike were trained in their own countries. Special counterinsurgency curricula were established at Fort Bragg, North Carolina; Fort Gordon, Georgia; and at the Southern Command's Fort Gulick in the Canal Zone. Over 20,000 Latin American officers underwent training in Panama alone during the 1960s. A 1,000-man unit of the Special Forces, assigned to Fort Gulick, formed the Mobile Training Teams sent to the Latin American countries to provide antiguerrilla training. In addition to scheduled training missions, the Green Berets were ready for emergency training and advising of counterinsurgency units such as those created in Bolivia in 1967 to fight Che Guevara. The Inter-American Defense College, founded in 1962 at Fort McNair in Washington, D. C., offered annual ten-month courses on social, economic, and political problems of the Americas as well as military matters for 40 to 60 officers of colonel rank or above. Periodic service chiefs' conferences and frequent joint tactical exercises such as the Unitas naval operations further refined the training for military operations. The United States also expanded its resident military missions in Latin America in the 1960s.

An explicit goal in both the conventional and counterinsurgency training of officers was to draw U.S. and Latin American military personnel closer together, both personally and ideologically. In arguing for the creation of the Inter-American Defense College, DeLesseps Morrison, Kennedy's ambassador to the OAS, said that the school would be "both a weapon in the struggle against Castro and a means for indoctrinating key Latin American officers in the political and social mores of the United States."[5] Precisely for that reason, several Latin American governments opposed the college's founding. Periodic Service Chiefs' Conferences served the same purpose, while a new Foreign Area Specialist Program, established in 1961, gave selected U.S. officers two and a half years of graduate training in language and area studies to enhance their effectiveness at building bonds with their southern counterparts. The expanded in-country missions were particularly useful in building close personal and professional relationships and thus in developing strong influence over the Latin American officers. A former member of the mission in the Dominican Republic reported that the Dominican military "is clearly sitting around waiting for the MAAG (Military Assistance Advisory Group) to tell it what to do. And it is also clear that the president [of the Dominican Republic] has less power over the Dominican military than the MAAG does. The 65-man MAAG mission lives, eats, sleeps with those guys."[6] A related function of the buildup of training and material aid was to bind the Latin American militaries more closely to U.S. weaponry, serving not only the interests of the U.S. weapons industry but also making it difficult to switch to alternate sources of supply and hence alternate political influences.

In responding to the buildup of revolutionary threats in the hemisphere, the United States doubled its annual military assistance budgets for Latin America from an average of $58 million from 1953 through 1961 to $129 million from 1962 through 1965. These figures do not include the cost of AID's police training program and some other military expenses. Yet the Military Assistance Program and AID budgets do not tell the entire story of the U.S. military response to the Cuban Revolution. The military options also included sponsorship of insurgency against established governments, including those of Salvador Allende in Chile and the Sandinistas in Nicaragua. The assiduous cultivation of the Latin American officer corps provided a safety net, an assurance that the ultimate arbiter of power in each country would be pro-United States and opposed to revolution.

While the general policy was to prepare the Latin American armed forces to handle their own insurgencies, Washington was ready to use U.S. forces when national forces appeared incapable of doing the job alone. Thus in addition to their training functions, Green Berets conducted clandestine missions in various countries during the 1960s; several died in counterinsurgency operations in Guatemala. The overt use of U.S. troops was a last resort, but the invasions of the Dominican Republic in 1965 and Grenada in 1983 removed any doubt that the United States would go to war if necessary to defend its hegemony in the hemisphere.

THE ALLIANCE FOR PROGRESS

The Alliance for Progress was the United States' most highly publicized response to the Cuban Revolution. In contrast to the economic, diplomatic, and military measures against Cuba, which were premised on the notion that Castro's actions to export revolution were responsible for radicalizing the Latin American political climate in the early 1960s, the Alliance was anchored in the acknowledgment that the real threat from Cuba was the power of its example to incite demands for change. Announced by President Kennedy in March 1961 and formally established five months later at Punta del Este, Uruguay, the Alliance for Progress was designed to preempt the revolutionaries by attacking the conditions that made revolution appealing to the masses. Specifically, it called for a range of social reforms to create more just societies, economic development to eliminate poverty, and the strengthening of democracy where it existed and its establishment where it did not. Overall, according to the document that created it, the Alliance for Progress was to be "a vast effort to bring a better life to all the peoples of the continent."[7]

The Alliance for Progress grew out of a mounting awareness in the United States that the condition of Latin America was a source of anti-Americanism and of potential for revolution. After crowds greeted Vice-President Richard Nixon with tomatoes and riots on his 1958 Latin American tour, the Eisenhower administration appointed the Rockefeller

Commission to study the causes of such hostility toward the United States. In a December 1958 speech, Senator John Kennedy called in general terms for a special aid program for Latin American development. A cadre of academic specialists and diplomats also lobbied persuasively for a program of development aid tied to reform.

Latin Americans themselves had urged the United States to underwrite a program similar to the Marshall Plan to fund rapid economic development. Among them, Brazilian President Jascelino Kubitschek called in 1958 for an "Operation Pan-America" and Fidel Castro, at a 1959 meeting of Latin American governments in Buenos Aires, called on the United States to invest $30 billion in Latin America's development in the coming decade. But it was the radicalization of the Cuban Revolution and the impact of fidelismo upon the hemisphere that prompted action, which began with Eisenhower's "Act of Bogotá" of September 1960 committing $500 million for social and economic development. During his presidential campaign, Kennedy elaborated upon his earlier idea and appointed a Latin American Task Force under the leadership of Adolf Berle to formulate plans for a cooperative hemispheric venture.

The Alliance for Progress was an inter-American agreement based on U.S. funding of a major part of a minimum of $20 billion in development aid needed over the next decade and on the commitment of the Latin American countries to undertake reforms and invest more of their own resources in social and economic development. The Charter of Punta del Este spelled out ambitious goals, including: a minimum annual per capita economic growth rate of 2.5 percent; more equitable distribution of national income; tax reform; comprehensive agrarian reform; elimination of adult illiteracy and provision of a minimum of six years' schooling for all children; a series of public health measures to raise life expectancy; and increased low-cost housing and public services. In relation to the promotion of democracy, President Kennedy called the Alliance "a plan to transform the 1960s into an historic decade of democratic progress."[8] In order to receive funding, all countries were required to formulate long-range economic and social development plans, preferably within 18 months of the signing of the charter.

Launched with great fanfare and lauded as a new Marshall Plan, the Alliance for Progress proved far less successful than its European predecessor. To be sure, some noteworthy accomplishments came from the Alliance during the 1960s. Between 1961 and 1968, the United States and its European allies committed an average of $2 billion per year in development aid, primarily in loans; actual disbursements under the Alliance were $1.1 billion per year and factoring in debt service, the net annual inflow of development capital was $638 million. While substantially less than projected, this amount was sufficient to make a difference, as evidenced in potable water projects, housing developments, clinics, and roads throughout Latin America funded by the Alliance, dedicated with appropriate ceremonies, and marked with plaques bearing the Alliance emblem. Supplementing the Alliance proper, the Peace Corps, established by Kennedy in 1961, sent some 16,000 volunteers to Latin America during its first decade.

Two countries stand out during the 1960s as showcases for the Alliance for Progress approach. Venezuela under the AD administrations of Rómulo Betancourt (1959–64) and Raúl Leoni (1964–69) and Chile under Christian Democrat Eduardo Frei (1964–70) came reasonably close to the model set forth in the Punta del Este Charter for social reform and economic development within a democratic framework. Both countries carried out structural agrarian reform that attacked the predominance of the traditional hacienda while distributing land to tens of thousands of rural workers; both invested heavily in social services in the countryside and in city slums; and through tax reform, minimum wages, and supportive labor legislation, both made serious attempts at income redistribution. In both countries, political participation was expanded by the incorporation of previously disenfranchised peasants and urban marginals. In sum, while not meeting every one of the Alliance's goals, Venezuela and Chile made sufficient progress so as to provide two credible models of a reformist alternative to the Cuban Revolution.

Venezuela and Chile were notable exceptions to the general rule of failure. Across Latin America, the 1961–68 period witnessed an annual per capita income growth rate of 1.8 percent — a quarter below the minimum goal. Income redistribution in most countries favored the wealthy few at the expense of the multitudes of poor. Most countries made a mockery of agrarian reform — the most emotion-laden social and political issue of the 1960s. In order to receive Alliance funds they drew up plans, established agrarian reform bureaucracies, and sometimes set up pilot projects or colonization zones in marginal areas; outside of Chile and Venezuela, however, efforts to meet the Alliance goal of "effective transformation . . . of unjust structures and systems of land tenure" were textbook cases of tokenism.[9] The strengthening of democracy also proved illusory: From a high point of civilian, constitutional governments when the Alliance for Progress was announced in 1961, Latin America a dozen years later was dominated by men in uniform as at no time since the Great Depression triggered coups throughout the region.

Beyond failing in its objectives, in its early years the Alliance for Progress actually tended to work against U.S. intentions. The massive propaganda attached to the launching of the Alliance and the very attractiveness of its goals undoubtedly contributed to the growth of expectations underlying the turmoil of the early 1960s. The visibility of the Alliance in political rhetoric, ceremonial dedications, and new government departments and initiatives was a constant reminder that the United States itself was publicly committed to change and betterment for the masses. Thus while intended to counter the Cuban Revolution, the Alliance initially added its own fuel to the destabilizing influence of fidelismo by contributing to a revolution of rising but unfulfilled expectations.

Underlying the failure of the Alliance were two conditions deeply embedded in Latin American reality and in the history of United States-Latin American relations. Despite the Kennedy administration's efforts and the financial incentives offered, no Latin American government could be persuaded to take the goals of the Alliance for Progress seriously. Dictators were not interested in stepping aside to watch democracy take root and flower; oligarchs were not anxious to share power with slum dwellers; the wealthy did not rush forward to reduce their share of the national income; landowners did not push legislation to dismantle the land tenure system they controlled. Nor were the Chilean and Venezuelan governments, which carried out progressive reform programs, persuaded by the Alliance for Progress; AD and Chile's Christian Democrats were genuinely reformist parties whose principles and programs antedated the Cuban Revolution and the Alliance for Progress. As for the other countries, rather than reform themselves out of existence the elites turned to other measures to fight the impact of the Cuban Revolution; in these efforts, they enjoyed the support of the U.S. government.

The second broad reason for the failure of the Alliance was that when confronted with a choice between placing its faith in the anticipated but unproven long-term benefits of reform and the short-term security of a military government willing to crack down on subversives the United States invariably opted for the latter. The incompatibility between military governments and the Alliance for Progress was explicit in the goal of strengthening democracy; the incompatibility was implicit in the area of social reform, which the militaries usually viewed as closely akin to communism. Kennedy himself faced the dilemma of dealing with military overthrows of civilian governments six times when coups replaced the constitutional regimes of Argentina, Peru, Guatemala, Ecuador, the Dominican Republic, and Honduras. While some of these governments, most notably those of Guatemala and Peru, were anything but progressive, the extension of diplomatic recognition and aid to the new military governments called into question the seriousness of Kennedy's commitment to ending the era of the strong men. And the termination of the Ecuadorean administration of Carlos Arosemena and especially the Honduran regime of Ramón Villeda Morales and the Dominican government of Juan Bosch were clear setbacks to the process of social reform.

Kennedy's responses to the resurgence of military rule were inconsistent. He repeatedly spoke out against coups and denounced them when they occurred: He lamented the Peruvian overthrow, saying that "this hemisphere can only be secure and free with democratic governments"; the State Department chastised the Ecuadorean officers, proclaiming that "military seizures of power should not become an acceptable substitute for constitutional procedures."[10] U.S. actions varied from immediate recognition of the junta that ousted Argentine President Arturo Frondizi to the withholding of diplomatic recognition and aid to the juntas that overthrew Bosch and Villeda Morales for eleven and a half and ten and a half weeks, respectively. Kennedy's assassination during the suspension of relations with Honduras and the Dominican Republic prohibits solid conclusions as to his final disposition toward military regimes. On the one hand, he extracted at least vague assurances of future elections before recognizing the juntas in Peru, Guatemala, and Ecuador, thus keeping alive the U.S. commitment on paper to constitutionalism. On the other hand, his failure to marshal all available resources to prevent coups — especially evident in the Dominican Republic case — made it appear that Washington's traditional anti-leftism outweighed Kennedy's commitment to strengthening political democracy, thus compromising the credibility of the Alliance for Progress.

THE END OF THE ALLIANCE

Kennedy's inconsistent attitude toward military governments was followed by the Johnson administration's explicit policy of recognizing and supporting any military regimes that served the purposes of the U.S. government. The Mann Doctrine was authored by Assistant Secretary of State for Latin America Thomas Mann in March 1964, on the eve of the U.S.-supported coup in Brazil. It held that U.S. diplomatic recognition and offers of assistance would not be based on a regime's origin; elected governments and military regimes would be judged on their merits, not their provenance. The Mann Doctrine amputated one of the three legs on which the Alliance rested, and given the predominantly conservative outlook of the Latin American military, it implied that the United States had lost interest in the social reform goals of the Alliance as well. With two of its three goals contravened by the Mann Doctrine, the tottering Alliance for Progress expired as a coherent policy a few months into the Johnson administration, although it continued to be funded and to finance development projects through the 1960s.

Two of President Johnson's actions telegraphed the message that the United States would not tolerate suspect governments, no matter how closely their goals and policies matched the objectives of the Alliance for Progress. First was U.S. involvement in the overthrow of the Goulart government in Brazil. Washington had been wary of Goulart since his accession to the presidency in 1961 because of his association with leftists, his calls for Alliance for Progress-style reforms, expropriations of some U.S. holdings, a law limiting remittances on foreign investments, and Goulart's resistance to breaking relations with Cuba. Supplementing U.S. economic and diplomatic pressure, the CIA had carried out a covert campaign since 1962, first to moderate Goulart and later to weaken him in preparation for an overthrow. Encouraged by the announcement of the Mann Doctrine, the military wasted no time and, with the full knowledge and support of the Johnson administration, overthrew Goulart on March 31 while a U.S. carrier task force stood offshore to lend assistance if requested. Johnson congratulated the officers within four hours of their seizure of power, and Ambassador Lincoln Gordon declared the coup "the single most decisive victory for freedom in the mid-twentieth century."[11] The military regime immediately broke relations with Cuba and welcomed new foreign investment; in response, the aid pipeline resumed its flow and American largesse poured in to support what its perpetrators called the Brazilian "revolution."

In April 1965, President Johnson emphatically revealed the true face of U.S. policy for containment of the Cuban Revolution when he ordered U.S. troops to the Dominican Republic to prevent the overthrow of the conservative government of Donald Reid Cabral by supporters of former President Juan Bosch. Bosch, running in the first post-Trujillo election, had won 62 percent of the vote in 1962 with promises of Alliance for Progress-style reforms and had taken office in February 1963. When he set out to implement agrarian reform and build up the weak labor move-ment, Bosch encountered resistance from the Dominican right and mili-tary, from U.S. economic interests on the island, and from Ambassador John Bartlow Martin, who accused the president of being soft on "Castro-Communists."[12] Facing the choice between Bosch's somewhat erratic attempts to build a democratic society on the ruins of Trujillo's three decades of dictatorship and the short-term security of a military-conservative coalition certain to protect U.S. investments and act against suspected revolutionaries, Kennedy vacillated. After weakening Bosch's government by reducing aid and discouraging his reforms, the Kennedy administration stood by in September 1963 when the military overthrew him, then denounced the coup and suspended diplomatic recognition and aid. This "hands off" stance contrasted sharply with the overt intervention of the United States in Dominican politics during the previous three years, when Washington used economic and diplomatic pressure and threats of military intervention to eliminate Trujillo and shape an acceptable post-Trujillo regime.

The events that led to U.S. intervention began on April 24, 1965, when a group of military officers rebelled to restore Bosch to the presidency. The fighting quickly spread to the civilian population, and after four days the rebels appeared to be gaining the upper hand. At this juncture, President Johnson ordered the landing of U.S. troops under the pretext of ensuring the safety of U.S. nationals. A few days later, Johnson declared that the action had been taken to prevent "the establishment of another Communist government in the Western Hemisphere."[13] The communists that U.S. sources detected were a small minority of the civilians involved in the revolt, while the leadership of the pro-Bosch movement was non- or anticommunist. The allegation of large-scale communist participation in the uprising and hence the likely communist control of the restored Bosch regime was not consistent with the facts as established in subsequent U.S. congressional hearings.

After the invasion, the United States pressured the OAS into an ex post facto endorsement of the intervention and persuaded Brazil, Nicaragua, Honduras, and Costa Rica to send token contingents of troops to join the 22,000 U.S. soldiers in a "collective" OAS peacekeeping exercise. The United States ended the first full-scale military intervention by U.S. troops in Latin America since 1927 after restoring order and arranging for a caretaker government and subsequent elections.

NOTES

1. Edward González, *Cuba Under Castro: The Limits of Charisma* (Boston: Houghton Mifflin, 1974), 69.

2. Quoted in Walter LaFeber, *The American Age: United States Foreign Policy at Home and Abroad Since 1750* (New York: W. W. Norton, 1989), 560–61.

3. Graham H. Stuart and James L. Tigner, *Latin America and the United States*, 6th ed. (Englewood Cliffs, N.J.: Prentice-Hall, 1975), 804–5.

4. Quoted in Che Guevara, *Guerrilla Warfare*, B. Loveman and T. M. Davies, eds. (Lincoln: University of Nebraska Press, 1985), 26.

5. John Child, *Unequal Alliance: The Inter-American Military System, 1938–1978* (Boulder, Colo.: Westview Press, 1980), 75.

6. Michael T. Klare, *War Without End: American Planning for the Next Vietnams* (New York: Vintage Books, 1972), 308.

7. "Declaration to the Peoples of America," in *Department of State Bulletin* XLV, no. 1159 (11 September 1961), 462.

8. *Department of State Bulletin* XLIV, no. 1136 (3 April 1961), 472.

9. "Declaration to the Peoples of America," 462.

10. *Historical Study: U. S. Policy Toward Latin America: Recognition and Non-Recognition of Governments and Interruptions in Diplomatic Relations, 1933–1974* (Washington, D. C.: Department of State, Bureau of Public Affairs, June 1975), 81, 86.

11. E. Bradford Burns, *A History of Brazil*, 2d ed. (New York: Columbia University Press, 1980), 504.

12. Abraham F. Lowenthal, *The Dominican Intervention* (Cambridge, Mass.: Harvard University Press, 1972), 27.

13. Cole Blasier, *The Hovering Giant: U. S. Responses to Revolutionary Change in Latin America, 1910–1985* (Pittsburgh: University of Pittsburgh Press, 1985), 246.

5

Rural Guerrilla Warfare

Guerrilla warfare takes its name from the Spanish response to Napoleon's 1808 invasion of Spain when after the defeat of the army, Spanish irregular forces harassed and skirmished with the Napoleonic army for several years. "Little war" (*guerra*, the Spanish term for war, modified by the diminutive) was not new in 1808; it was a strategy as old as the earliest, unrecorded use of unorthodox methods of fighting by weaker groups against a regular army. Wars of irregular forces against regular armies were certainly known in Latin America prior to Castro's defeat of Batista; the early nineteenth-century wars of independence, Cuba's own independence wars, and the Mexican Revolution of 1910, for example, involved extensive use of guerrilla methods, and Augusto C. Sandino's resistance to the U.S. Marines occupying Nicaragua from 1927 to 1933 was the United States' first encounter with guerrilla warfare in Latin America. But it was not until the Cuban Revolution that guerrilla warfare became the preferred method of insurrection in Latin America.

The wave of guerrilla outbreaks that swept Latin America in the wake of Castro's victory was inspired by the Cuban example, as portrayed in the myth of the heroic guerrilla and by the symbol-laden installation of a guerrilla government in which khakis, boots, and beards were the official dress. Successors of the first guerrillas were able to rely on more than enthusiasm: They had the writings of Che Guevara as a practical guide to the conduct of guerrilla warfare. Having overall responsibility for carrying out the revolution in Cuba, Fidel left the field of guerrilla warfare to Che, whose first loyalty was to the cause of revolution rather than to his adopted island nation. While always acknowledging Fidel's preeminent role in the Cuban guerrilla war, with the publication of his *Guerrilla Warfare* in 1960 Che assumed the mantle of spokesman for the Cuban Revolution in matters of insurrection in Latin America.

CHE GUEVARA ON GUERRILLA WARFARE

Che's *Guerrilla Warfare* can hardly be called a major theoretical contribution to the study of guerrilla warfare. In the areas of strategy and tactics he adds little to the insights of Mao Zedong and Vietnamese General Vo Nguyen Giap, who wrote about rural-based guerrilla warfare from their experiences. The bulk of the book is a "how-to" manual, based on the Cuban experience, describing the organization, training, supply, and operation of a guerrilla *foco* — the guerrilla force itself. *Guerrilla Warfare* is replete with homilies on the spiritual and physical requirements for guerrilla fighters; advice on selecting knapsacks, shoes, and weapons; instructions on tactics for fighting the national army; and descriptions of the various stages through which the successful foco develops.

The real importance of *Guerrilla Warfare* is its validation of the Cuban Revolution as the model for the Latin American revolution. Building upon the official story of guerrilla preeminence in the fight against Batista, Che's work reduced the lessons of the Cuban Revolution to axioms: "1) Popular forces can win a war against the army; 2) It is not necessary to wait until all conditions for revolution exist; the insurrection can create them; 3) In underdeveloped America the countryside is the basic area for armed fighting."[1] This message, offered in authoritative fashion by a participant and with the obvious blessing of Fidel, added the patina of intellectual legitimacy to the multiple signals coming from Cuba that Castro's exploit could be replicated. In Che's words, "of these three propositions the first two contradict the defeatist attitude of revolutionaries or pseudo-revolutionaries who remain inactive and take refuge in the pretext that against a professional army nothing can be done, who sit down to wait until in some mechanical way all necessary objective conditions are given without working to accelerate them."[2]

While goading the Latin American left to take action, *Guerrilla Warfare* placed strict limitations on the applicability of the Cuban model. In a crucial caveat, Che qualified the ability of the insurrection to create conditions necessary for revolution: "When a government has come into power through some form of popular vote, fraudulent or not, and maintains at least an appearance of constitutional legality, the guerrilla outbreak cannot be promoted, since the possibilities of peaceful struggle have not yet been exhausted."[3] Given the unusually large number of elected civilian governments, guerrilla war would have had little application in 1960 outside the dictatorships of Trujillo, Duvalier, Somoza, Stroessner, and the Salvadoran military.

A year after the publication of *Guerrilla Warfare,* Che began to modify his position on the ability of the insurrection to create the conditions for revolution by declaring that the objective conditions — things such as poverty, oppression, class conflict — were in place throughout Latin America. Glossing over the problem of constitutional governments and the existence of possibilities for peaceful struggle, Che now declared that the subjective conditions — the belief that revolution could occur and the will to undertake it — could be created by the insurrectional foco.

By 1963 Che finished his theoretical formulation of the guerrilla's role in sparking revolution. In "Guerrilla Warfare: A Method" he attacked head-on the problem of how to proceed in those countries with elected and potentially responsive governments. Reflecting a firming-up of his Marxist theoretical underpinnings, he now identified the constitutional governments as "dictatorships of the exploiting classes."[4] Propped up by U.S. imperialism, those governments had no more real legitimacy than did the Caribbean-style dictatorships. The function of the guerrilla foco was to drive the bourgeois-landowner state into the use of force, unmasking the true face of the oligarchic regime. Thus the foco itself would start the revolutionary process by turning the constitutional government into a repressive dictatorship against which popular opposition could be generated. By elaborating the concept of *foquismo,* or the primacy of the guerrilla foco itself in the revolutionary process, Che was able to apply his version of the Cuban model to virtually any Latin American country.

Che gave fair warning that the guerrilla struggle would be long and hard. In his 1966 "Message to the Tricontinental," Che predicted that "many shall perish" in the cause of the Latin American revolution.[5] His descriptions of the qualities of the guerrilla fighter portray a superman with a social conscience who is ready to die for the cause. Besides the obvious difficulties of launching and sustaining a foco, Che admitted the importance to the Cuban Revolution of that "telluric force called Fidel Castro."[6] He also pointed out the great advantage to Cuba of being the first guerrilla war to succeed: It had had the support of some of the bourgeoisie; and not knowing the true implications of the revolution, the United States had been disoriented.

Despite these warnings, Che was not entirely candid in laying out the difficulties facing guerrilla fighters. Explicit in *Guerrilla Warfare* and other writings is the official version of the struggle against Batista, the myth of the heroic guerrilla. Accordingly, despite repeated assertions that his analysis is based on the Cuban experience, Che focuses on the guerrilla foco itself, to the virtual exclusion of the broader anti-Batista struggle. After stating that "the struggles of the city masses of organized workers should not be underrated," *Guerrilla Warfare* devotes no more than 2 percent of its text to the "external front," or the urban resistance, which, it adds, should be strictly controlled by the "central command."[7] Because of the extreme popularity of the Cuban Revolution and the stature of Che Guevara, millions of Latin Americans took his words as gospel. Thus in portraying the myth of the heroic guerrilla as fact, Che was not only distorting Cuban history; he was presenting a flawed model to the revolutionaries of Latin America — one that would lead many to their deaths.

MAJOR GUERRILLA MOVEMENTS OF THE 1960s

The first couple of years after the fall of Batista witnessed a rash of guerrilla outbreaks throughout Latin America. Inspired by Castro's success, armed bands in many countries took to the mountains in emulation of the Cubans. These quixotic ventures usually fizzled as the would-be revolutionaries encountered the reality of hunger, the elements, peasant hostility, and, if this was not enough to make them abandon the quest, army bullets. While exacerbating the general climate of instability that fidelismo created, the first, naive wave of guerrilla warfare did not seriously threaten any established government.

The failed naive phase of guerrilla warfare was followed by a different kind of guerrilla movement in the early and mid-1960s. The new movements were less impulsive in their origins, better prepared, and more committed to the hard work and time necessary to overthrow a government. While none was successful, the guerrillas in Guatemala, Venezuela, Colombia, and, to a lesser extent, in Peru were powerful enough to require major governmental commitments of force and resources for their suppression. In the cases of Guatemala and Colombia, despite some changes in leadership and title, the guerrillas operated continuously into the 1990s.

Guatemala offered generally good conditions for guerrilla warfare in the early 1960s. It had appropriate terrain, oppressive rural social and land tenure systems, and a government that, although elected, was headed by a conservative general and closely overseen by the military. Between 1944 and 1954, the reform governments of Juan José Arévalo and Jacobo Arbenz had introduced far-reaching reforms that challenged the heretofore untouched hegemony of landowners and foreign capital. After organizing some 200,000 urban and rural workers and expropriating 600,000 hectares of land for redistribution — some of it belonging to the United Fruit Company — Arbenz was overthrown in 1954 by a surrogate CIA invasion force headed by Colonel Carlos Castillo Armas. Castillo Armas quickly restored the status quo ante through violent repression. Having experienced the beginnings of reform, some workers, intellectuals, and peasants were predisposed to a resumption of the struggle under the influence of fidelismo; having experienced more recently repression and retribution in the form of killings, torture, and persecution under Castillo Armas, many more were reluctant to risk their lives in a cause that might not be winnable.

The Guatemalan guerrilla movement grew out of a failed November 1960 coup by young nationalist army officers who, beyond their commitment to reform, objected to the open use of Guatemala as the CIA's training ground for Cuban exiles later to be sent to the Bay of Pigs. After going into exile, Marco Antonio Yon Sosa and Luis Turcios Lima returned to set up a foco composed of a mix of officers, nationalists, reformers, communists, and peasants.

The Rebel Armed Forces (Fuerzas Armadas Rebeldes, FAR), founded in 1962, was able to win some skirmishes and was a contributing factor in the overthrow of President Ydígoras Fuentes in 1963. Yet in the next few years the FAR and other guerrilla groups such as the 13th of November Revolutionary Movement (Movimiento Revolucionario 13 de Noviembre, MR-13) encountered serious obstacles in peasant indifference, troops trained in counterinsurgency, contingents of Green Berets in combat, and disunity within their own ranks. Severe government repression against all potential collaborators — peasants, left and moderate politicians, students, and union leaders — also hampered the guerrillas' efforts. As part of the policy of intimidation through terrorism, government troops and private right-wing death squads — such as the National Organized Anti-Communist Movement (Movimiento Anti-Comunista Nacional Organizado, MANO) and the New Anti-Communist Organization (Nueva Organización Anti-Comunista, NOA) — assassinated selectively in the cities and conducted large-scale massacres in the countryside, including the killing of 3,000–5,000 peasants in the Zacapa-Izabal area. Stymied in their attempt to establish a secure zone of operations, the guerrillas kept their visibility by killing Green Berets, kidnapping officials, and killing U.S. ambassador John Gordon Mein during a kidnap attempt in 1968.

After losing its original leaders in 1966 and 1970, the FAR disappeared. However, by 1970 the deadly cycle of guerrilla activity and government terrorism was entrenched. With military men holding office or closely supervising weak civilian governments, there has been no realistic possibility of structural reform through electoral means. Thus when new guerrilla outbreaks occurred after 1970, government and private death squads swung into action, seeking to deny guerrillas support through assassinations and rural massacres — practices that continued into the 1990s. The intensification of conflict and repression under the governments of General Romeo Lucas García (1978–82) and General José Efraín Ríos Montt (1982–83) caused unprecedented numbers of casualties. The common people of Guatemala, especially the largely Indian peasantry, have borne the cost of the standoff between guerrillas and government. Some 150,000 Guatemalans had abandoned homes and land and fled to Mexico by the mid-1980s; more had sought refuge in the United States, and by 1990 at least 150,000 — the vast majority of apolitical people caught in the violence — had been killed in Guatemala's vicious cycle of repression and rebellion.

Guerrilla activity in Venezuela developed in a very different political context. After living under military dictatorships during most of its republican history, Venezuela had established civilian government under AD leader Rómulo Betancourt in February 1959, just six weeks after Castro's victory over Batista. AD was committed to a broad program of reforms, including agrarian reform. Its ambitious goals frightened the right, while for the fidelistas AD moved too slowly to implement reforms that were too modest. Moreover, after a friendly beginning of their relationship as Latin America's newest reformers and as sworn enemies of the Trujillo dictatorship in the Dominican Republic, Castro and Betancourt soon parted ways over their differing attitudes toward reforms and elections. After the falling out, Fidel actively supported the overthrow of Betancourt in a concerted attempt to derail the leading reformist alternative of the early 1960s to his style of revolution.

Venezuela's guerrillas were a heterogeneous grouping of university students, former AD members, ex-communists, and dissident military officers. Between 1962 and 1965 the Venezuelan Communist Party embraced the armed struggle as well. The attack on AD began with urban actions that included street demonstrations, strikes, sabotage, and assassinations. Guerrilla focos were operating in the Andean terrain of nine states by 1961, but until the founding of the Armed Forces of National Liberation (Fuerzas Armadas de Liberación Nacional, FALN) in 1963 cooperation among the groups was haphazard. Despite the improved coordination that followed, counterinsurgency tactics, longstanding peasant support of AD, and the government's agrarian reform program worked against the guerrillas' attempts to establish a liberated zone.

The focos and their urban counterparts suffered a severe setback when, ignoring the guerrillas' assassination threats, over 90 percent of eligible voters turned out in the 1963 presidential elections won by AD's Raúl Leoni. Leoni's offer of amnesty further undermined the guerrillas, as did the Venezuelan Communist Party's abandonment of the fidelista line in 1965. These developments isolated FALN leader Douglas Bravo and his collaborators, reducing the guerrilla movement to a nuisance. Nonetheless, periodic skirmishes continued until 1969, when the new Christian Democratic (COPEI) government of Rafael Caldera offered another amnesty that further thinned guerrilla ranks. This action, combined with the disheartening death of Che Guevara in 1967, spelled the end of the Venezuelan guerrillas as an effective force.

Guerrilla warfare in Colombia, a complex phenomenon with unique characteristics, antedated the Cuban Revolution. Rural violence between supporters of the dominant Liberal and Conservative Parties is a long tradition in Colombia, with its roots in the nineteenth century. The assassination of populist leader Jorge Eliécer Gaitán in 1948 touched off severe urban rioting which spread to rural areas, exacerbating the endemic violence and ushering in an era known straightforwardly as "La Violencia" (The Violence). Despite strenuous efforts and some success, the weak Colombian state proved incapable of quelling the violence. By 1962, the government estimated that some 160 guerrilla bands with 3,000 members were active; moreover, several "independent republics" or liberated zones existed in the countryside, immune to Colombian government authority.

By the time of the Cuban Revolution, then, Colombia had been in the grip of La Violencia for a decade. When they appeared, fidelista groups promoted several minor focos, but it was not until 1964 that the first significant, expressly revolutionary guerrilla organization, the Army of National Liberation (Ejército de Liberación Nacional, ELN), emerged from an amalgamation of existing guerrillas with revolutionaries from the cities. The communist party founded the Colombian Revolutionary Armed Forces (Fuerzas Armadas Revolucionarias Colombianas, FARC) in 1966 on the basis of the independent peasant republic of Marquetalia, and Maoists established the Popular Liberation Army (Ejército Popular de Liberación, EPL) two years later. Father Camilo Torres, Latin America's best known guerrilla priest, fought briefly with the ELN before falling in action in 1966.

Despite the advantageous situation they inherited, the Colombian guerrillas did not enjoy great success. While the Liberal and Conservative governments that alternated in power through the 1960s were unresponsive to demands for reform, the intermittent surfacing of populist leaders demonstrated that the legal struggle was not exhausted in Colombia. Partially offsetting the socially retrograde land tenure system were extensive vacant lands and government colonization programs in the hinterlands, which relieved some pressure for agrarian reform. Although not seriously threatened by the guerrillas through the 1960s, the Colombian government was unable to defeat them with a concerted military campaign. Guerrillas remained active into the 1990s, intermingling in many cases with the cocaine traffickers.

Peru was a fourth country to experience significant guerrilla activity in the 1960s. Peru offered good terrain in the Andes and the upper Amazonian jungle for Che's version of guerrilla war. It had an impoverished, largely Indian rural population, an extremely skewed land tenure pattern, and a labor system on traditional Andean haciendas that resembled serfdom. Peru also had a history of rural uprisings against landowners and government authorities. On the other hand, when the major focos were launched Peru had a relatively popular elected president in Fernando Belaúnde Terry, a moderate reformer who favored a mild version of agrarian reform.

Dissident communists and former APRA members organized most of the guerrilla activity. Héctor Béjar, a former communist, founded the National Liberation Army (Ejército de Liberación Nacional, ELN) in 1963. It went into action in May of that year, crossing into Peru from Bolivia in an attempt to link up with Hugo Blanco's peasant movement in the Valley of La Convención. Army troops defeated the ELN near Puerto Maldonado and killed or dispersed its fighters.

After several trips to Cuba, former APRA member and MIR leader Luis de la Puente Uceda went underground in 1964 to prepare for guerrilla war. Both MIR and ELN launched focos in 1965. MIR created three separate units in different parts of the Andes. One located on the border with Ecuador did not take action. Another foco at Mesa Pelado near La Convención lasted two months in the face of the Peruvian army's elite counterinsurgency troops, trained and advised by U.S. Green Berets. The third MIR foco near the jungle town of Satipo achieved some minor victories and survived seven months before the army destroyed it. The ELN's foco in the Ayacucho region faced a similar situation; after a few successful attacks, it succumbed by the end of 1965. The strategy of multiple focos had failed to take root in Peru.

The main guerrilla movements of the 1960s, then, were partial or complete failures. At best they caused significant concern and expenditure for the governments of their countries and survived to continue fighting in the 1970s and 1980s, even into the 1990s; at worst they were snuffed out quickly and easily. Their failure is easy to understand through a comparison of the focos of the 1960s with the Cuban original. After the open discussion in the wake of Castro's triumph about the guerrilla method, the appearance of focos in any country was no surprise. Except in Venezuela, these focos lacked solid urban support to form resistance units, carry out propaganda, and provide supplies and recruits for the guerrillas. In contrast to Fidel's forces, the 1960s focos faced counter-insurgency forces whose training and equipment benefitted from the U.S. experience in Vietnam. And ignoring Che's caveat in *Guerrilla Warfare,* they all sought to overthrow elected governments, two of which — Betancourt's in Venezuela and Belaúnde's in Peru — were reformist and popular. In launching his Bolivian foco, Che Guevara intended to reverse the sagging fortunes of Latin America's guerrillas.

CHE IN BOLIVIA

Che Guevara was a highly visible figure in revolutionary Cuba. He was a member of Fidel's inner circle and the most powerful man in Cuba after Fidel and Raúl Castro. He was president of the National Bank of Cuba from November 1959 to February 1961, minister of industries from then to April 1965, a member of the executive committee of the ruling party, and a colorful and charismatic leader in his own right. Che's intractable radicalism, expressed in his establishment of moral incentives for labor and his strident criticism of the Soviet Union's relations with the Third World, eventually proved counterproductive to economic development and damaging to Cuban-Soviet relations. Thus with Fidel's blessing, Che left Cuba in April 1965 to pursue his true vocation of transnational revolutionary. After spending a few months with a guerrilla foco in the Congo, he returned to Cuba in March 1966 to develop his plans for promoting the Latin American revolution.

Che's guerrilla war in Bolivia was the centerpiece of a broad Cuban plan to reinvigorate the flagging momentum of revolution in Latin America. Despite Castro's untiring efforts to support the insurrectionary movements that his revolution had inspired, little had been accomplished in the seven years since his triumph, and prospects for revolution seemed to be dimming. While most Latin American countries experienced guerrilla movements, only four had given rise to credible focos, none of which had achieved much success. Complicating the picture was the further fragmentation of the Marxist left, not only among communists, Trotskyists, and fidelistas but by 1966 including the pro-Chinese communists and a plethora of splinter groups formed to fill the leftover theoretical interstices. Rounding out the bleak panorama facing Fidel and Che was the strident determination of the United States to stop revolution, demonstrated by U.S. support of the 1964 Brazilian coup, the 1965 invasion of the Dominican Republic, and the Pentagon's extensive and effective counterinsurgency program.

True to his character and consistent with his past behavior, Fidel responded to adversity by setting higher goals — in this case, continent-wide or even worldwide revolution. Given the growing U.S. involvement in Vietnam, Che and Fidel reasoned that the outbreak of revolutionary movements around the world might tie down U.S. military forces and ultimately stretch them to the breaking point, dealing a death blow to U.S. imperialism. In Che's words, the world's exploited masses could anticipate "a bright future should two, three, or many Vietnams flourish throughout the world with their share of deaths and immense tragedies, their everyday heroism and their repeated blows against imperialism, impelled to disperse its forces under the sudden attack and the increasing hatred of all peoples of the world."[8] To generate enthusiasm and organizational support for the emerging concept of coordinated anti-imperialist insurrection, Fidel held two important congresses in Havana within 18 months. The Tricontinental Congress, meeting in January 1966, brought together progressive governments and movements from throughout the Third World to promote anti-U.S. action. The OLAS conference, held in July 1967, was designed to cement the support of Latin America's revolutionary groups for the continental revolution.

Fidel and Che also put out a renewed call for revolution through French philosopher Régis Debray, who published *Revolution in the Revolution?* in 1967. Debray's message was simple: The failure of attempts at revolution since 1959 was due to deviations from the Cuban model — heresies such as "armed self-defense," "armed propaganda," and the subjection of the guerrilla foco to a political party. He vigorously attacked the thesis of "Cuban exceptionalism" — the notion that the Cuban Revolution was a unique phenomenon that could not be repeated elsewhere in Latin America.[9] Debray assured his readers that the correct application of Che's foco principle would yield results. He implored revolutionaries to rise above the ideological and strategic hairsplitting that divided the left and to take action in a continental insurrection against the United States and its puppets.

In order to implement the renewed push for revolution and the continental strategy, Fidel and Che devised a plan based on an extrapolation of Che's principle that the initial foco can spawn a second and then multiple fronts. A single foco, led by Che himself with veteran Cuban guerrillas and Fidel's material and moral support, would provide training and inspiration for fighters from around the hemisphere. They in turn would establish new fronts in their own countries as conditions permitted until all of Latin America would be aflame with revolution. Che initially looked to his Argentine homeland as the location of his foco but, finding little appropriate terrain, he shifted his attention to Bolivia. Cuban agents contacted Mario Monje, leader of the Bolivian Communist Party, in early 1966 and scouted the country for a base of operations.

Analysis of the failure of Che's Bolivian foco and hence of his ambitious continental strategy must begin with the question of his choice of Bolivia. Bolivia was suited in some ways to Che's purposes: It was extremely poor, heavily rural, and Indian; it had been ruled since November 1964 by a general. The largest sector of the industrial labor force, the tin miners, were well organized and militantly leftist. Situated in the heart of the Andes and bordering five South American countries, Bolivia was especially appealing as the nerve center for the continental revolution. Although Bolivia's excellent terrain was remote from the bulk of the population living on the altiplano, it appeared very suitable for purposes of launching multiple focos in several countries.

Bolivia's recent history, on the other hand, militated against Che's choice. As a result of the 1952 revolution and the subsequent thorough agrarian reform, Bolivia had no significant land problem. Despite the prevailing rural poverty, the peasantry had become essentially conservative in defense of its newly-won land. Che may also have underestimated the popularity of the government of General René Barrientos. Although by 1966 Che had embraced foquismo, or a belief in the ability of the foco to create conditions for revolution irrespective of the type of government in power, he may have interpreted the regime as a Caribbean-type reactionary regime that might be more vulnerable than an elected government to insurrection. Although he had overthrown a constitutional government in 1964, Barrientos had been elected president in 1966 with 62 percent of the vote. He was something of a populist who spoke Quechua and constantly visited remote Indian settlements to firm up his support among the rural population.

In launching his foco, Che faced two challenges common to most guerrilla movements of the 1960s but exacerbated by time and place. The United States had developed its counterinsurgency units beginning in 1961; by the time they were needed in Bolivia the U.S. forces were highly skilled at the rapid creation and subsequent advising of counterinsurgency units because of several years of training missions and military action in Latin America and additional experience in Vietnam. The universal problem of urban support was exacerbated in Bolivia by two factors. First, the foco was a Cuban operation, directed by Che; while he expected to recruit Bolivian cadres for work in the "external front" as well as the foco, his insistence on controlling the operation discouraged recruitment efforts by Bolivian Marxist groups. Second, the fragmentation typical of the Latin American left was extreme in Bolivia. While Che's agents initially dealt with Monje of the Bolivian Communist Party, they found his party caught in the common vacillation between legal and armed struggle; thus Monje's promises of fighters and urban cadres were often cancelled by the central committee. Yet when the Cubans tried to deal with more committed fidelistas such as Moisés Guevara, the communists threatened complete withdrawal. Advance man Pombo recorded the Cubans' frustration in his diary: " We asked them what they had done to date; they replied, 'Nothing.' We told them we could not sit around 20 years waiting for them."[10] On balance, the Cubans' belief in Bolivia's strategic value to the continental revolution outweighed the obvious problems of establishing a foco in that country.

Che entered the country disguised as a Uruguayan businessman in the first week of November 1966, four months after his advance party had arrived. Within days the Cubans proceeded to the large farm purchased in the rugged hills of Santa Cruz province where training was to start. The farm at Ñancahuazú met the basic requisites for a training camp: It was sprawling, relatively isolated, and contiguous to the zone selected for the foco. After the first month of secret training, however, the seemingly routine beginning disintegrated into a nightmare culminating in defeat and death. Read in juxtaposition with Che's *Guerrilla Warfare,* the diaries of Che and three Cuban companions, Rolando, Pombo, and Braulio, tell a tale of serious miscalculation and disregard for the rules; as the story unfolded, it was as though the master had not read his own guidebook.

A fundamental part of the problem was the terrain. It was remote and hilly and its vegetation was thick and spiny enough to require constant use of machetes for passage, but not sufficiently tall and dense to provide good cover for a guerrilla party. Nor were there prominent peaks for orienting Che's group. The dominant feature of the Ñancahuazú region was the Río Grande and its tributaries, which flowed between high banks forming steep canyons filled ordinarily from bank to bank with water. The scarcity of fords often necessitated the building of rafts for crossings, and incoming streams made travel along the rivers' banks difficult. The rivers took their toll in drowned men and lost supplies, and they turned out to be traps for the party — guerrillas or army — that found itself pursued into the canyons.

Che's *Guerrilla Warfare* describes foco operations in favorable and unfavorable terrain. The Ñancahuazú area is closer to the second category, raising doubts as to its selection as the launching pad for the continental revolution. Although Che prescribes tactics for successful operations in unfavorable terrain, it would seem that the choice of the Beni region, a jungle and mountain zone east of La Paz originally favored by the Cuban advance party, would have allowed greater possibilities for establishment of a liberated zone — a requisite to the foco's ultimate success. However, southeastern Bolivia offered far better access to neighboring countries than did the remote Beni; thus again the continental revolution apparently weighed more heavily in Che's calculations than did the success of the Bolivian foco itself.

The difficulty of the terrain and the guerrillas' ignorance of regional geography became manifest in February 1967 when the small group set out on a training march. The exercise, designed for 25 days, lasted 48 — twice as long as scheduled. The training march revealed two critical weaknesses in the foco, even before it planned to go into combat. In *Guerrilla Warfare,* Che posits that to compensate for the more open countryside and greater presence of roads in unfavorable terrain, "the mobility of this type of guerrilla should be extraordinary."[11] Frequently lost and slowed by the difficult riverine terrain, the foco at this early stage was anything but mobile; while *Guerrilla Warfare* suggested that a foco could march 30 to 50 kilometers per day, Che's band covered just a few kilometers on good days and almost nothing on bad days. The exercise also cost two men drowned and the loss of considerable equipment swept away by the currents.

Guerrilla Warfare also admonishes that "work on the masses . . . is even more important in the unfavorable zones."[12] While the seven-week march was not the definitive test, it was discouraging that not a single peasant joined the foco. Reflecting the demoralizing turns of events during the training march, Che's diary is full of pessimism: "A black day for me; I made it by sheer guts, for I am very exhausted" (February 23); "The men are getting increasingly discouraged at seeing the approaching end of the provisions but not of the distance to be covered" (March 7); "The morale of the men is low; Miguel has swollen feet, and there are several others in that condition" (March 15).[13]

Upon returning to the farm, tired and discouraged, the foco learned that the Bolivian army, informed by two deserters, had discovered and raided the training base. In response, Che decided to begin combat immediately before the army could organize an effective campaign against him. On March 23, the guerrillas ambushed a 32-man army patrol, killing or wounding 13 and capturing large amounts of arms and ammunition. While the victory was good for guerrilla morale, Che later lamented having engaged in combat so early, before even the semblance of a secure zone had been established.

A second successful engagement, in which the army suffered some 15 casualties, took place on April 10. In response, the government declared four southeastern provinces a "zone of emergency." A week later the foco accidentally split; despite weeks of searching for each other, wasting time, energy, and supplies needed for warfare, the band led by the Cuban Joaquín and the larger one under Che's command never linked up. During May and June a series of small, indecisive encounters took place as Che's band moved north without apparent plan. The military high point for Che came on July 6 when his group captured the small town of Samaipata on the highway linking the major cities of Cochabamba and Santa Cruz. After holding it for a few hours and acquiring some supplies, the guerrillas moved on. However, the capture of such a strategically important locale by the redoubtable Che Guevara, whose presence in Bolivia had just been announced, received worldwide news coverage. It also spurred the Bolivian command to commit two field divisions to the antiguerrilla campaign.

From this point onward, the diaries of Che and his three Cuban comrades reflect growing despair and a monotonous litany of problems: food and water shortages, exhaustion, sickness, loss of essential equipment, desertions, low morale, breaches of discipline, quarrels between Cubans and Bolivians, and a virtually total lack of support from peasants and urban cadres. All communication with Havana was lost. Three and a half months after entering combat, rather than preparing a second front the foco was reduced to a daily struggle for survival.

Central to the problems of the foco was the failure to gain the support of the area's peasantry. Che stated unequivocally in *Guerrilla Warfare* that "the guerrilla fighter needs full help from the people of the area"; he continues, "While [the enemy] must operate in regions that are absolutely hostile, finding sullen silence on the part of the peasants, the rebels have in nearly every house a friend or even a relative."[14] In the case of Che's Bolivian foco, the prescribed roles of army and guerrillas were reversed. Throughout the 11 months of its operation, not a single inhabitant of the area joined the foco; some were indifferent, others were hostile to the guerrillas and cooperative with the army, which had been carrying out civic action projects in the zone. Near the end of his venture, Che even complained that "the peasants do not give us any help and are turning into informers."[15] One of the most telling miscalculations was the language problem. Rather than Quechua, a widely spoken Indian language that most of the Bolivian guerrillas knew and the Cubans studied, the lingua franca of the zone was Guaraní, which no one in the foco spoke. In addition, the banner of agrarian reform was useless in the war zone, where land was unusually abundant.

Another critical weakness of Che's foco was the lack of reliable help from the Bolivian left. Given the failure of peasant recruitment, it was crucial to have recruits from the Bolivian cities to augment the core of Cuban veterans sent with Che. At the foco's maximum strength of 51, reached in March, 29 were Bolivians and the majority of the rest Cubans; of the 29 Bolivians, Che felt that many were uncommitted and unreliable. The presence of so many Cubans made it easy for the Bolivian government to depict the foco as a foreign invasion force, and the Cubans' beards, long hair, and speech confirmed the government's allegations to the peasantry of the zone. President Barrientos cleverly used the foreign invasion argument to firm up support at the national level, getting leaders of the powerful peasant militias to sign a "Peasant-Military Pact" against subversion in July 1967. Despite the excellent credentials and high rank of the Cubans sent to Bolivia — all were Sierra Maestra veterans and officers in the Cuban army, and four were members of the communist party's central committee — they could not build a successful foco without help from the Bolivian left and the peasantry.

Guerrilla Warfare insists that "a good supply system is of basic importance to the guerrilla band" and dwells on the need for proper equipment, clothing, and medicines.[16] The failure of supply during the final three months of Che's foco took a greater toll than the army did. Food was a constant problem. Since local support was not forthcoming, the diet was what the guerrillas could kill or pick. Che's entry for August 24 reveals the situation: "At dusk the *macheteros* returned with the traps; they caught a condor and a rotten cat. Everything was eaten together with the last piece of anteater meat."[17] Che's asthma medicine had been lost for some time, and as his attacks became more debilitating he had to resort to riding the horses and mules that were not eaten. Weapons and ammunition were in short supply as well.

In the monthly summaries that Che entered in his diary, he regularly noted the low quality of the army units sent against his foco. His analysis for September — "now the Army appears to be more effective in its actions" — reflected the integration of newly trained counterinsurgency ranger units into the forces arrayed against Che.[18] The United States had been involved in the fight against Che since the first reports of guerrilla activity, when the Pentagon had commissioned an infrared aerial reconnaissance of southeastern Bolivia that helped to locate the foco. In April 1967, a Special Forces Mobile Training Team from the Panama Canal Zone under the command of Major Ralph W. "Pappy" Shelton arrived to create counterinsurgency units. Some 650 rangers were in place by mid-August, and Che quickly detected the difference that they made. As his diary so poignantly reveals, Che was defeated by his own mistakes and miscalculations; but the Pentagon's counterinsurgency program clearly hastened his demise.

The end came for Che's guerrillas in two engagements when the army's noose finally closed on the foco. Both battles underscored the deadly potential of the rivers for trapping retreating units in exposed and inescapable gorges. Joaquín and his band were destroyed in the Vado del Yeso on August 31. After another five weeks of pursuit and skirmishes, the army pinned down Che's group in the Quebrada del Yuro on October 8, killing six and capturing Che. He was executed the next day by Bolivian officers in the presence of U.S. personnel.

RURAL GUERRILLA WARFARE AFTER CHE

Che's death transcended the eradication of a small foco in southeastern Bolivia; it was the apotheosis of the great apostle of guerrilla warfare and the burial of his plan for continental revolution. The death of the master at his own game, following upon the failures of dozens of less famous guerrillas, forced a reexamination of the foco thesis. Some revolutionaries turned to urban guerrilla warfare as the method of insurrection, while developments in Chile culminating in the election of Salvador Allende led others to reassess the possibilities of the electoral path to power. Yet while the Americans and their Latin American allies gloated over Che's demise and the fidelistas despaired, the defeat in Bolivia did not spell the end of rural guerrilla warfare in Latin America.

For the decade after 1967, few new rural focos were started. The surviving major guerrilla movements of the 1960s, those in Guatemala and Colombia, experienced periodic upswings in success but did not become serious threats to their countries' governments until the resurgence of the Guatemalan guerrillas in the late 1970s and early 1980s. A dozen years after Che's death, the 18-year struggle of the guerrilla-based Sandinista National Liberation Front (Frente Sandinista de Liberación Nacional, FSLN) against the Somoza dynasty finally succeeded. While it deviated from Che's model in significant ways, the Sandinistas' struggle reaffirmed the validity of rural guerrilla warfare as a primary means of insurrection and rekindled the hopes of Latin American revolutionaries. Two major rural guerrilla movements developed or intensified after the 1979 Sandinista victory, and both attained far more success than any of the focos of the 1960s. The insurgency in El Salvador began in the early 1970s, following over a decade of increasing tensions caused largely by the expansion of export agriculture at the expense of the small landholding peasantry. As land pressure increased, governments turned to heightened repression rather than agrarian reform to stem the rural unrest. The dominant landowner-military alliance was challenged in the 1972 elections by the rising reformist Christian Democratic Party. Its candidate, José Napoleón Duarte, won the election but after employing large-scale intimidation and fraud the government turned over the presidency to its candidate, Colonel Arturo Armando Molina. Many Salvadorans interpreted this election as the definitive closing of the possibility of reform through the political process and a few turned to guerrilla action.

The disunity of the insurrectionary forces, reflecting the fragmentation of El Salvador's political left, impeded the guerrillas for several years. By 1980, however, circumstances had changed. Another fraudulent election in 1977 confirmed the oligarchy's refusal to condone reforms, and the use of government-sanctioned death squads against peasants, leftists, and even priests and nuns increased. The 1979 Sandinista victory in neighboring Nicaragua provided encouragement and some material aid to the insurgents. The following year Archbishop Oscar Arnulfo Romero, an outspoken critic of the death squads and government violations of human rights, was assassinated, apparently by government agents. These developments led to the founding in 1980 of the umbrella Farabundo Martí National Liberation Front (Frente Farabundo Martí de Liberación Nacional, FMLN) to coordinate guerrilla activity.

Shortly after its inauguration, the Reagan administration issued a "White Paper" that, ignoring the indigenous roots of the rebellion and the government's glaring use of terrorism against the populace, declared the Salvadoran conflict a case of communist subversion directed by Moscow and abetted by Havana and Managua. Thus justifying intervention, the United States sent massive amounts of military and economic aid as well as contingents of military advisors, who virtually took charge of counterinsurgency operations from the Salvadoran military in order to prevent the government's collapse. Meanwhile, tacitly amending its interpretation of the causes of the war, the Reagan administration pressured the various short-lived juntas of the early 1980s into agrarian and other reforms to reduce the appeal of the guerrillas. The election of moderate reformer Duarte to the presidency in 1984 raised hopes for a peaceful solution, but the guerrillas continued fighting as, behind the scenes, the military continued to obstruct reform and use violence virtually at will against civilians as well as insurgents.

During the Duarte administration (1984–89), the civil war stabilized with the government holding the main cities and keeping the highways open by day, and the guerrillas controlling substantial territory and operating relatively freely at night, disrupting transportation and sabotaging utilities and military installations. The election of conservative President Alfredo Cristiani in 1989 seemed to reduce the prospects of either a guerrilla victory or a negotiated peace. However, following the Sandinistas' loss of power in Nicaragua and a thwarted guerrilla offensive in May 1990 that carried the fighting into the streets of San Salvador, representatives of the FMLN and the government began negotiating to end the war that had claimed at least 75,000 lives and created a million refugees since its escalation in 1980.

The second major rural guerrilla movement to develop since Che's death is the Sendero Luminoso, or Shining Path, in Peru. Sendero Luminoso traces its pedigree back to the fidelista mobilization of the 1960s, when it was founded in Ayacucho as a unit of the new National Liberation Front (Frente de Liberación Nacional, FLN). The movement has always been centered in Ayacucho, where its founder and leader, Abimael Guzmán Reynoso, held a teaching post in the University of Huamanga. A colonial university, Huamanga reopened after a long hiatus in 1959 with the mission of supporting development through educational outreach to the predominantly Indian population of the impoverished south-central Andean region.

Sendero Luminoso combines Maoist principles with a strong grounding in indigenist nationalism. The Maoist influence is evident in the movement's emphasis on long-term cultivation of support among the rural masses prior to launching armed action; the Ayacucho command broke with the FLN in 1965 over the decision to launch guerrilla focos that year. In 1970 the Ayacucho group formed the Communist Party of Peru in the Shining Path of Mariátegui (Partido Comunista del Perú en el Sendero Luminoso de Mariátegui). José Carlos Mariátegui, founder of Peru's original communist party in 1928 and the most influential social critic of twentieth-century Peru, advocated abolition of the existing land tenure system and a return to a hypothetical pure native Andean communism rooted in the communal village. Sendero Luminoso has demonstrated the appeal of

Mariátegui's ideas to the extremely downtrodden Indians of the Ayacucho region. Before taking up the armed struggle in 1980, Guzmán and his followers patiently built support among the highland Indian communities of Ayacucho and adjacent departments. The largely Indian, Quechua-speaking student body at Huamanga University imbibed the ideas of Sendero Luminoso in classes and study groups. The converts took the message of revolution back to the rugged countryside where they returned as agricultural technicians, nurses, and especially as teachers. The military government's agrarian reform of the 1970s, designed precisely to preempt revolution by creating new landowners, had a very limited impact in Ayacucho where overpopulation and lack of usable land limited benefits but not expectations. Thus after nearly two decades of preparation and following the failure of agrarian reform in the area, Sendero Luminoso took up arms in 1980.

Sendero Luminoso's plan involved four stages of armed struggle, progressing from attacks on symbols of state authority to the eventual encirclment of the major cities and seizure of power. By 1982 guerrilla war was well advanced, forcing the government to place three Andean departments under military jurisdiction. Sendero Luminoso also extended its activities into Lima and began coordination with the Túpac Amaru Revolutionary Movement (Movimiento Revolucionario Túpac Amaru, MRTA), founded in 1984, in bombings, sabotage, and assassinations. A favored tactic after 1985 was the assassination of town and village mayors affiliated with APRA, the party in power nationally. Sendero Luminoso and MRTA sought to disrupt the 1990 national elections, but despite an escalation of threats and assassinations the elections were held as scheduled.

At the outset of the 1990s the sui generis Peruvian guerrilla movement appeared to be at least holding its own. Sendero Luminoso held a large amount of territory in several Andean departments despite repeated military assaults and government repression. Both insurgents and government had committed massacres and thoroughly terrorized the inhabitants of the zone. Reliable estimates put the death toll of a decade of guerrilla warfare and government counterinsurgency at over 20,000. Two factors will be important in determining the course of conflict in the 1990s: the extent to which the strongly indigenist views of Sendero Luminoso are transplanted to the millions of inhabitants of Lima's teeming slums; and the ability of President Alberto Fujimori, elected in 1990, to revive the moribund Peruvian economy.

NOTES

1. Che Guevara, *Guerrilla Warfare*, B. Loveman and T. M. Davies, eds. (Lincoln: University of Nebraska Press, 1985), 47.

2. Ibid., 47–48.

3. Ibid., 48.

4. Guevara, "Guerrilla Warfare: A Method," in *Guerrilla Warfare*, 186.

5. Guevara, "Message to the Tricontinental," in *Guerrilla Warfare*, 208.

6. Guevara, "Cuban Exceptionalism?" in George Lavan, ed., *Che Guevara Speaks: Selected Speeches and Writings* (New York: Grove Press, 1968), 26.

7. Guevara, *Guerrilla Warfare*, 48, 130–31.

8. Guevara, "Message to the Tricontinental," in *Guerrilla Warfare*, 213.

9. Régis Debray, *Revolution in the Revolution? Armed Struggle and Political Struggle in Latin America*, tr. by Bobbye Ortiz (New York: Grove Press, 1967).

10. Pombo's diary, 24 September 1966, in Daniel James, ed., *The Complete Bolivian Diaries of Che Guevara and Other Captured Documents* (New York: Stein and Day, 1968), 274.

11. Guevara, *Guerrilla Warfare*, 69–70.

12. Ibid., 75.

13. James, ed., *Bolivian Diaries*, 116, 121, 124.

14. Guevara, *Guerrilla Warfare*, 50, 115.

15. James, ed., *Bolivian Diaries*, 219.

16. Guevara, *Guerrilla Warfare*, 120.

17. James, ed., *Bolivian Diaries*, 199.

18. Ibid., 219.

6

Urban Guerrilla Warfare

The death of Che Guevara and the defeat of his Bolivian foco cut short Fidel Castro's concerted efforts of 1966 and 1967 to revive the momentum of revolution in Latin America. The continental revolution, the two, three, many Vietnams strategy, even foquismo itself rang hollow after the apostle was added to the long list of martyrs to the cause of reproducing the Cuban Revolution. Yet within two years of Che's death, a new wave of insurrection rekindled the hopes of the revolutionaries and the fears of Washington and its Latin American allies.

Urban guerrilla warfare, an adaptation of Che's approach to the seizure of power, was in full swing in Uruguay, Chile, Brazil, and Argentina by 1969. Even in Brazil, where the urban guerrillas were least successful, they were more effective than most of the rural focos of the 1960s had been. Urban guerrilla warfare was far more threatening to the governments of Uruguay and Argentina than rural focos had been anywhere outside of Cuba. Thus the rise of urban guerrilla warfare and its early successes in some of Latin America's largest and most developed countries breathed new life into the faltering Latin American revolution.

Although at variance with Che's prescriptions, urban guerrilla warfare represented a revival and continuation of the influence of the Cuban Revolution. The most prominent of the Brazilian urban guerrillas, Carlos Marighela, led the Brazilian delegation to the OLAS meeting in Havana; having absorbed the fidelista message of the conference, upon his return Marighela broke with the Brazilian Communist Party and took up the armed struggle against the military government. The Tupamaros consciously based their movement on Che's foco principle and set out to create revolutionary conditions in Uruguay through revolutionary action. In Argentina, several of the urban guerrilla organizations traced their lineage to earlier, failed rural focos. One Argentine leader explicitly linked

Che's death to the guerrillas' turn to the cities: "Che was killed. Therefore, we had to change our way of thinking."[1]

Although seemingly abrupt, the transition from rural to urban guerrilla warfare had antecedents in the early and mid-1960s. Two movements of that period made extensive use of urban armed units even while concentrating on the countryside. During the height of the Venezuelan guerrilla movement in 1962 and 1963, a major portion of the insurrection was concentrated in the cities, especially Caracas. Clandestine urban cadres organized combat units to conduct sabotage, demonstrations, assassinations, and other activities culminating in the unsuccessful effort to disrupt the 1963 elections. The Guatemalan guerrillas for a while also had urban units to complement the activities of their primarily rural forces, and some urban activity often accompanied the predominantly rural struggle in other countries. In the area of theory, at least one writer began a vigorous advocacy of urban-based revolutionary war while rural focos were still in vogue: Abraham Guillén, an exiled veteran of the Spanish Civil War living in Argentina and Uruguay, published his *Strategy of the Urban Guerrilla* in 1966, prior to Che's Bolivian venture.[2]

STRATEGIES OF URBAN GUERRILLA WARFARE

Unlike the major authors of tracts on rural guerrilla war, none of the writers on the urban guerrilla was the protagonist of a successful movement. In contrast to Mao, Giap, and Che Guevara, who wrote up their experiences and presented them as theories and models for emulation, those who wrote on the urban guerrilla drew on historic cases, on critiques of Che's foco theory and the attempts to apply it, and on their own unsuccessful or unfinished experiences. Thus no theorist of urban guerrilla war wrote with the authority of a Mao, a Giap, or a Guevara, and consequently no source comparable to the corpus of Che's works existed to guide the revolutionaries in Latin America's cities.

Abraham Guillén was the most prolific and probably the most widely read author on the urban guerrilla. He based his message partially on urban insurrections in Europe, particularly on the Paris Commune of 1871 and the Russian Revolution of 1917, and on the 1936 Madrid resistance to Franco in which he had participated. Guillén was also a close observer of the Latin American scene who carefully analyzed the failures of the rural foco strategy in the countries where it had been applied. After moving from Buenos Aires to Montevideo, he became acquainted with the Tupamaros during their formative phase. Thus his thoughts on the urban guerrilla reflect a synthesis of study, experience, and observation.

Although Guillén's revision of Che is quite thorough, the two agreed on the continental strategy of revolutionary linkage. Guillén wrote that "to the 'holy alliance' of the indigenous oligarchy and yanqui imperialism we must answer with an offensive of Latin American liberation on all fronts, in all countries, in the cities and the countryside, through a revolutionary war on a continental scale."[3] He went further, proposing the creation of mechanisms to hasten pan-Latin American cooperation in pursuit of revolution. Borrowing from APRA founder and ideologist Víctor Raúl Haya de la Torre, he posited the creation of continent-wide mass organizations, including labor unions, parties, youth organizations, and a Latin American liberation front.

Guillén's differences with Che are fully aired in writings that preceded as well as followed Guevara's death. The Spaniard felt that Che's faith in the ability of the foco to create conditions for revolutions was misguided: "Foquismo . . . is petty bourgeois in origin as well as outlook — evident in the token number of workers and peasants in the guerrillas' ranks. Actually, it is an insurrectional movement for piling up cadavers, for giving easy victories to the repressive generals trained by the Pentagon."[4] A strong mass line was necessary for victory, specifically "an antioligarchical and anti-imperialist popular front based on a program of liberation that brings together workers, peasants, the proletarianized middle class and even a section of the native bourgeoisie fearful of being pushed to the wall by imperialism; [otherwise] the guerrilla will lose the war . . . from failure to obtain the support of the great mass of the population of an underdeveloped country."[5] Guillén inserted a caveat similar to the one that Che had placed in *Guerrilla Warfare*: Revolution could only succeed in a country where the ruling class had lost its prestige and legitimacy as the result of some profound crisis or serious economic decline.

Guillén categorically rejected the primacy of the rural struggle. Referring to the failure of the Peruvian focos of 1965, he wrote: "To organize a small revolutionary army and to isolate it from the popular masses in a mountainous terrain, without a territorial organization to support it, is to expose it to implacable destruction."[6] In another piece, he argued: "It would be absurd in our epoch of highly developed urban populations to launch the principal front of a revolution in small villages or mountains under conditions in which peasants are no longer a majority and there are few logistical resources for modern warfare."[7] For Guillén, any country with an urban majority — nine of the twenty Latin American countries by 1970 — must have the main revolutionary movement in the cities; rural guerrillas should operate also, where feasible, but always in a supporting role. Despite pretensions to broader application, Guillén seems to have had Argentina and Uruguay, and possibly Chile, primarily in mind as locations for urban guerrilla movements. Argentina and Uruguay were preponderantly urban, had large capital cities that dominated national life, and lacked the mountain and jungle terrain favored by rural guerrillas, although Argentina's Andean regions offered enough potential to have attracted a few short-lived rural focos during the 1960s.

Despite the availability of writings on theories and strategies of urban guerrilla warfare, the urban fighters seemed to be guided above all by pragmatic considerations. After Che's death and the eclipse of the rural foco, Southern Cone revolutionaries were better able to focus on the situation in their own countries. No longer blinded by the myth of rural guerrilla invincibility, they could see more clearly that with their huge urban populations and flat, open terrain, the Cuban model had never been relevant to their situation. The urban guerrillas took guidance from Guillén, Marighela, and others, but unlike the practitioners of the rural foco, they had no single annointed theoretician whose words rang with the authority of victory. Strategies and tactics were usually flexible, based on trial and error. One Argentine urban guerrilla stated straightforwardly: "We put things into practice before we made up theories about them"; a Uruguayan counterpart confirmed this approach, arguing that "there is no better revolutionary theory than that derived from revolutionary actions themselves."[8] Freedom from the constraints of dogma may have given the urban guerrillas an advantage over their rural counterparts who read and sought to emulate Che.

THE TUPAMAROS OF URUGUAY

In a widely circulated interview conducted in 1967, a leader of Uruguay's Tupamaros paraphrased Fidel Castro: "Each revolutionary, each revolutionary group has only one duty: *to prepare* to make the revolution."[9] As much as anything, the emphasis on preparation for revolutionary action set the Tupamaros off from other Latin American guerrilla movements, both rural and urban. From its first action in July 1963 — the theft of some guns from the Swiss Rifle Club in Nueva Helvecia — fully four years of intense preparatory work went by before the guerrillas launched full-scale war on the government.

The Tupamaros are best known for having pioneered urban guerrilla warfare in Latin America. Despite earlier instances of important urban components of guerrilla movements, the Tupamaros were the first to reject Che's tenet of the primacy of the rural struggle. Although stressing the need for rural warfare as a complementary action, to the Uruguayan guerrillas the urban theater was the decisive one — the site where the revolution would be won or lost.

The Tupamaros did not generate a theory or grand strategy of urban guerrilla warfare. To a certain point, Abraham Guillén may have been writing for the Tupamaros, but not as an authorized spokesman. Nonetheless, writings and interviews reveal that the Tupamaros embraced urban guerrilla warfare as a matter of expediency. In the words of one leader, without urban warfare "those countries lacking the geographical conditions favorable to rural guerrilla warfare . . . would have to discard armed struggle in the process of a revolution."[10] Uruguay, a small country of 72,000 square miles and a population of 3 million, is flat and largely devoted to pasture. It has the least hospitable terrain in all of Latin America for rural focos, so poor that it falls short of the conditions Che described as "unfavorable terrain." Despite having an economy based on meat and wool exports, Uruguay in 1979 was Latin America's second most urbanized country, after Argentina. Eighty per cent of its population lived in cities and towns and half resided in Montevideo, a city of 1.5 million. As one Tupamaro put it, "we have a big city with more than 300 square kilometers of buildings, which allows for the development of an urban struggle."[11]

Despite reversing the fields of action, the Tupamaros shared two fundamental concepts with Che. They identified with the foco principle, "the principle that revolutionary action in itself . . . generates revolutionary consciousness, organization, and conditions."[12] They also adhered to the notion of continental revolution and maintained a Committee on International Affairs that developed contacts with revolutionary movements and friendly governments in Latin America and throughout the world.

The challenge facing the guerrillas was formidable, in large part because Uruguay, along with Chile, was the bastion of constitutional government in South America. Often called the "Switzerland of South America" because of its prosperity, political stability, and experimentation with a Swiss-type plural executive system, Uruguay boasted a tradition of civilian government based on regular elections, broad participation, a two-party system, and well developed individual liberties. Uruguay was Latin America's most advanced welfare state, having nearly three-quarters of its labor force covered by the social security system.

What the Tupamaros saw and hoped to exploit was what they called the Uruguayan crisis. The economy by the 1950s was becoming stagnant; heavily dependent on its raw material export base, Uruguay had exhausted the growth potential of import-substitution industrialization without having modernized its rural sector, whose productivity was far lower than that of the similar Argentine rural economy. A secular decline in wool prices exacerbated these conditions. The result of this economic conjuncture was inflation, rising unemployment, and a pronounced deterioration in living standards through the 1960s for the Uruguayan middle and working classes and the development of a marginal sector of slum-dwelling unemployed.

The Tupamaros' analysis also detected a growing hollowness of Uruguayan democracy. An unusual form of proportional representation kept third parties from making gains against the historically dominant Colorados and second place Blancos. While there had been no interruption of constitutional continuity, there was mounting evidence of corruption and of citizen cynicism in the 1960s. The economic decline led to a dramatic growth in labor unrest and strikes, to which the government responded with states of siege in 1965, 1967, 1968, and 1969. The Uruguayan situation probably served Guillén as the model of a ruling class that had lost its prestige and legitimacy in a setting of economic decline.

All in all, the Tupamaros concluded that whereas a prosperous and democratic Uruguay had been the exception, "the process of the deterioration of its economy . . . gradually included Uruguay in the rest of the Latin American scene. Therefore, objective conditions in Uruguay are no longer different from those in the rest of Latin America."[13] Their job was to create the subjective conditions through revolutionary action and the building of mass support in a polity where the legal struggle was far from exhausted, as reflected in the continuing electoral process and heightened strike activity.

Preparations for the revolutionary struggle began in 1963 with the assault on the Swiss Rifle Club led by union organizer and Socialist Party member Raúl Sendic. Originally named the National Liberation Movement (Movimiento de Liberación Nacional, MLN), the Tupamaros attracted dissidents from Marxist and left groups who embraced the activist fidelista approach to revolution. The MLN made a virtue of the diversity of its members' ideological and party backgrounds. In a marked contrast to most countries, where insurrectionary movements reflected the fragmentation and mutual animosity of the left, the Uruguayan guerrillas lived by their slogan, "nonsectarian armed struggle," with few exceptions. The MLN later adopted its popular name, derived from the Inca noble Tupac Amaru II who in 1780, in highland Peru, led the greatest indigenous rebellion in the history of the Spanish empire in the Americas.[14]

During their four years of underground preparation the Tupamaros carefully avoided confrontations with superior government forces — confrontations they would lose. They escalated their actions gradually, from break-ins to bank robberies to bombings, but always eschewing fights with police and troops and avoiding any killings. The Tupamaros' reputation as romantic, benign revolutionaries was based on their restraint and on their Robin Hood-style actions to benefit the poor, such as a Christmas Eve "Hunger Commando" hijacking of a food truck and distribution of its contents in the slums. Concurrent with their visible actions the Tupamaros were active with clandestine recruitment. Consisting largely of middle-class students and professionals, the movement also included workers, military, and upper class elements who lived apparently normal lives but for their clandestine activities. They also established an infrastructure to sustain the armed struggle: supply networks, safe houses, even underground clinics equipped for emergency surgery as well as long-term recuperative care.

As their numbers and facilities grew, the Tupamaros developed an elaborate organization designed to maximize fighting potential while insulating the movement against detection and destruction. Following the concept of compartmentalization, the structure consisted of a central executive committee and columns of 30 to 50 people, each containing cells of between 5 and 10 members. Although coordinated from above, each column was designed to be self-sustaining in the case of trouble at the top; thus the columns were equipped to gather intelligence, maintain supplies, and undertake armed or propaganda action independently, making it theoretically possible for one surviving column to regenerate the movement. Outside the underground itself were support committees that helped in recruiting, securing supplies, and providing needed skills.

The emerging guerrilla movement suffered a serious setback in December 1966 and January 1967, when an unintended encounter with police led to arrests and the discovery of safe houses and supplies. The organization proved resilient, however, and by 1968 the Tupamaros escalated their pressure, moving from the "Robin Hood" stage of self-publicity and exposing the regime to a more aggressive phase of direct challenges to government authority. The first kidnapping was in August 1968 when the Tupamaros seized unpopular industrialist and government official Ulysses Pereira Reverbel and held him for four days. In July

1969 they drew their first blood, attacking and killing some police. By September 1969 they had established a clandestine radio.

"Operation Pando," an event commemorating the second anniversary of Che Guevara's death, was the Tupamaros' real coming-out party. On October 8, 1969, some 50 Tupamaros occupied Pando, a city of 60,000 inhabitants, for several hours. Having arrived individually or in small groups by private and public transportation, in a carefully coordinated action the guerrillas captured the main public buildings, robbed the banks, and harangued the populace. A policeman and 3 guerrillas were killed and 16 Tupamaros were captured, but the demonstration of guerrilla power was a sobering challenge to the authority of the state.

By November 1969, while continuing their food distribution in slums, bank robberies, bombings, and kidnappings, the Tupamaros assumed the state function of dispensing justice. This included assassinations of police accused of torturing arrested guerrillas and the arrest and — on several occasions — the trial of government and foreign officials for complicity in counterinsurgency activities. Dan Mitrione, an instructor in AID's Office of Public Safety police counterinsurgency training program in Uruguay, was seized in July 1970 and held in the guerrillas' "People's Prison" for the release of 150 political prisoners. The maneuver backfired, however, as President Jorge Pacheco Areco refused to negotiate, declared a state of siege, and launched an intense search for People's Prison. The government operation netted nine leading Tupamaros, including Raúl Sendic. The guerrillas retaliated on August 9 by executing Mitrione, whom they accused of teaching sophisticated torture techniques to the police. Full-scale war was on.

For the next two years, the Tupamaros' fortunes fluctuated between spectacular successes and severe setbacks. In November 1970 the guerrillas carried out the largest bank robbery in Uruguayan history. They seized British Ambassador Geoffrey Jackson the following January and held him in People's Prison. In July 1971, 38 Tupamaros escaped from Women's Prison, followed in September by the escape of 106 Tupamaros, including Sendic, from Punta Carretas Prison. Maintaining a sense of humor despite the earnestness of the war, escaping guerrillas painted on the tunnel they had dug: "MLN (Tupamaro) Transit Authority: Please keep to your left."[15] Three days after the Punta Carretas escape, the guerrillas released Geoffrey Jackson.

Influenced by the recent electoral victory of Salvador Allende in Chile, the Tupamaros declared their support for the leftist Broad Front coalition in the national elections scheduled for November 1971 and in September called a truce with the government. The election's results belied the Tupamaros' strategy: The Broad Front received only 18 percent of the vote and conservative Colorado Juan María Bordaberry won the presidency. The Tupamaros broke their truce in December 1971, when a column occupied the city of Paysandú and carried out coordinated actions in nearby towns. It appeared that the guerrillas were on the verge of opening a rural front in preparation for a final assault on the government.

Shortly after the Paysandú action the government's counterinsurgency program, aided and advised by U.S. officials, began to bear fruit. Earlier government actions — periodic states of siege, closure of left parties and press organs, enhanced police and military presence — had proven ineffectual against the guerrillas. As the Tupamaros' strength and aggressiveness grew, the authorities developed progressively tougher responses. Government-sponsored or -tolerated paramilitary death squads, similar to those in Brazil, Guatemala, and later in Argentina and El Salvador, targeted guerrillas and leftists in general. The abduction of Ambassador Jackson brought the most energetic and repressive measures to date. With congress granting a state of siege, 10,000 troops and police cordoned off areas of the capital and conducted building-by-building searches for People's Prison. The Pacheco government placed the military in charge of all guerrilla activity in September 1971. On April 15, 1972, the day after the Tupamaros executed four men for involvement in the death squads, the Bordaberry government declared a "state of internal war" and began a census of householders and the registration of all Montevideo residents in an effort to force guerrillas out of safe houses and discourage all collaboration with them. All news of the guerrillas and the counterinsurgency drive was censored.

The government's all-out campaign, combined with valuable information extracted from captured Tupamaro leader Héctor Amodio Pérez, soon brought results. After discovering People's Prison in May 1972, the government announced on July 15 that it had captured over 600 Tupamaros, killed 100, and located 70 of their safe houses in the past three months. On September 1, counterinsurgency forces wounded and captured Raúl Sendic. Guerrilla actions continued, but at a greatly diminished pace.

Following their successes in counterinsurgency, the military and the Bordaberry administration met increased levels of political opposition from civilians demanding relaxation of security measures and opposing a restrictive new education law designed to control student activism. The military reacted harshly to criticism of its involvement in death squads and alleged brutal treatment of prisoners. Facing a wave of labor unrest and political protest, Bordaberry acceded to the gradual militarization of his government until the culminating coup of June 1973, when he closed congress and municipal governments and began to rule by decree with a military-civilian cabinet. With its now unfettered power turned on the guerrillas, the government quickly ended the era of significant Tupamaro action.

A postmortem on the Tupamaros suggests that several factors contributed to their defeat. The Uruguayan case did not appear to bear out Che's concept that the foco would create conditions for revolution by forcing governments to become repressive. Rather, after the struggle became intense and bloody, the guerrillas appear to have lost much of the support that they had enjoyed during their earlier Robin Hood phase. The effectiveness of the government response helped to deny the guerrillas the wide backing they needed. U.S. aid in counterinsurgency strengthened the government's response and helped to turn the tide against the guerrillas. Finally, the government displayed a determination to win the war, whatever the cost in political and individual rights. The ultimate defeat of the Tupamaros, however, should not obscure the fact that theirs was the most promising insurrection since Castro's. In contrast to the many rural focos of the 1960s, the Tupamaros seriously threatened to topple the government of their country and seize power. Defeat of the Tupamaros required an all-out government effort and cost Uruguay a decade of repressive military-based dictatorship and the loss of its distinctive political tradition. The success of the Tupamaros helped sustain the hopes for revolution in Latin America and inspired emulation in Brazil, Chile, and Argentina.

URBAN GUERRILLAS IN CHILE AND BRAZIL

The urban orientation of guerrilla warfare in Chile was essentially a practical matter. The western slope of the Andes that forms Chile's borders with Argentina and Bolivia offers very little cover and the forested areas of the south are too accessible for long-term covert activity. By contrast Santiago, a city of 2.2 million in 1965 and the country's economic and administrative center, appeared to offer an attractive setting for armed insurrection. Urban guerrilla warfare in Chile was primarily the work of the Movement of the Revolutionary Left (Movimiento de Izquierda Revolucionaria, MIR), a group founded in 1966 by students at the University of Concepción. MIR went into action the following year against the reformist government of Eduardo Frei, beginning with a campaign of nonlethal bombings directed at U.S.-connected installations in Santiago and broadening in 1968 to include Chilean targets such as newspaper and party offices. Between November 1969 and June 1970, MIR escalated its attacks to include armed assaults, bank robberies, and airplane hijackings, the latter causing the first fatality attributed to the guerrillas. MIR also cultivated support in slum areas through organizational work and donations of expropriated money.

In its first three years of activity, MIR appeared to follow the Tupamaro pattern of a measured escalation of actions designed to demonstrate its power while avoiding premature confrontations with superior government forces. The possibilities of success for the urban guerrilla approach in Chile, however, were not fully tested owing to the suspension of MIR's antigovernment actions during the 1970 presidential campaign. Despite its conviction that the revolution could not be won at the ballot box, MIR agreed to the suspension in order to avoid creating a major law and order issue that would work against leftist candidate Salvador Allende.

After Allende's election, MIR switched roles, becoming an ally of the government but not always a welcome one. It operated on the fringe of power and beyond the limits of strict legality to foster mobilization by promoting seizures of land and factories and generally pushing to radicalize the government's policies. MIR simultaneously prepared for the civil war or military coup that it was certain would come. Its organization was badly damaged in the 1973 coup that overthrew Allende, severely limiting its ability to mount effective action against the military government of General Augusto Pinochet.

Like Chile, Brazil experienced a relatively brief period of warfare in the cities. Yet between 1969 and 1971 the Brazilian urban guerrillas made headlines as a result of their bold moves, which included bank robberies, kidnappings, assaults, and prison breaks. Of the various forms of resistance to the military government installed in 1964 and its successors, the urban guerrilla movement was the most dramatic and, while it lasted, the most threatening to the regime.

The context within which the Brazilian urban guerrillas developed was diametrically opposite that in which the Tupamaros and Chile's MIR evolved. The 1964 government that replaced Goulart was reasonably moderate in comparison with later regimes. It did not abolish civilian institutions but rather sought to dominate through reserving the presidency for a military man, strengthening presidential powers at the expense of congress and the states, and taming the politicians. However, periodic confrontations proved that even the purged politicians were insufficiently pliable, requiring the military to assume more direct control. By 1967 it was apparent that existing political channels were ineffective, leading some to conclude that the armed struggle offered the only hope for change.

Beginning with a foco launched in the Serra de Caparão in early 1967, a variety of fidelista groups attempted to pursue rural guerrilla warfare. All of these focos succumbed quickly to the swift actions of the Brazilian army. By 1968, the underground resistance had begun preparations for armed action in Brazil's cities. In early 1969, following a harsh crackdown that ended all pretense of civilian participation in government, the urban guerrillas swung into action.

Carlos Marighela was the leading Brazilian theoretician of the urban guerrilla. In assessing the possibilities of insurrection against Brazil's firmly entrenched military regime, Marighela concluded that the cities offered the best possibilities for successful action. In addition to São Paulo and Rio de Janeiro, with 8.4 and 7.2 million inhabitants respectively, Brazil in the late 1960s had four other cities of over a million people and five more of over half a million. Overall, Brazil was 55 percent urban. While it possessed seemingly unlimited jungle terrain, most of that was remote from major population centers, making communications and supply extremely difficult. The quick defeats of rural focos convinced Marighela that the cities were the appropriate starting point, but he believed that guerrilla activity would later shift to the countryside and finally produce a field army capable of defeating the government's forces. Thus in contrast to Guillén, Carlos Marighela reaffirmed Che's belief in the primacy of rural struggle in Brazil: "(a) The city is the area of complementary struggle, and the whole urban struggle whether on the guerrilla or mass-movement front, must always be seen as tactical struggle. (b) The decisive struggle will be in the rural area."[16]

Marighela's *Manual of the Urban Guerrilla,* a training guide for city fighters similar to Che's handbook for rural guerrillas, describes the purposes, organization, and activities of the urban guerrillas. It offers detailed instructions on the use of arms, ambushes, sabotage, escapes, and other practical advice for urban guerrillas. Ultimately, however, the success of the urban fighter rests on the same two assumptions that pervade Che's analysis of the rural guerrilla: the support of the populace and the superior qualities of the revolutionary. "The urban guerrilla is characterized by courage and a spirit of initiative. He must be a good tactician and a good shot, and make up for his inferiority in weapons, ammunition, and equipment by his skill and cunning." But above all, "his moral superiority is incontestable."[17] As to popular support, "when they see that the revolutionaries' firepower is being directed against their enemies, the masses — hitherto helpless against the dictatorship — will recognize the guerrillas as their ally and come to their support."[18]

The truncated history of the Brazilian urban guerrillas demonstrates little of either the guerrillas' superiority or the growth of popular support. In contrast to the Tupamaros, the Brazilian guerrillas were divided into various independent groups; despite efforts to unite, their fragmentation reduced their effectiveness. During the period of greatest activity, 1969 through 1971, the movement's successes, however spectacular, were outstripped by its failures. Major bank robberies, raids on military and police barracks, kidnappings of the U.S., West German, and Swiss ambassadors, and the exchange of these officials for political prisoners were among the high points of the guerrillas' successes. These accomplishments, however, were outmatched by the deaths of Marighela and other guerrilla leaders, mass arrests of guerrillas and sympathizers, and the decimation of entire organizations. Like so many of the rural focos, the Brazilian urban guerrillas took actions that were too bold, actions certain to elicit strong retaliation, before they had the numbers, training, and organization to survive the government's counteroffensive. The Brazilian case also demonstrates the difficulties of challenging a dictatorship that recognizes no limitations on its use of force.

ARGENTINA'S URBAN GUERRILLAS

Despite the predominance of flat, open terrain in Argentina, the Andean foothills in the country's northwest offer some prospects for rural guerrilla warfare. Thus, in common with most of the hemisphere, Argentina was the scene of rural guerrilla outbreaks following Fidel's seizure of power in Cuba. Movements launched in 1959 and 1963 were easily defeated, and another rural foco met an early demise at its training camp in Tucumán province in 1968. Thereafter, influenced by the death of Che and by the successful operations of the Tupamaros in neighboring Uruguay, the Argentina revolutionaries turned to the cities as the site of the armed struggle. In addition to greater Buenos Aires, whose 10 million people accounted for some 40 percent of the national population, Córdoba, Rosario, and Mendoza each had approximately three quarters of a million inhabitants by 1970.

During their first few years, most of the Argentine urban guerrillas were at least nominally Peronist while most were also Marxist. This ideological and programmatic blend reflected recent Argentine political history, which had been dominated by Juan Perón. After his overthrow in 1955, stable government had proven impossible because of the continuing deep division over Perón and his millions of loyal followers, including the great bulk of Argentina's 2.5 million trade union members. The political rights of Peronists, their parties and unions, and ultimately the matter of Perón's return to power were at question, and neither the military establishment nor civilian politicians could agree on how to deal with the issue. Thus from 1955 on, civilian and military governments using either repression or conciliation toward the Peronists alternated in power, with none achieving peace and stability.

For the guerrillas, who came into existence during the hard-line regime of General Juan Carlos Onganía (1966–70), the return of Perón was a strategy for achieving what they hoped would be revolution from above — a hope based on Perón's repeated declarations of his intention to establish a "socialist fatherland." Because most of them were Peronist, the urban guerrillas were programmatically in the mainstream of Argentine politics even while, in terms of strategy, they occupied a fringe position within the heterogeneous Peronist movement. Thus in contrast to their Brazilian and Uruguayan counterparts, many of the Argentine guerrillas shared considerable common ground with unionists and politicians, and their actions were designed to strengthen those bonds and move the working class to greater militance. Their armed actions were also designed to make the country even more ungovernable than it had been since 1955, leaving the return of Perón as the only option for restoring political peace. In pursuing a broadly popular and concrete objective — the return of Perón — and by virtue of being an element of the political mainstream, the Argentine urban guerrillas were in a much better position to succeed than were the guerrilla movements, both rural and urban, that sought the far more ambitious objective of system overthrow.

The Argentine urban guerrillas went into action in the wake of the "Cordobazo," a May 1969 workers' uprising in the industrial center of Córdoba that spread to several other cities. Encouraged by this display of antigovernment militance, nearly a dozen urban guerrilla bands were operating before the end of 1970. The five major groups were the Marxist-Leninist Armed Forces of Liberation (Fuerzas Armadas de Liberación, FAL); the Trotskyist People's Revolutionary Army (Ejército Revolucionario del Pueblo, ERP); the Marxist-Leninist-Peronist Revolutionary Armed Forces (Fuerzas Armadas Revolucionarias, FAR); the Peronist Armed Forces (Fuerzas Armadas Peronistas, FAP); and the Peronist Montoneros. While each operated independently, with some territorial division among themselves, there was considerable exchange of information among the groups as well as some coordinated operations.

The guerrillas' tactics reflected the influence of the Tupamaros and included expropriations of money and arms, kidnappings of representatives of foreign companies, dispensation of revolutionary justice, Robin Hood-style actions to help the poor, and bold moves to reveal the government's weaknesses. Unlike the Tupamaros, who progressed through stages as they built strength, the Argentine guerrillas burst upon the scene after some underground preparation employing the whole gamut of actions. Robin Hood actions were important as linkage with the poor. Among those were giveaways of stolen milk, meat, blankets, and toys in slums and the donation of 154 ambulances purchased with money extorted from Ford Motor Company. The kidnapping of Stanley Sylvester, British consul and manager of Swift and Company in Rosario who had recently laid off 4,000 workers, was a major coup; in exchange for his release, the company rehired the workers with compensation, improved working conditions, and distributed food in the city's slums.

Concurrently, the guerrillas mounted a campaign of escalating violence between 1970 and 1973. They administered "revolutionary justice" in the assassinations of many, including ex-President Pedro Aramburu (1955–58), who had attempted to de-Peronize the political system and labor unions; General Juan Carlos Sánchez, whose energetic strike-breaking and repression in Rosario had made him a hated figure; and Admiral Emilio R. Berisso, in reprisal for a government massacre of captured guerrillas. Executives of foreign-owned companies, including Fiat, Coca-Cola, and Kodak as well as Swift and Ford, were kidnapped and ransomed or persuaded to pay huge sums as insurance against abduction. Following the example of Operation Pando, the guerrillas occupied at least two small cities. In addition, there were constant bank robberies, attacks on elite establishments such as country clubs and race tracks, assaults on police stations and military bases, and even an attack on the presidential residence. While the urban fighters suffered some reverses, their successes far outweighed their losses during the early 1970s.

These guerrilla successes were an important factor in the return of Perón. Faced with economic crisis, labor militancy, and an escalating guerrilla war, the military government of Alejandro Lanusse in desperation called for elections in 1973 that would be open to Peronists but not to Perón. After a transitional Peronist government that cleared the way for Perón's candidacy, the aging leader won the presidency in September 1973 with 62 percent of the vote. Perón's return, however, quickly disillusioned the Peronist left, including the guerrillas. Perón aligned himself with the rightist bloc of his movement, which included the bulk of the unions, and turned on the left, confirming the suspicions of some guerrillas that their hopes for a revolution from above had been misplaced. During Perón's brief government (October 1973–July 1974), some urban guerrillas resumed armed action. After his death and the accession of his widow, Isabel Perón, virtually all guerrillas returned to combat, in pursuit now of a socialist revolution from below. Thus after 1973 the guerrillas were no longer in the mainstream of national politics; like their counterparts throughout Latin America, they were a decidedly fringe, extremist element. Being in tune with the masses had contributed to the guerrillas' success; leading the masses toward true revolution was a much more difficult challenge.

The repression of the left that Perón had begun increased during the government of Isabel Perón (July 1974–March 1976). In addition to regular police and military crackdowns the Argentine Anticommunist Alliance (AAA), a private death squad under military sponsorship, published death lists and assassinated a range of leftists, including the brother of former president Arturo Frondizi. By April 1975, it was estimated that AAA was killing five people daily, including Chilean and Uruguayan leftists who had fled the 1973 military coups in their countries. The primary remaining guerrilla groups, ERP and the Montoneros, responded in kind, targeting military men and police for assassination and attempting to build support in the mainstream Peronist movement by carrying out Robin Hood actions. ERP kidnapped Esso executive Victor Samuelson and received $14 million ransom for his release in March 1974; the following year, the Montoneros received $60 million for the Born brothers, members of one of Argentina's richest families. These ransoms financed the fierce war that grew even more intense after the military overthrew Isabel Perón to assume direct rule in March 1976.

Under the regime of General Jorge Videla, no holds were barred in the fight against subversion, and the "dirty war" got dirtier. Thousands of noncombatants were assassinated and "disappeared" at the hands of the military and their collaborators. Despite some spectacular assassinations and acts of sabotage, the guerrillas were unable to mobilize popular support against the government. Information extracted under torture led to the discovery of the ERP's network of safe houses and the detention of 200 of its fighters in May 1977. This blow caused the leadership to order its members to flee the country. The Montoneros fought on until November 1979, when their remaining cadre went into exile. The Montoneros admitted losing 5,000 fighters killed, detained, or disappeared after resuming the insurrection in September 1974, leaving only some 500 survivors to escape the country. The military government's use of terror to isolate the guerrillas from potential supporters and the guerrillas' mistakes in strategy and tactics, which reinforced their separateness from the Peronist masses, defeated one of Latin America's two most success-ful urban guerrilla movements.

Despite its ultimate failure as a method of insurrection, urban guerrilla warfare had significant influence beyond the borders of the countries in which it was employed. By demonstrating that a different type of armed struggle had potential for success, the urban guerrillas ushered in a new, more pragmatic and mature stage in the quest for revolution in Latin America. While still inspired by Castro's achievements in Cuba, by the late 1960s Latin America's revolutionaries were able to see through the blinders imposed by the rigid Cuban model of foco-driven rural guerrilla warfare. The most successful of the rural guerrilla movements that began or prospered after the death of Che — the Sandinistas in Nicaragua, the FMLN in El Salvador, and the Sendero Luminoso in Peru — modified or abandoned the foco principle and incorporated lessons from the urban guerrillas. Even more radical departures from Che's formula were soon to come when revolutionaries in Peru and Chile abandoned insurrection altogether, at least temporarily, to lead or collaborate in carrying out revolution from above. Thus the urban guerrillas succeeded where Fidel and Che failed in 1967; they revived the flagging momentum of revolution in Latin America but, ironically, they did it by burying the gospel of rural foquismo in the unmarked Bolivian grave of the apostle.

NOTES

1. Héctor Víctor Suárez, "The Revolutionary Armed Forces: With Che's Weapons," *Granma Weekly* (Havana), 17 January 1971, quoted in James Kohl and John Litt, eds., *Urban Guerrilla Warfare in Latin America* (Cambridge, Mass.: MIT Press, 1974), 379.

2. Abraham Guillén, *Estrategias de la guerrilla urbana* (Montevideo: Ed. Manuales del Pueblo, 1966).

3. Abraham Guillén, quoted in Donald C. Hodges, ed. and tr., *Philosophy of the Urban Guerrilla: The Revolutionary Writings of Abraham Guillén* (New York: William Morrow, 1973), 230.

4. Ibid., 269.

5. Ibid., 253.

6. Ibid., 233.

7. Ibid., 254.

8. Suárez, "Revolutionary Armed Forces," in Kohl and Litt, *Urban Guerrilla Warfare*, 380; and M. L. N. Tupamaros, *Actas Tupamaras* (Buenos Aires: Schapire Editor, 1971), 7.

9. "30 preguntas a un Tupamaro," *Punto Final* (Santiago, Chile), 2 (58) (2 July 1968), quoted in Antonio Mercader and Jorge de Vera, *Tupamaros: estrategia y acción* (Montevideo: Editorial Alfa, 1969), 55 (italics added).

10. Leopoldo Madruga, "Interview with Urbano," *Tricontinental Bulletin* (Havana), nos. 57-58 (Dec. 1970–Jan. 1971), in Kohl and Litt, *Urban Guerrilla Warfare*, 285.

11. "30 preguntas a un Tupamaro," 57.

12. Ibid., 49.

13. Madruga, "Interview with Urbano," 283.

14. The term "Tupamaro" also has a specifically Uruguayan context. The Spanish and creole elites applied it to the gaucho fighters for Uruguayan independence, especially the followers of José Artigas, as a term of condemnation for rebellion, à la Tupac Amaru, against royal authority and elite rule.

15. Kohl and Litt, *Urban Guerrilla Warfare*, 173.

16. Carlos Marighela, *For the Liberation of Brazil*, tr. by John Butt and Rosemary Sheed (Harmondsworth, Eng.: Penguin Books, 1971), 47.

17. Ibid., 64.

18. Ibid., 48.

The Peruvian Military Reformers, 1968–75

When the Peruvian armed forces seized power on October 3, 1968, for the second time in six years, few domestic or foreign observers guessed that the impending military interregnum would differ significantly from previous periods of military rule. The radical language of the coup manifesto, denouncing "powerful economic forces . . . motivated by overwhelming greed, [which] retain political and economic power, and frustrate the popular desire for basic structural reforms" was generally considered window dressing.[1] Yet within a year, the government headed by General Juan Velasco Alvarado had attracted attention by its bold beginnings in reform, and by the early 1970s it was clear that the Peruvian military was committed to a thorough structural transformation of the country.

The anomaly of the Peruvian armed forces' bucking the prevailing hemispheric trend to lead what they called a "revolution" made the Velasco government the subject of intense international scrutiny. As a result of its sweeping reforms in domestic and foreign policy, the Peruvian regime was taken as a model by military men in several Latin American countries who formed "peruanista" factions within their institutions. By the time of Velasco's removal from office in 1975, Peru had undergone more significant change than any Latin American country since the Cuban Revolution, with the possible exception of Chile under Allende; while many of Velasco's reforms were reversed by subsequent governments, others, including land reform, endured to mark the seven years of Velasco's presidency as an important watershed in Peru's modern history.

Coming after a decade of frustration for Latin America's revolutionaries, whose attempts to replicate the Cuban Revolution had met abject defeat, the Peruvian military regime offered new hope for change. Disillusioned by their own failures at insurrection and attracted by the government's reforms, some of Peru's fidelistas supported the Velasco regime and a few, including former foco leader Héctor Béjar, became important collaborators. Fidel Castro praised the Velasco government for its reforms and its anti-imperialist stance. Thus the Peruvian government, especially in conjunction with the Allende government in Chile, elected in 1970, opened a new perspective on revolution in Latin America: the prospect of revolution, or at least structural reform, from above. While the purists might reject halfway measures, Fidel's implicit blessing of the Peruvian military regime and the frustration of a decade of failed insurrection made the notion of revolution from above an appealing one for much of the Latin American left. The return of Perón in 1973, the populist administration of Luis Echeverría in Mexico (1970–1976), the nationalist government of Omar Torrijos in Panama (1970–1981), the leftist military government of Juan José Torres in Bolivia (1970–1971), and the "peruanista" military regime of Guillermo Rodríguez Lara in Ecuador (1972–1976) suggested that the Peruvian armed forces had initiated a new if transitory phase in the politics of change in Latin America.

One of the salient traits of the Peruvian military government was its sui generis nature. The regime that called itself the "Revolutionary Government of the Armed Forces" has been identified by scholars as revolutionary, reformist, corporatist, nationalist, state capitalist, populist, fascist, modernizing, and experimental. Of its various characteristics, the most visible thread linking the main pronouncements and policies of the Velasco government is its unrelenting nationalism. As one would expect, an institution whose ostensible duty is defense of the homeland will be inherently nationalistic. In the broadest sense, the military accepted the mission of nation-building, of creating a true country out of the hollow shell of a republic. Its social reforms were designed to bring the excluded majority of Peruvians — those marginalized by race, language, geography, and poverty — into the national mainstream. Its economic and diplomatic policies attempted to achieve true independence for a country long subject to an exaggerated dependency. Its moves to strengthen the state were likewise motivated by nationalism, by the impulse to transform a state subservient to national and foreign capital into a state sufficiently powerful to represent the broader interest of the nation under construction over the narrow special interests that had held sway.

BACKGROUND TO THE
MILITARY GOVERNMENT

Peru in the 1960s was a textbook case of a country ripe for revolution or reform. Whether viewed through the lenses of fidelismo or those of the Alliance for Progress, Peru exhibited most of the problems and hallmarks of underdevelopment and social atavism. Although Peru ranked eighth in Latin American per capita income at $338 per year in 1960, distribution of this modest income was extremely skewed. Forty percent of Peru's 10 million people in 1960 spoke Quechua, Aymará, or another native tongue as their first language. Adult illiteracy was over 50 percent nationally, and much higher in the Indian strongholds of the Andes. Peru's land distribution was characterized by extremes: 1.2 percent of the country's largest landowners owned 75 percent of usable surface, while 84 percent held 6 percent of the land in plots averaging under two hectares. Millions of rural Peruvians, in addition, were landless. The country's formal economy was based on agricultural and mineral exports, much of those controlled by foreign interests, mainly U.S. On the positive side, Peru's exports were more diversified than those of most hemispheric countries, a fact that insulated the country somewhat against world market price swings. The dynamic new fish meal industry had become the largest export sector by the 1960s.

Peruvian thinkers had been highly critical of the country's condition, especially of the land tenure system and the plight of the Indian, since Manuel González Prada wrote at the turn of the twentieth century. José Carlos Mariátegui, founder of Peru's communist party, wrote *Seven Essays on Peruvian Reality* in 1928.[2] A critical examination focusing on land, Indians, and dependency, Mariátegui's analysis remained essentially accurate in the 1960s. The struggle to rectify those conditions gave rise to the APRA, the prototype of Latin America's democratic left, in the 1920s. However, a blood feud between the army and APRA, stemming from a 1932 uprising involving excesses on both sides, combined with skillful political manipulation by Peru's elites, kept the APRA from power and thus postponed substantive reform until it was long overdue. By the 1950s APRA itself, having been driven underground by more than one government, had opted for restoration of its legal status in exchange for moderating its position on reform.

Signs of peasant, labor, and student unrest appeared in the 1950s and proliferated in the early 1960s as the Cuban Revolution and the Alliance for Progress accelerated the incipient mass awakening. In common with most of Latin America, Peru experienced the formation of fidelista parties and factions, new demands for radical change, the growth of peasant organization and militancy, and a general intensification of political unrest. Responding to Hugo Blanco's peasant movement in the Valley of La Convención, all major candidates in the 1962 national elections called for agrarian reform; after the military annulled those elections to forestall a possible APRA victory, the 1963 campaigns reiterated the major parties' commitment to land redistribution. With the victory of moderate reformer Fernando Belaúnde Terry, some 300,000 individuals from approximately 400 Indian communities carried out their own agrarian reform by occupying dozens of haciendas; many were never removed. Meanwhile, guerrilla focos were launched, and quickly defeated, in 1963 and 1965.

Against this backdrop of heightened demands for change and a broad consensus on the need for at least moderate reform, a stalemate in national politics led to the continuing postponement of meaningful reform. Sacrificing principle for political expediency, Apristas in congress allied themselves with their erstwhile enemies, the party of ex-dictator Manuel Odría, to block or water down Belaúnde's moderate reform proposals. In addition to this paralysis of the political system, economic problems, labor unrest, and continuing rural agitation plagued the Belaúnde administration. The outcome of negotiations with International Petroleum Company (IPC), an Esso subsidiary, Peru's primary oil producer, and a major symbol of U.S. imperialism to many Peruvians, severely weakened the government. In August 1968 it announced but did not divulge the terms of the Pact of Talara, the proposed resolution of a long-standing dispute over the company's legal status and exploitation rights. When the content of the agreement leaked out, revealing major concessions to the company and a scandal involving a missing page of the document, Belaúnde's government was damaged beyond repair. The more nationalist and reformist factions of the officer corps seized the opportunity to remove an inept civilian government and install an administration committed to their views. This action also foreclosed the possibility of an APRA victory in the upcoming national elections.

The military's intervention under those circumstances did not portend the changes in store. The new government's first action, the outright expropriation of IPC, was interpreted as merely the culmination of a process botched by Belaúnde rather than the opening salvo in a vigorous campaign of economic nationalism. While there were numerous precedents in Latin America of military men as reformers — among them Marmaduke Grove, who led the Chilean Socialist Republic of 1932; the Toro and Busch governments in Bolivia in the 1930s; Juan Perón in

Argentina in the 1940s and 1950s; and the Arbenz regime in Guatemala in the early 1950s — military-dominated governments usually upheld the status quo. Following a spate of uprisings by leftist officers in the early 1960s, of which only the October 1960 coup in El Salvador succeeded, the climate of military politics in the era of the Cuban Revolution was decidedly conservative. Although the 1962–63 military junta had shown flexibility in establishing Peru's first agrarian reform in the agitated Valley of La Convención, that had been an emergency response to a grave situation and did not appear to presage the aggressive reformism of the government installed in 1968.

Explanations of the Peruvian military's radical departure from precedent and from the general pattern of military politics in the 1960s and 1970s include several factors. Strong representation in the officer corps of men of provincial middle-class origin is cited as evidence that the military was essentially a middle-class institution with no binding ties to the Peruvian oligarchy. The advanced training offered in the Center for Advanced Military Studies (Centro de Altos Estudios Militares, CAEM) included a large dose of social sciences focused on Peru and taught by civilians from a progressive perspective. This instruction contributed to the military's belief that its job of providing national security went beyond military questions to encompass the development and modernization of a backward country. The equation of national security with modernization and development flowed naturally from the study of Peruvian history: Peru's loss to Chile in the War of the Pacific (1879–83) was generally attributed to the country's backwardness, above all to the marginal condition of its Indian majority. Field experience in civic action and counterinsurgency provided the officer corps with first-hand knowledge of social conditions in the poorest areas of the country and made it aware of the threat posed by rural mobilization fostered by those conditions. Frustration with civilian politicians for failing to resolve the country's pressing problems was a factor encouraging the military to suppress established institutions following the 1968 coup rather than follow its normal pattern of calling for elections to replace the overthrown government.

While the foregoing considerations provide important insights into the Peruvian military's course of action after 1968, they also describe to some degree the characteristics and experience of the militaries of several other countries — militaries that did not embrace reform as their response to the impact of the Cuban Revolution. Two other significant factors help to set Peru's military apart from other cases and explain its unique behavior. One was the composition of the group that organized the coup and subsequently ran the government. The coup instigators were progressives who sought substantive change in Peru's economy and society; after installing themselves in power, they were able to keep the influence of conservative officers to a minimum. While the president and cabinet-level officials were generals, a large cadre of colonels who were committed to quite radical change had been prime movers in the coup; they assumed a direct role in government through the Advisory Committee to the Presidency (Comité de Asesores a la Presidencia, COAP), which exercised strong influence over policy formulation. Within a year or two, most of those colonels were promoted and placed in positions of greater authority. With the conservatives neutralized, General Velasco mediated constantly between the radicals and the more moderate nationalists, balancing the radicals' demands for a fundamental redistribution of wealth and power in Peru versus the moderates' desire to strengthen national capitalism through policies designed to increase productivity. While the government's policies normally reflected some compromise, Velasco's personal inclinations cemented the ascendancy of the more radical faction throughout most of his presidency.

Another factor in the Peruvian military's orientation emerges from a comparison with the four other militaries that assumed long-term power in the 1960s and 1970s, abolished civilian institutions, and governed as institutional military regimes, but which adopted right-wing policies and extreme repression to accomplish their missions. The military governments that took power in Brazil in 1964, Uruguay and Chile in 1973, and Argentina in 1976 were established in the face of immediate threats of revolutionary takeover — at least from the military's viewpoint. In Brazil and Chile, soldiers removed presidents they saw as moving dangerously far to the left; in Uruguay and Argentina, the militaries acted to counter urban guerrilla insurgencies that threatened to topple civilian governments and seize power. In each case the immediate threat to national security was translated as communism or Castroism, and the military's task in restoring peace was in part to destroy Marxist influence in all its forms. In Peru, by contrast, despite rising levels of turmoil and mobilization, the military faced no immediate threat of revolution; rather, it faced an inept civilian government and supporting institutions that failed to enact the reforms deemed necessary to prevent revolution. The Peruvian officers, then, had the luxury of reflection and deliberation in formulating policies after seizing power, rather than having to strike swiftly and decisively at revolutionary forces that appeared as immediate threats to vested interests.

THE RESHAPING OF PERUVIAN SOCIETY

When the military took power it had no blueprint for achieving its broad nationalist objectives, despite later allegations of a secret "Plan Inca" laying out the reform program. Thus it took several years and a series of reform measures before the Velasco government's vision of a new Peru came into focus. Because of the relatively closed nature of discussion and planning within the military institution and the time lags separating the several phases of reform, observers at various points believed that the "revolution" had run its course. But despite hiatuses between the announcement and implementation of the successive reform measures, the Velasco government displayed a constantly deepening commitment to radical change.

The military launched its program of transformation with the agrarian reform law of June 24, 1969. Announcing it on the newly-proclaimed "day of the peasant," Velasco called the measure "a law which will end forever an unjust social order."[3] Action of some sort on agrarian reform was not unexpected. The military's 1962 program in La Convención and Belaúnde's 1964 law had legitimized the issue, while widespread frustration over the slow pace of land distribution had plagued the latter years of Belaúnde's administration. Critics of Peru's land tenure system for nearly a century had focused on the inefficiency and social injustice of the highland haciendas, and the 1962 and 1964 laws had been aimed at eliminating or modernizing some of those holdings.

To the shock of virtually all observers, Velasco first applied agrarian reform to the modern export-producing plantations on the coast. When the government moved within days after issuing the law to expropriate the capital-intensive holdings of the Grace Company and several of Peru's most powerful families, Velasco's commitment to radical change became clear. Expropriation of coastal plantations, some of which included industrial components such as cane-based paper mills and distilleries, was not a blow for economic modernization; in fact, previous plans had specifically exempted coastal plantations because of the danger of disrupting export earnings as well as the political power of the owners. This was a blow directed at Peru's oligarchy and an important segment of foreign capital, and also at the APRA, the military's historic enemy, much of whose strength lay in the agricultural workers' unions of the north coast sugar zone.

When agrarian reform reached the Andes, some months after the law's enactment, the primary emphasis was on ending a backward system of land tenure and social domination. The typical Andean hacienda was undercapitalized and underproductive; it was worked by a resident labor force paid primarily in land use rights and by seasonal labor drawn from nearby Indian communities and from pockets of landless peasants. In the Andean regions, the challenge to agrarian reformers was not simply redistribution of land; in contrast to the highly productive coastal agriculture, land in the Andes would have to receive major investment in order to afford even a modest living for its inhabitants.

In both regions, reformed agricultural property was placed under cooperative ownership rather than being distributed in individual holdings. This reflected the regime's emphasis on cooperatives, worker self-management, and the communitarian approach to restructuring society. On the coast, conflict ensued along several axes over which groups were to be included in the cooperatives and with what rights: field versus industrial workers; unskilled versus skilled workers; workers versus professionals, such as accountants, agronomists, and chemists; and resident versus nonresident workers. In the Andes, resident workers of expropriated haciendas were challenged by neighboring Indian communities, which were often overpopulated and which had historic claims against haciendas for stealing their land; landless seasonal workers also pressed claims to land.

These competing claims for land unleashed a wave of mobilization in the countryside that the authorities only gradually brought under control. One effect of the competition for land was a progressive deepening of the reform process as expropriations were extended beyond the limits of the law to satisfy the manifest land hunger. Most reformed holdings on the coast were organized into individual Agricultural Production Cooperatives (Cooperativas Agrícolas de Producción), run by elected worker committees but with final authority residing in a manager appointed by the government. In the Andes, the competing claims were commonly resolved by the creation of Agricultural Societies of Social Interest (Sociedades Agrícolas de Interés Social), which integrated hacienda and community lands in a single extensive production unit. In order to address income disparities among land recipients in a broader area, some region-wide units were created to transfer resources and income from the wealthier to the poorer holdings.

By the end of the Velasco presidency, the traditional hacienda and the large private coastal hacienda had virtually disappeared. By the end of the 1970s, some 400,000 families — between a quarter and a third of the rural population — had received land, most of them in cooperative ownership. Approximately 8.5 million hectares, generating 60 percent of the country's agricultural income, had been expropriated; much of the remainder belonged to Indian communities. Inevitably, such an ambitious agrarian reform did not serve all those in need of land. Nonresident landless peasants were the most often neglected, and many of them simply switched bosses from hacienda owners to cooperative members. In some areas, including the south-central Andean department of Ayacucho where Sendero Luminoso has its stronghold, population pressures were such that land-short Indian communities could not be given additional land. In general, technical support for improved crop and livestock yields lagged far behind goals. But when all the shortcomings are listed, it remains that in less than a decade the military accomplished much of what critics had called for since the nineteenth century, and more. They not only reformed the Andes, but they also redistributed the heretofore sacrosanct modern sector of the agricultural economy, using agrarian reform to attack the Peruvian power structure.

Another redistributive reform, the General Law of Industries of July 1970, applied the principle of worker self-management that undergirded agrarian reform to the industrial sector. Manufacturing firms with six or more workers or a gross annual income of over a million soles (approximately $25,000) were required to establish a *comunidad industrial* (industrial community) consisting of all permanent employees. The industrial community received 15 percent of the company's pre-tax net income each year with which to purchase shares in the firm until the workers achieved 50 percent ownership of total shares. In addition, workers received 10 percent of annual pre-tax profits as profit sharing. As of September 1974, 3,446 industrial communities had been established with approximately 200,000 members. Another 100,000 workers participated in similar communities in the fishmeal, mining, and telecommunications sectors.

The industrial community was designed to increase productivity by tying worker income to company profits and to dampen class conflict and wean workers away from unions by extending the benefits of ownership. Inevitably, as with agrarian reform, this radical departure from the status quo generated conflict between labor and management and among workers of differing skills, pay levels, and longevity. Effective worker self-management required education of the labor force in all aspects of the company's operations. Many owners found ways to underreport profits through transfers, inflation of costs, and other devices, so as to contribute less to the workers than was owed. Partly for this reason, industrial communities owned on the average only 8 to 9 percent of their companies by mid-1974.

The most sweeping formulation of worker ownership and self-management was that contained in the Velasco government's Social Property Law of May 1974, the result of over four years of preparation and extensive intramural and public debate. Reflecting the influence of Christian Democratic notions of communitarianism and of the Yugoslav practice of worker self-management — two Yugoslav consultants helped prepare the draft — the social property law laid the basis for what the regime hoped would become the dominant sector within a pluralistic economy. The social property sector would consist of firms in almost any line of production or business composed solely of workers who would run each firm through a democratic process. Ownership of the firm, however, would reside in the entire social property sector, and part of the income of each firm would be applied to a fund for creating new worker-managed companies. Overseeing the sector was a government-appointed council with power over wages, establishment of new companies, and general administration.

With the social property law, the government's concept of the pluralistic Peruvian economy was finally defined. The four elements would be the state sector, consisting primarily of mining, petroleum, and basic industries; the reformed private sector featuring industrial communities; the private sector of small firms and companies of any size not required to have industrial communities; and social property, which would encompass existing and future cooperatives in agriculture as well as the new firms to be created throughout the economy. While it was possible to convert a reformed private firm to social property, the Velasco government favored development of the social property sector through creation of new enterprises. Given the government's control over credit resources, the bulk of new investment would be channeled into the social property area, which would be the primary engine of growth and become the largest sector within 15 years.

The social property law represented the most radical expression of the Peruvian military experiment. It was to be the centerpiece of the new Peru, which would be "neither capitalist nor communist" and would afford full participation to all citizens. While the government made a start in creating social property firms, even under the most favorable circumstances its projection of the sector's growth to dominance was unrealistic. The replacement of Velasco in 1975 effectively killed the drive to make social property a reality. Although by this time some innovative region-wide cooperative ownership arrangements had been established under agrarian reform, the push for completely collective sector-wide ownership ended after Velasco's removal.

Secondary means of redistributing resources toward the poor majority of Peruvians included the expansion and transformation of the educational system and new policies for the urban squatter communities. The Velasco government emphasized basic literacy, bilingual education for the speakers of Indian languages, and vocational and technical education to counter the traditional orientation of Peruvian education toward the liberal arts and law, which reformers blamed for perpetuating the values of Peru's exploitive class system. Velasco also hoped that educational reform would "forge a new kind of man within a new morality that emphasizes solidarity, labor, authentic liberty, social justice, and the responsibilities and rights of every Peruvian."[4] Because of its democratic and practical orientation, the educational reform encountered stiff resistance from two bastions of privilege, universities and private schools.

The military government saw the mushrooming population of the squatter settlements or barriadas surrounding Lima and provincial cities as both a problem and an opportunity. To alleviate conditions as well as cultivate support, especially among the 900,000 barriada dwellers who constituted a fourth of Lima's population, the government gave priority to setting up self-help programs, extending utilities to the zones, and granting titles to plots that normally were occupied in illegal land invasions. Symbolizing the new approach was a new name for the barriadas: *pueblos jóvenes* or new towns.

THE QUEST FOR NATIONAL SOVEREIGNTY

To complement its restructuring of Peruvian society, the Velasco government implemented a series of measures designed to achieve Peruvian sovereignty, both economic and political. These measures included the transformation of the Peruvian state from a pliant tool of vested national and foreign interests into a powerful entity capable of defining and implementing national goals and policies. Second, the regime established new guidelines for foreign investment that would ensure national control of key sectors of the economy. Third, Velasco's government worked to end Peru's notable subservience to the United States by charting an aggressively independent course in foreign relations.

By Latin American standards, the pre-1968 Peruvian state was very weak economically. Private capital dominated every sector of the economy, with foreign investment playing a major or decisive role in most areas including mining, agriculture, petroleum, communications, utilities, and even retailing. The telephone company, most other utilities, and Peru's national and international airlines were privately held; Peru was one of three countries in the world, along with the United States and Canada, where all major railroads were not state-owned. Even the Central Bank, the government's main source of leverage over the economy, was under the control of private banks. If it were to achieve the economic power to transform Peruvian society, the government would have to enhance the state's role in the economy.

Strengthening of the state's economic role flowed from three policies. Agrarian reform and creation of the industrial communities weakened the economic power of both national and foreign private capital. Nationalization of private investments outside of agriculture put direct ownership of major economic sectors in state hands. And new restrictions on foreign investment kept international capital from regaining the enormous influence that it had enjoyed before 1968.

In nationalizing petroleum and expropriating the coastal haciendas, the Velasco government made impressive progress in its first year toward breaking the economic power of the national oligarchy and major foreign investors. In 1970 the regime turned its attention to the remaining sectors of the economy. The key provision for promoting state economic power was the General Law of Industries, which also established the industrial community. This law reserved natural resources and "basic industries" for state ownership. Enactment of the law launched a phase of negotiations with owners, both foreign and national, over the terms of expropriation and compensation. Within five years, the government had taken ownership of the fishmeal industry, most mining and metal refining, railroads and the international airline, some pharmaceutical firms, most electric utilities, cement plants, most banking and insurance, and the telephone and cable companies. It also established a state import-export monopoly over key commodities and invested as a partner with private capital in numerous enterprises, including television and radio stations. While the state sector grew quickly and impressively, the government retained flexibility by working out operating agreements with private firms in some activities, including oil exploration. By 1975, the state's share of total national investment had risen from 13 percent a decade earlier to nearly 50 percent, moving Peru toward the levels of state economic involvement found in Mexico, Chile, and Argentina.

Even while expropriating the "commanding heights" of the economy, the military government pursued new foreign capital to meet Peru's development needs, but under radically different terms of investment that came to be known as the "Velasco Doctrine." President Velasco first announced a new attitude toward foreign investment in a 1970 speech:

"We are not a weak group of nations at the mercy of foreign capital. They need our raw materials and our markets. And if we need capital goods and advanced technology, the evident bilaterality of these needs must lead to new arrangements that protect the present and future interests of Latin America."[5] The Velasco Doctrine essentially sought to foster development without the dependency concomitant to foreign investment in the Third World. Translated into policy, the Velasco Doctrine was one of the military government's most innovative and widely admired policies; it became Decision 24 of the Andean Pact, the six-member regional common market headquartered in Lima.

Under the new rules, foreign capital was invited to invest in needed areas on a temporary, phase-out basis, preferably in partnership with national capital; when the total investment had been recovered and a reasonable, agreed-upon profit had been made, the majority share of the foreign investment would become state property. The final regulation of the Andean Pact allowed a maximum annual profit repatriation of 14 percent of total investment and required divestment to reduce the foreign share of joint ventures to less than 50 percent within 15 years. Thus, rather than rejecting foreign investment, the Peruvian government sought to shape it into a positive force for the country's development. Despite the new restrictions and U.S. pressure against the international lending agencies, foreign capital flowed readily into the country until near the end of the Velasco presidency.

The political aspect of state development involved a similar approach: weakening autonomous political and economic organizations capable of challenging the state and replacing them with government-controlled entities designed to incorporate and represent the populace along economic and functional lines. Such corporatism has deep roots in Latin America, both in Iberian colonial institutions and in twentieth century responses to the emergence of class conflict and radical politics. The Velasco government went beyond the normal corporatist objective of subordinating independent organizations, such as parties, labor unions, and economic interest groups, to the state. It attempted to use the corporate structure as a tool for integrating the previously marginalized majority — especially campesinos and barriada dwellers — into the national polity and, in the process, turning them into active supporters of the government.

Consistent with its rejection of unnecessary repression, the government normally tolerated institutions that were too strong to take on or too weak to cause problems. It did not challenge the church as an institution. The political parties and national labor confederations retained considerable freedom of action so long as their opposition to the government was restrained, while the regime worked to weaken them by wooing away their constituencies through reform and playing rivals off against one another. On the other hand, the government did not tolerate open challenges or covert attempts to sabotage its policies. It abolished the national teachers' union, for example, for striking in defiance of the regime and replaced it with a government-sponsored union. The National Agrarian Society (Sociedad Nacional Agraria), the interest group of large-scale agricultural producers, was abolished in 1972 for opposing agrarian reform; its members were merged with the peasant syndicates into the government-controlled National Agrarian Confederation (Confederación Agraria Nacional), which officially represented the entire agricultural population. Although not abolished, the Sociedad Industrial Nacional was reorganized so as to be more pliant to government wishes.

The capstone of the government's corporatist endeavors was National System to Support Social Mobilization (Sistema Nacional de Apoyo a la Movilización Social, SINAMOS), founded in 1971. SINAMOS was to be a vast organization, running from local units to the national level, to support the military government in the aftermath of the dismantling or marginalization of the major parties and unions. It was intended to decentralize decision making and provide access to government for the marginal populations that the military was attempting to integrate into national life as well as for those groups, such as labor and professionals, whose existing associations were being suppressed. The challenge was to grant the organizations enough freedom of action so that they could attract members while ensuring that they did not become independent groups capable of acting against government interests.

Predictably, the creation of such a vast program designed to achieve a delicate balance between co-optation and the fostering of grass-roots democracy caused considerable reaction and chaos. Because of the great expectations raised for their betterment, peasants, squatters, and workers proved more inclined to press for additional benefits than to express their gratitude to the government for gains already made. APRA, with its hundreds of thousands of loyal members and its control over major labor and professional groups, also proved resilient to governmental pressure and stood as an important obstacle to the success of SINAMOS-backed organizations. Overall, SINAMOS failed to develop the degree of support the government desired, resulting in the debilitating irony that Peru's first government devoted to structural reform was one without a broad base of organized popular support.

The final nationalist goal of the armed forces in office was to establish an independent foreign policy, distancing Peru from its traditional close alliance with the United States. One step in asserting its independence was the establishment of diplomatic relations with the Soviet Union, China, Cuba, and other socialist countries. Peru also signed a trade pact with Moscow and acquired significant amounts of Soviet arms, giving the Soviet Union its first military presence in the hemisphere outside of Cuba. Widely admired within the Third World for its reforms and its innovative reformulation of the rules of foreign investment, Peru quickly assumed a leadership role in the Nonaligned Movement.

The Velasco government displayed its independence of the United States in other ways as well. In the early months of the regime, Velasco denied compensation for IPC's expropriated properties, alleging that the company owed Peru $690 million in excess profits and unpaid taxes, and defied Washington to implement economic sanctions. Enforcement of Peru's claim to 200 miles of territorial waters against U.S. fishing boats also strained relations, as did Washington's suspension of military aid and Lima's subsequent expulsion of the U.S. military mission in Peru. These provocations were somewhat offset by moderation on other fronts. Apart from the IPC case, reasonable offers of compensation followed most expropriations of U.S. properties. For its part, Washington failed to apply the Hickenlooper Amendment, which required the cutting of aid to countries failing to pay for nationalized U.S. investments, preferring a quiet financial pressure that eventually took a toll on Peru's economy. U.S. restraint was largely explained by a situation that was unique in the era of the Cuban Revolution: A military regime was carrying out reforms that, if conducted by a civilian government, would have led Washington to orchestrate a quick overthrow to save the country from communism. The fact that the radicals were in uniform thus had a moderating effect on the U.S. response to a reform process that many considered a revolution.

FALL OF THE VELASCO GOVERNMENT

By 1974 a number of general trends and specific circumstances had converged to weaken the Velasco regime. One long-term trend that affected the government was a rising level of conflict expressed in strikes, anti-regime demonstrations, and riots. Much of the conflict was generated by the reform process itself, which unleashed demands for change but rarely satisfied any important group. Agrarian reform, for example, might have been expected to produce a fairly contented group of new landowners who would form a solid core of support for Velasco. Rather, as discussed above, agrarian reform produced several axes of conflict among would-be beneficiaries and fully satisfied few, leaving much of the countryside in a state of mobilization. Workers belonging to industrial communities might also have been expected to support the government, but rather than demonstrating gratitude they tended to vent their dissatisfaction with the slow pace of accumulation of worker shares in their firms; in 1972, as an example, the Confederation of Industrial Communities demanded the immediate granting of 50 percent worker ownership rather than following the gradual process defined by law, and forced the resignation of the relevant government official. Adding to the problem of unmet expectations was the fact that the government had created organizations at every level, designed to generate support, that served instead as vehicles for expressing discontent and mobilizing people against the government. APRA, which had a pervasive presence in most important economic sectors, also worked to undermine the government while building its own clientele.

Economic problems had become serious by 1974. Peru's balance of trade suffered in 1972 when the fishmeal industry, the leading export sector, nearly collapsed as a result of climatic changes affecting the Humboldt Current. Peru also fell victim to the 1974–76 world recession. The government had borrowed heavily to finance state-led development, with good results to 1974; then, along with several other Latin American countries, Peru found itself deeply in debt but, with the prices of its exports down, unable to pay its obligations. This led to the imposition of austerity measures in 1975 that exacerbated the endemic conflict affecting the country.

The year 1974 was the high water mark of reform and the beginning of a reaction against the regime's more radical policies and their proponents. Even some of the regime's supporters regarded the social property law of May as too radical and unworkable. While the effect of that law was to be gradual, the effect of a July decree expropriating the Lima press was immediate. Expropriation of the press met two government objectives. On one hand, the participatory system would be strengthened by the granting of newspapers to labor, agricultural cooperatives, professionals, and the other main sectoral organizations that the regime had created. At a practical level, the move would silence the increasingly strident criticism that the press was aiming at Velasco. This measure was widely viewed as a step toward totalitarianism on the part of a regime that heretofore had been surprisingly tolerant of dissent. An unexpectedly violent reaction to the press expropriation forced the government into a more repressive posture and hastened its demise.

As the popular unrest, economic problems, and reactions to reform took their toll on the regime, the declining health of General Velasco provided the opportunity for open discussion of the succession and a considerable amount of jockeying for position within the armed forces. Velasco's health problems had forced him to relinquish power for three months in February 1973, and after his return he was a partial invalid. Further deterioration in 1975, combined with the mounting problems besetting the government, opened the way for a peaceful coup led by heir-apparent General Francisco Morales Bermúdez, a member of the moderate faction of Velasco's supporters. The new government reflected a shift in power within the officer corps away from the radicals, who were associated with turmoil and economic difficulties, toward those espousing the more moderate developmentalist line.

After initially proclaiming itself the continuation of Velasco's revolution, the Morales Bermúdez government quickly moved to end the more radical policies of its predecessor. While the distribution of expropriated agricultural land continued, the social property sector was allowed to go bankrupt and a modification of the 1970 Industrial Law exempted all but the largest firms from worker co-management. Recognizing the failure of SINAMOS and the urgent need for civilian support, Morales Bermúdez turned to the military's historic enemy, APRA, which in exchange for major concessions exercised its discipline to curtail the level of antigovernment agitation. Facing a crisis of debt payments, the new regime was also forced to deal on unfavorable terms with foreign banks, which in exchange for emergency loans received an unprecedented degree of control over the Peruvian economy. Thus, ironically, the successor to the government that proudly had led the Third World in the quest for more equitable relations with the capital-exporting countries delivered Peru into a position of even greater dependency than before 1968.

Around the time that they took power, the leaders of the Velasco government estimated that the thorough transformation of Peru that they envisioned would require until at least 1990, or 22 years. The experiment in revolution from above ended after only seven, long before all the country's pressing problems could be addressed and before the main reform programs that the military implemented could have a chance to bear fruit. In common with the contemporary right-wing military regimes in South America, which also had long-term objectives for societal transformation in a different direction, the Peruvian military government succumbed to political failures and to economic forces largely beyond its control. It is impossible to determine whether the vision of a new Peru that General Velasco and his more radical collaborators had — a vision of a country neither capitalist nor communist, based on full citizen participation and anchored in economic independence — could have been achieved under even the most favorable circumstances. Nonetheless, the Peruvian military government of 1968–75 had the distinction of leading one of Latin America's most ambitious and sincere attempts to cope with underdevelopment and social injustice in the twentieth century.

NOTES

1. Quoted in George D. E. Philip, *The Rise and Fall of the Peruvian Military Radicals, 1968–1976* (London: The Athlone Press, 1978), 13.

2. José Carlos Mariátegui, *Seven Interpretive Essays on Peruvian Reality*, tr. by Marjory Urquidi (Austin: University of Texas Press, 1971). The "interpretive" is added to the title in this edition.

3. Quoted in Susan C. Bourque and David Scott Palmer, "Transforming the Rural Sector: Government Policy and Peasant Response," in Abraham F. Lowenthal, ed., *The Peruvian Experiment: Continuity and Change under Military Rule* (Princeton, N.J.: Princeton University Press, 1975), 179.

4. Velasco Alvarado, 8 February 1971 speech, quoted in Robert S. Drysdale and Robert G. Myers, "Continuity and Change: Peruvian Education," in Lowenthal, *The Peruvian Experiment*, 254.

5. Velasco Alvarado, 6 April 1970 speech, quoted in Shane Hunt, "Direct Foreign Investment in Peru: New Rules for an Old Game," in Lowenthal, *The Peruvian Experiment*, 312.

8

Chile Under Allende:
A Peaceful Road to Socialism?

The election of Salvador Allende as president of Chile in September 1970 attracted immediate, worldwide attention. For the next three years, events in Chile were observed, analyzed, and recorded by legions of journalists, social scientists, and political operatives from around the globe. Allende, a member of Chile's Socialist Party and leader of a Marxist-dominated coalition of six parties, had campaigned on the promise to move Chile as quickly as possible to socialism. His election presented a situation unique not only to Latin America, but to the world. In contrast to the member parties of the Socialist International, such as the British Labour Party, the German Social Democratic Party, the Venezuelan AD, or the Peruvian APRA, and to the proponents of Arab socialism, Allende was a traditional Marxist who believed that socialism meant state ownership of the means of production and distribution — not merely a welfare state. In contrast to the countries where socialism had been established — the Soviet Union, Eastern Europe, China, other Asian countries, and Cuba — Allende had taken power without insurrection or military conquest. Besides being a freely elected president, Allende professed allegiance to Chile's well-established pluralist political system — a further contrast with the one-party dictatorial socialist states. Thus Chile provided the laboratory test for the question that heretofore had remained hypothetical: Is there a peaceful road to socialism?

The election of Allende revived the hopes of Latin America's revolutionaries and the worries of the conservatives as well as the U.S. government. Together with the Peruvian experiment next door, Allende's election gave credence to the notion that revolution, after all, might be achieved by means other than armed insurrection, which had proved extremely difficult after 1959. Even Fidel Castro had to reassess. Without discarding the established Cuban line, he gave his implicit blessing to the Chilean path by visiting the country for nearly a month in 1971.

Combined with his praise for the Peruvian military, Fidel's endorsement of Allende and his apparent retreat from rigid adherence to the Cuban model seemed to offer an opening for a reconciliation of the Latin American left, which the Cuban Revolution had splintered. Even though it was widely acknowledged that the Chilean political system was unique within Latin America and that a Marxist electoral triumph was highly unlikely in any other country, the United States feared that a second socialist country in the hemisphere, in combination with a radical regime in Peru, might create an effective anti-U.S. axis in Latin America. Among the implications of Allende's election, according to the CIA, were a threat to "hemispheric cohesion" and "a definite psycho-logical advance for the Marxist idea."[1]

CHILE AND THE CUBAN REVOLUTION

Along with Uruguay, Chile was the most stable of Latin America's constitutional democracies. The Chilean pattern of elected civilian governments developed in the nineteenth century, at a time when government in most of Spanish America alternated between chaos and authoritarian stability. Incorporation of the urban middle and working classes into the political system was accomplished during the 1920s and 1930s, occasioning a period of instability and the last direct military intervention before 1973. By 1938, when Chile became the only Latin American country to elect a Popular Front government, the party system had evolved into three well-defined blocs: a Marxist left composed of the Communist and Socialist parties; the middle-class Radical Party in the center; and the historic Liberal and Conservative parties on the right. Presidents were elected from the center or right, while congress reflected a fairly stable balance among the three blocs, with the Radicals normally holding the swing vote.

Featuring a tradition of civilian rule, respect for civil liberties, and competitive elections, the Chilean political system in the late 1950s still excluded large segments of the adult population. The rural labor force and smallholders continued to be under the control of large landowners, who either barred them from the electoral process or manipulated their votes in favor of Conservative or Liberal candidates. Literacy requirements, difficult voter registration procedures, and the absence of effective organization also marginalized residents of the burgeoning shantytowns of Santiago and Valparaíso. The exclusion of these broad sectors made the Chilean political edifice less solid than it appeared — a weakness readily exposed by the influence of the Cuban Revolution.

In common with the rest of Latin America, Chile experienced the impact of the Cuban Revolution in several ways, including a rise in demands, the radicalization of existing political groups, and a leftward shift of the political agenda. The influence of greatest consequence for Chile was the development of political consciousness and organization, leading later to a broad mobilization, among the marginal groups — especially rural labor. Attempts to organize rural labor were not new in the 1960s: The left had tried to unionize agricultural workers since the 1920s, with little success. After the Cuban Revolution and the rise of agrarian reform as a pan-Latin American issue, the Marxist parties set out more aggressively to organize rural unions and proselytize landless workers and smallholders. Their efforts paralleled those of the Christian Democratic Party (PDC), a dynamic new political force founded in 1957 that espoused a program of structural reform and sought to develop support among the marginal groups.

Despite legal obstacles and the determined resistance of landowners, Marxists and Christian Democrats made rapid headway in breaking landowners' control of the peasantry, to the point that by 1961 the Conservative and Liberal parties joined the Radicals in calling on the right-wing government of Jorge Alessandri, elected in 1958, to undertake a moderate, preemptive agrarian reform. The resulting 1962 agrarian reform law, which made inefficiently worked large properties subject to expropriation and subdivision, had predictably little effect on the structure of rural property; but it was an accurate reflection of the rapid leftward shift of the terms of political debate in Chile.

EDUARDO FREI AND THE "REVOLUTION IN LIBERTY," 1964–70

Against the backdrop of a groundswell of demand for change and a strong sympathy for the Cuban Revolution, the half-hearted preemptive strategies of the Alessandri government proved ineffectual. This was demonstrated conclusively in the results of a March 1964 congressional by-election in heavily rural Curicó province, a traditionally safe stronghold of the right, where the dramatic rise of the Marxist and PDC vote among agricultural workers and smallholders buried the right's candidate. Sensing the collapse of landowners' control of the rural vote and with it the eclipse of the right's electoral strength at the national level, the Conservatives and Liberals took a drastic step to avoid a potential Marxist victory in the September 1964 presidential election. Realizing that a three-candidate field could open the way for Socialist candidate

Salvador Allende, they broke an electoral alliance with the Radical Party and freed their supporters' votes. For most, this meant voting for Christian Democrat Eduardo Frei, a reformer but a lesser evil than Allende. Frei welcomed the right's support but rejected its efforts to moderate his reformist campaign platform.

In the absence of a rightist candidate, the 1964 presidential election offered voters only two viable options: change or more change. Salvador Allende, running for the third time as the candidate of the predominantly Marxist Popular Action Front (Frente de Acción Popular, FRAP), promised to move the country toward socialism by nationalizing the key sectors of the economy, including the U.S.-owned copper mines, increasing state investment, raising taxes on the wealthy, creating a mixed agricultural economy, and promoting unionization. Frei's program was similar and equally ambitious but, reflecting the Christian Democratic ideology, less statist; hence its slogan, "Revolution in Liberty." Frei promised an agrarian reform that would create 100,000 new landowners in six years, huge investments in education and housing, Chileanization or government co-ownership of copper, profit-sharing in industry, and a plan called "people's development" (*promoción popular*) to provide organization and political input for slum dwellers, peasants, women, and other underrepresented groups.

The choice facing the Chilean electorate — two candidates promising revolution — reflected the radicalization of Chilean politics since the last presidential election in 1958. While neither candidate's program mentioned it, the 1964 election was also a referendum on the Cuban Revolution. With Fidel now firmly in the Soviet camp, Frei supporters were quick to suggest that an Allende victory would lead Chile inexorably to domination by Moscow. Allende supporters pointed to Frei's ties to the United States and the similarity between his program and the Alliance for Progress, which they deemed a Yankee plot to thwart social reform and national liberation. More clearly than in any other Latin American election of the 1960s, the 1964 Chilean race was in effect a contest between the Cuban and the U.S.-promoted models of reform and development. The CIA funneled over $2.6 million into Frei's campaign — over half the total cost — apparently without the candidate's knowledge or approval, and Frei supporters brought in Fidel Castro's estranged sister Juana to testify to the horrors of communism. Frei won, as expected, receiving 55.6 percent of the vote to Allende's 38.6, with 4.9 percent going to the Radical Party's candidate.[2]

Frei's greatest challenge as president was to satisfy the urgent demand for social reform and economic improvement that had been heightened by the Cuban Revolution and by the campaign promises to the rural workers and urban shantytown dwellers. It was an implicit assumption that if the Christian Democratic-Alliance for Progress approach did not satisfy the demands unleashed, Allende and his Marxist alternative would become all the more attractive by the next presidential election in 1970. With this knowledge, the United States contributed generously to the Frei government through Alliance for Progress funds and an array of other grants and loans.

Eduardo Frei left office with a solid record of accomplishment. He achieved the Chileanization of the copper companies, gaining 51 percent government control with options to purchase the remaining 49 percent. The government also acquired all or part of the U.S.-owned telephone and telegraph companies. In the area of promoción popular, it established thousands of organizations, such as the ubiquitous Mothers' Centers (Centros de Madres), to foster self-help projects and articulate the interests of the poor. For a large part of the rural population, Frei's unionization and minimum wage laws brought about material improvement and social and political liberation from landowner control.

The Christian Democrats could not reach their ambitious goals, however, in every area. Inflation remained a problem, and owing to a severe drought and some disinvestment in agriculture, economic growth failed to reach the government's projections. Although falling short of his goals in education and housing, Frei made impressive progress in both areas. In agrarian reform, he made a substantial beginning in dismantling the hacienda system but established less than a third of the promised 100,000 new small farms.

Despite a record of reform that would have qualified as radical prior to 1959, the Frei government failed to satisfy the aspirations of Chile's mobilized lower classes for change and improvement. This was especially true in the rural sector, where the very success of Frei's union law had given workers the means of pressing their growing demands for land, with which the agrarian reform did not keep pace. Frustrated by what they considered the slow pace of reform, the PDC left wing broke off in 1969 to form the Movement for Unitary Popular Action (Movimiento de Acción Popular Unitaria, MAPU).

At the same time, the government that was too moderate for the left alarmed the right. Perhaps most worrisome to the upper classes were their perceptions that the Christian Democrats lacked a firm commitment to capitalist private property and that the government's expropriations of rural properties were politically motivated. They also experienced under Frei, for the first time, a government that did not automatically interpret and apply the law in their favor and defend their interests against redistributive threats. Thus increasing pressure from the left began to be matched by a resurgence of the right as vested interests and some of the middle classes decided to stiffen the fight against reform so as to keep Chile, as they saw it, from going into the abyss.

After a disastrous 1965 congressional election in which the combined Liberal and Conservative share of the vote fell to 12 percent, leaving them with 7 of 45 senate seats and only 9 of 147 seats in the chamber of deputies, the historic parties dissolved themselves in 1967 to reappear as the National Party. After a strong showing in the 1969 congressional election, the right adopted a more aggressive posture and decided to take a stand in 1970 by running its own presidential candidate, despite the increased risk of a Marxist victory. It was this return to the normal three-bloc presidential election that opened the way for Salvador Allende.

THE ELECTION OF ALLENDE

Salvador Allende was the 1970 presidential candidate of a coalition considerably broader than the one he had headed in 1964. Besides the Socialists and Communists, the People's Unity (Unidad Popular, UP) included four non-Marxist parties whose presence in the coalition was designed to allay fears of a rigidly Marxist regime: the Radical Party, now stripped of its former power but still commanding some middle class votes; MAPU, the former Christian Democratic left; and two smaller groups, Independent Popular Action (Acción Popular Independiente) and the Social Democratic Party (Partido Social Democrático). Allende promised an acceleration of the reforms already underway and extensive nationalizations to move Chile toward socialism. As before, the United States spent millions of dollars to stop Allende.

The right backed former president Jorge Alessandri, a respected and pragmatic conservative. Alessandri's candidacy was labeled "independent" so as to avoid too close an identification with the historic right and to appeal to middle class voters disillusioned with the leftward shift of both the PDC and the Radicals. While not rejecting the continuation of all reform, Alessandri made clear his intention of curbing the more radical changes instituted under Frei.

The Christian Democrats selected Radomiro Tomic of the party's left-center bloc as their candidate. Tomic saw Allende as his chief rival, and accordingly designed a campaign to compete for the left vote. He called for a significant deepening of reform, including the nationalization of copper, completion of agrarian reform, and expropriation of substantial parts of the economy. In adopting his left strategy, Tomic distanced himself from Frei, who, despite the wear of nearly six years as president, remained Chile's most popular politician. Some analyses suggest that Tomic's strategy cost him middle class votes with no compensating increase in working class support, strengthening Alessandri without significantly hurting Allende.

The polls indicated a close race between Alessandri and Allende, with Tomic trailing. With Alessandri leading on election eve, Allende's victory was a mild surprise. Allende received 36.5 percent of the vote to Alessandri's 35.2, with Tomic getting 28.0 percent. Two reactions to Allende's victory captured the ambivalent attitudes of the right. The Santiago stock market fell overnight by half, indicating deep-seated fear of Allende; and two impeccably tailored elderly gentlemen who had voted for Alessandri, interviewed at random for international television, responded stoically, "One must know how to lose."[3] This combination of fear and resignation guided the behavior of the Chilean right for the first year of the Allende administration.

The election results showed that after six years of substantive reform a large majority of Chileans supported an acceleration of change: By nearly two to one they voted for programs that went well beyond Frei's 1964 platform. Although Allende's percentage of the vote would make him a minority president, this condition was the norm given Chile's multiparty system and the absence of a runoff provision; Frei, who had obtained a majority owing to the absence of a rightist candidate, had been the only exception to the rule since 1942. While being a minority president was not usually a serious handicap, Allende's ambitious program of reform would require a congressional majority, which he lacked. Thus Allende would have to translate the mandate of the Chilean electorate for change into votes in the next congressional elections. His task was to woo the large segment of Tomic supporters, mostly middle and working class, to the UP, and in doing so he faced three obstacles. The 30-month hiatus between presidential and congressional elections would diminish almost any president's ability to translate his own early popularity into congressional votes. The high degree of party loyalty characteristic of the Chilean electorate, moreover, would complicate Allende's task. Finally, the most fundamental problem would be to preserve the commitment of Tomic's middle class constituency to reform in the context of the promised transition to socialism.

Allende's first challenge came from the U.S. government, supported by elements of the Chilean right. Having spent millions of dollars and employed all sorts of dirty tricks over the years to prevent Allende's election, the United States turned to blocking his installation as president. There was no grace period of watching and waiting to see what Allende would do or trying to moderate him after he took office. President Richard Nixon and Secretary of State Henry Kissinger, both reportedly infuriated at Allende's victory, set out immediately to prevent his inauguration, scheduled for November 3. Kissinger saw Chile partially in geopolitical terms: "In a major Latin American country you would have a communist government, joining, for example, Argentina, which is already deeply divided, along a long frontier; joining Peru, which has already been heading in directions that have been difficult to deal with; and joining Bolivia, which has also gone in a more leftist, anti-U. S. direction. . . . So I do not think we should delude ourselves that an Allende take-over in Chile would not present massive problems for us."[4] International Telephone and Telegraph (ITT), which feared the loss of its large Chilean investments, encouraged these efforts; ITT president Harold Geneen constantly badgered the White House for action and spent over a million dollars of corporate funds to keep Allende from office.

One of Washington's approaches to blocking Allende, known as "Track I," invoked a legal means of denying him the presidency. By the 1925 constitution, congress actually elected the president when no candidate received an absolute majority of the popular vote — the normal condition in Chile. In the past, congress had always elected the candidate receiving the relative majority of votes, but given the situation in 1970 this congressional power offered an attractive option to the Chilean right and the Nixon administration. Rightist politicians approached the popular President Frei, asking his aid in persuading PDC congressmen to vote for Alessandri; by this scheme, Alessandri would resign after his inauguration and Frei, who was legally barred from succeeding himself, could then be a candidate in new elections. The United States pressured the Christian Democrats in every way possible and authorized the payment of bribe money to supplement its efforts at persuasion. The Track I option disappeared, however, when Frei refused to participate in the scheme and Allende accepted a set of constitutional amendments known as the "Statute of Democratic Guarantees." The PDC-sponsored guarantees were designed to strengthen the legal status of private education, the press, parties, unions, and the military against any possible totalitarian tendencies that Allende or his government might harbor. Satisfied that the constitutional amendments protected liberal democracy, the Christian Democrats voted for Allende.

Concurrently with the political maneuvering, Washington pursued "Track II," a plan for a military coup to forestall Allende's assumption of power. Despite the long odds, in view of the Chilean military's record and repeated statements of adherence to the constitution, the CIA made contacts within the armed forces while planning economic sabotage and propaganda to prepare the climate for a transitional military government. With constitutionalist General René Schneider as army commander-in-chief, the problem was to find an officer of sufficiently high rank to mobilize the number of troops needed for a successful coup. After much fumbling, and even after the CIA had given up, a group of military personnel and anti-Allende civilians took action, accidentally killing General Schneider in an attempt to kidnap him. Rather than serving its intended purpose, the coup attempt backfired, generating support instead for the constitutional position and Allende's election. The period between Allende's popular election on September 4 and his inauguration on November 3, normally a time of festivities and of high hopes for the winner, was instead a continuous crisis. It was also a harbinger of what Allende could expect from his domestic and foreign enemies.

THE REVOLUTION OF RED WINE AND EMPANADAS, NOVEMBER 1970–OCTOBER 1971

In a press conference early in his administration, Allende promised "a revolution *a la chilena* with red wine and *empanadas* (meat pies)."[5] His reference to the festive diet of the Chilean *pueblo* was an apt metaphor for his first year in office, which was characterized by an atmosphere of enthusiasm and optimism within the government and a broad spectrum of the population. Among the president's early initiatives were redistributive measures and populist gestures designed to cement the loyalty of the working class: free milk for school children and nursing mothers, rent reductions, and rescheduling construction of the Santiago subway so as to serve working class neighborhoods first. Workers also benefitted from some old-fashioned pump priming based on an expanded public works program, increased social security and pension payments, and a modification of the wage and salary adjustment mechanism, adopted in the 1940s to cope with Chile's permanent inflation. The middle classes benefitted from the elimination of taxes on modest incomes and property — a measure compensated by increasing taxes on the wealthy. With money in their pockets from a 25 percent increase in real income, workers went on a year-long consumption spree that touched off a minor boom in industry and services and raised the level of employment.

"We must make haste — slowly," is an aphorism attributed to Salvador Allende at the outset of his presidency.[6] Despite opposition control of congress, movement toward fulfilling UP's campaign program of structural reform was anything but slow during Allende's first year. The only major policy for which Allende obtained congressional support was the nationalization of all remaining U.S. interests in copper, which passed by unanimous vote. For the rest of his programs Allende had to rely on the extensive powers of the presidency and on clever use of laws and regulatory powers. In nationalizing the economy, he found that many foreign and domestic companies were willing to accept very low buy-out offers in the climate of economic and political insecurity that followed Allende's inauguration. In addition, he discovered and used an obscure 1932 emergency decree-law that empowered the government to expropriate any enterprise not meeting rigid production criteria. The UP government also manipulated the long-established system of wage and price controls in ways designed to force targeted companies toward bankruptcy and used to its advantage existing law allowing the government to assume the management of firms undergoing labor conflicts.

Extensive nationalizations in banking, insurance, communications, transportation, textiles, cement, and other manufacturing sectors, combined with the copper nationalization, gave the state control of the "commanding heights" of the economy within Allende's first year. With legislation and machinery already in place for agrarian reform, the UP government accelerated the pace of expropriations and found a loophole that allowed it to create embryonic state farms in place of the small private holdings that the Christian Democrats had fostered. Meanwhile, Allende reestablished diplomatic relations with Cuba during his second week in office, thus becoming the first head of state to resume ties severed as a result of the 1964 OAS action.

The April 1971 municipal elections reflected the success of Allende's first five months as president. Because of the extreme centralization of Chilean government, municipal elections were always considered a referendum on the national government rather than a contest over local issues. The UP improved its electoral performance by 13.2 points, from the 36.5 percent that Allende received in September to 49.7 percent, including 1 percent for an independent pro-government party, in April. The combined opposition received 48 percent — the rest being blank or invalid ballots — allowing the UP to claim an absolute majority of valid votes.

In terms of voter support, April 1971 was the high point for the UP. Allende was unfortunate that congressional elections, held every four years, were not scheduled until April 1973; in contrast, Frei had had the advantage of congressional elections within five months of his inauguration, allowing him to translate his personal popularity into a majority in the chamber of deputies and to ensure enactment of his legislative program. Although Allende did not enjoy a similar opportunity, critics point out that his campaign promise to revamp Chilean government institutions by strengthening presidential powers, creating a unicameral legislature, and reforming the judiciary might have been enacted if he had taken the risk of a plebiscite following the UP victory in April 1971.

By the end of Allende's first year there were signs of trouble for his government. On the economic front, Allende's expensive programs of nationalizations and pump priming had used up a large portion of Chile's foreign currency reserves. Delay in compensating the copper companies — ultimately, the refusal of all compensation — provided a ready excuse for a U.S. credit boycott that forced the government to find alternate sources of foreign loans. Insecurity of rural property led to serious disinvestment in crops and herds in the private sector.

There were also signs of increased political trouble for the regime. Spurred by Allende's victory and by elements of the left, illegal property seizures increased in the cities as well as the countryside. A PDC victory in a Valparaíso congressional by-election in July 1971 was the government's first electoral reversal. Although both parties denied collusion, the National Party had declined to nominate a candidate for the seat, launching an undeclared right-center alliance that soon became explicit. Just as the opposition alliance was forming, Senator Carlos Altamirano of the Socialist Party's extreme left wing — a bloc that flirted with insurrection even while participating in the political system — became secretary-general of Allende's own party. The ingredients of confrontation and polarization were in place, and a PDC proposal for a constitutional amendment to limit Allende's powers of expropriation, introduced in October 1971, set the climate for the ensuing period of escalating conflict between government and opposition.

CONFRONTATION AND POLARIZATION, OCTOBER 1971–SEPTEMBER 1972

Allende's fight to succeed as president was an uphill battle from the beginning, and by his second year in office the problems that would bring about his overthrow were out in the open. Perhaps his most fundamental difficulty was that the UP controlled only one branch of government. Congress was the obvious target, but the passage of time diminished the prospects of achieving a congressional majority in 1973.

The judiciary presented many problems for Allende. Its lack of sympathy with UP objectives was especially significant given the refusal of congress to pass the government's bills; being forced to enact its program by stretching existing laws and powers and constrained by the primacy of capitalist definitions of property in a transition to socialism, the UP was constantly frustrated at the judiciary's ability to slow or halt its progress. Judicial reform figured in the UP electoral program and Allende formally proposed it to congress, but to no avail.

Finally, there was the ultimate arbiter of politics, the armed forces. Despite Chile's long history of rarely interrupted civilian government, everyone knew that the armed forces, by action or inaction, would determine whether Allende would finish his six-year term. Allende's task in relation to the military was to keep it loyal to its tradition of nonintervention; to accomplish that, the president would have to avoid a major crisis of the kind that would make the military's intolerance of disorder override its commitment to nonintervention.

As its second year in office began, the UP was faced with mounting economic problems as well as increasing intransigence by the opposition and the United States. The primary economic problem was inflation, a chronic condition in Chile but one that by 1972 was moving well beyond the 1960s range of 8 to 46 percent and would reach over 300 percent by September 1973. The inflationary spiral resulted largely from the government's massive spending on property acquisitions, subsidies to nationalized firms, and on wages, but was greatly compounded by congressional refusal to approve budgets. In order to maintain the momentum of his first year, Allende turned increasingly to the government printing presses that churned out enough currency to pay the bills but also to stimulate inflation and devaluation.

Besides the stiffening of domestic opposition, Allende had to deal with a Nixon administration firmly committed to his overthrow. In addition to the credit boycott, Washington funneled money through the CIA to opposition parties and to *El Mercurio,* the conservative dean of Santiago newspapers that the UP was harassing in the hope of bankrupting it or convincing its publisher, Agustín Edwards, to capitulate. Between September 1971 and April 1972, the Nixon administration authorized the expenditure of over $2.5 million for the above purposes — part of the $8 million total spent to destabilize the Chilean government — while instructing the CIA to explore every possible avenue to a coup. The U.S. press, while not consistently supportive of the Nixon position, did its part to shape U.S. public opinion against Allende by focusing on matters such as meat rationing, without noting that Chilean governments had controlled supplies and prices of basic foods since the 1930s.

The UP's political fortunes also took a turn for the worse in the months following Allende's first anniversary in office. Fidel Castro came for an announced ten-day visit in November 1971 but stayed three and a half weeks. The visit had some improbable and light moments, such as Fidel's visit to the annual livestock show of the very conservative and elite National Society of Agriculture (Sociedad Nacional de Agricultura), but his very presence in Chile conjured up visions of Marxist dictatorship. Fidel's customary bombastic discourse did not help, either: After he labeled the opposition "fascist," the right and center press and parties accused Castro of interference in Chile's internal affairs.

The power struggle between president and congress reached a new level in January 1972 with the first of several congressional impeachments of cabinet ministers. In the same month the opposition retained two congressional seats in by-elections; more troubling for the government than the failure to gain those seats was the decline of 5.5 percent in the UP vote since the previous April. In March 1972, 13 cases of arms from Cuba labeled as works of art were discovered to have been imported without customs inspection upon the approval of the minister of the interior. Since the arms were not for the military, this caused a furor about the government's suspected involvement in arming popular militias and led to an opposition-introduced arms control law that Allende signed over the objections of some of his coalition partners.

Underlying the increasing confrontation and polarization were a growing mass mobilization and the government's ambivalent attitude toward controlling it. Throughout rural Chile, unauthorized worker occupations of estates led to frequent violence as landowners armed themselves and banded together to defend their properties. While this phenomenon had begun under the Frei government, its exacerbation after the 1970 election created chaos in the countryside and disrupted production. The promoters of these seizures were generally UP members or sympathizers, sometimes agrarian reform officials themselves, who sought to radicalize the revolution with all possible speed. In Santiago and other cities, similar extralegal expropriations were proceeding apace, especially in the industrial belt of the capital where workers and left activists seized dozens of factories.

This "hypermobilization" of the rural and urban working class posed a difficult dilemma for the Allende administration. On one hand, Allende had constitutional responsibility as president to enforce the law, which of course guaranteed private ownership rights until a valid expropriation order was given, and he repeatedly stated his commitment to the rule of law. On the other hand, the workers were Allende's constituency, and for ideological as well as practical reasons he was understandably loathe to use the force of a "people's" government against the people. The government's responses to the wave of unauthorized seizures of factories and haciendas reflected Allende's vacillation over property rights and the rule of law. Some properties were returned to their owners, usually after promises to the occupiers of expeditious legal expropriation; many were not returned at all; and in some cases the government expelled the workers by force.

The government's inconsistency reflected more than sentimental considerations about the use of force on the people. More basically, it was the product of the deep division within the UP coalition and within Allende's own Socialist Party over strategy and tactics for making the revolution. On the left, a strong minority of the UP and its allies advocated pushing ahead with all speed to break the back of capitalism and install a true people's government before the opposition could regroup and react. The left believed that stimulating rather than restraining the popular mobilization would help accomplish this goal and that the government itself should encourage extralegal acts rather than enforce bourgeois law.

The left wing of the Socialists, led by party Secretary-General Carlos Altamirano, had long expressed disdain for Chile's political institutions and had argued the need for insurrection at the appropriate time. After the departure of its own conservative wing in 1971, MAPU, itself the former PDC left, generally supported the Altamirano position. Outside the government but tacitly allied with it was the MIR, the urban guerrilla organization that had given up insurrection during the 1970 presidential campaign. The MIR operated openly on the fringe of government, fostering takeovers, developing shantytown organizations, forming worker militias, proselytizing the populace, and generally pushing Allende as hard as it could toward ever bolder steps.

The more conservative majority of the UP consisted of the Communists, the Allende Socialists, the Radicals, and the smaller groups. Their position was to push vigorously toward socialism primarily through legal means, by extending state control and redistributing income. They were not willing to take the risk, which the UP left and the MIR implicitly accepted, of provoking an armed reaction against the government; they preferred consolidation of gains at a certain point, if necessary, over continual confrontation. These deep divisions within the UP were aired and debated but not resolved at a conference in February 1972, and the schisms persisted to the end.

The government's vacillation on the rule of law was a major factor in the UP's political failure. To succeed, the government had to preserve its half of the electorate until the 1973 congressional election. The PDC's hold on significant portions of the working class — a majority of the rural unions, several skilled workers' unions, and women — meant that Allende's chances of converting the lower class majority of Chileans into a UP electoral majority were slim. Therefore he had to rely on a significant portion of Chile's large middle classes for electoral support.

The middle sectors tended to view rising levels of confrontation and the government's vacillation on law enforcement with apprehension, and the opposition press constantly fed their fears with reports and photo spreads of land seizures, worker marches, MIR activities, and discoveries of arms caches. Accelerating inflation and shortages of food and consumer goods further eroded support for or tolerance of Allende among the middle classes, and the leveling tendency, reflected in the integration of the historically separate white and blue collar workers' social security systems, undoubtedly reinforced a growing disenchantment with the government. Substantial parts of the middle class revealed their antigovernment sentiments in October 1972 when a truck owners' strike, called to protest a government plan to nationalize the trucking sector, precipitated action by Chile's economic and professional associations, or *gremios*.

COUNTERATTACK AND OVERTHROW, OCTOBER 1972–SEPTEMBER 1973

The gremio movement had begun during the Frei administration, when the virtual eclipse of rightist political power impelled Chile's economic elites to seek alternate means of defending their interests. While long-established organizations such as the Sociedad Nacional de Agricultura, the Society for Industrial Development (Sociedad de Fomento Fabril), and the Central Chamber of Commerce (Cámara Central de Comercio) had acted as pressure groups for many years, heightened threats to their interests in the 1960s stimulated the expansion of membership and coordination of efforts across sectoral lines. In the process of expansion, the large capitalists set aside their traditional disregard for their lesser counterparts and espoused the commonality of interests among all merchants, from the major import-export houses to the humble shopkeeper, all farmers, manufacturers, and professionals. Thus by the time of Allende's election, hundreds of thousands of small farmers, artisans, taxi owners, and market stall operators were organizationally affiliated with Chile's traditional elites in the multiclass gremio movement, a loose confederation of interest groups dominated by the elites and coordinated by a central command.

The October 1972 truckers' strike launched a mass movement of opposition to Allende based on strategies and tactics borrowed from labor unions and left parties. Described as "the mass line of the bourgeoisie," the movement featured a "bosses' strike" or lockout by business owners and a shutdown of transportation, professional services, shops of all kinds, and even strikes by some 100,000 PDC-controlled agricultural workers.[7] Accompanying these actions were housewives' "marches of the empty pots," student demonstrations, and general street agitation normally associated with the left. Government supporters responded by occupying some of the factories and businesses from which they were locked out. The elite organizations of large-scale entrepreneurs cleverly remained in the background during the strike, leaving the spotlight to leaders of the middle-class associations who could more effectively portray the action as a broad-based, popular rejection of Marxism.

This innovative approach to upper- and middle-class self-defense was very effective. The shutdown of provisioning to the cities necessitated establishment of emergency supply networks involving additional regulations and demonstrated the government's vulnerability to coordinated private sector action. The strike was resolved after four weeks, but only by the appointment of three military officers to Allende's cabinet.

The president invited the military into his cabinet to restore order and to build confidence in the regime by presiding over and ensuring the fairness of the March 1973 congressional elections. While the military's objective was to contribute to stability and thus to reinforce its ability to remain out of "politics," the generals and admirals inevitably became involved in controversial, politically charged policies. Many officers disliked the resulting identification of the armed forces with UP policies, and as the government's problems continued to mount, they came increasingly to reject participation, preferring to let the government sink on its own until public opinion would welcome a coup. After the initial three military ministers resigned in March 1973, the council of generals rejected Allende's requests for renewed military participation in his government. Only in the desperate days of August 1973 did they agree to hold office again. This involvement led to a bizarre scene at the home of army commander Carlos Prats, where wives of anti-UP officers picketed in protest of the military's role in government. While military participation gave Allende a short respite after the gremios' strike, it resolved no major problem and ultimately discredited the noninterventionist position within the officer corps.

The March 1973 congressional elections followed an acrimonious campaign. Prior to the election, Allende, recognizing the slim chance of victory, had stopped talking about a congressional majority and claimed that 40 percent of the vote would be an endorsement of UP rule. The National Party, aiming by now at Allende's removal, called for the opposition to achieve the two-thirds of congress needed to impeach the president. The outcome allowed both sides to claim victory: 44.0 percent of the valid vote for UP candidates to 55.7 percent for the opposition. The UP's total was 7.5 percentage points above Allende's 1970 figure but nearly 6 below the 1971 municipal election results. The few seats that the UP gained did not change the majority and since virtually every vote now was party line, the 1973 election cemented the deadlock between president and congress, reinforcing the polarization of Chilean politics.

The president's annual address to congress on May 21 gave Allende a final opportunity to recount his government's accomplishments. Judged against the UP campaign platform the achievements of two and a half years were impressive. Expropriation of 3,570 rural properties, amounting to 35 percent of Chile's total agricultural surface, had left only a small number of holdings exceeding the legal maximum. The government had nationalized over 200 of the country's largest enterprises, which accounted for 30 percent of Chilean production, exceeding Allende's goal of 91 companies listed after his election. A third of wholesale distribution and 90 percent of bank credit were under state control, and income redistribution had proceeded effectively. In sum, Allende had moved Chile well along the road toward socialism.

While emphasizing the UP's successes, Allende's speech also acknowledged that Chile had entered a stage of crisis. By May 1973 the Chilean economy was near collapse, beset by runaway inflation, rapidly declining production, shortages of essential goods, lack of new investment, and mounting deficits. Rising street violence, numerous incidents of assassination and sabotage, the arming of workers and of the right wing Fatherland and Liberty (Patria y Libertad), and the establishment of neighborhood vigilance patrols reflected the growing instability that was rapidly undermining Chile's institutional foundations. The sense of crisis was so great that by the next month the military was working out plans for a coup and the UP moving to counter it. The small, easily suppressed rising of Santiago's Second Armored Regiment on June 29 served notice that the brink had almost been reached.

On July 25 the gremios launched another national strike, this one clearly designed to shut down the economy as long as necessary to secure Allende's removal. Several additional groups, including large contingents of PDC-controlled labor, joined forces with the gremios that had conducted the October 1972 movement. Rejecting all attempts at conciliation, the gremios continued their action until, caught between the antigovernment mobilization and the counteractions of its own supporters, the Allende government witnessed its authority virtually evaporate.

In the midst of escalating violence, economic paralysis, and political deadlock, the armed forces in August received a provocation that hastened their preparations for removing Allende. Naval intelligence reported a plot by sailors in Valparaíso and Talcahuano to rise against their commanders and accused the MIR, Socialist Senator Carlos Altamirano, and MAPU Deputy Oscar Garretón of promoting the planned revolt. Coinciding with that revelation was Allende's first use of his commander-in-chief's powers over military retirements and promotions to place officers of his confidence in strategic positions in the military hierarchy. Although unrelated to the naval plot, this reversal of Allende's hands-off policy, motivated by his growing sense of danger, could be interpreted by the officer corps as coordinated subversion from above and below. As with their Brazilian counterparts in 1964, the perception of tampering with military discipline was the final straw for the Chilean officers. The last serious obstacle to the coup disappeared when constitutionalist General Prats, rebuffed by his colleagues, resigned as army commander on August 22. Any lingering hesitation vanished on September 9, when Socialist Party leader Carlos Altamirano made a radio-broadcast speech defying the military to prosecute him for subversion and rejecting all compromise with the opposition. When it came on September 11, a week before Chile's national holiday, the coup was efficient and brutal.

Although the train of events of Allende's final weeks appeared to make the coup unavoidable, different decisions at critical junctures throughout the UP administration might have postponed or prevented the denouement of September 11, 1973. If Allende had held the plebiscite on his proposed institutional reforms soon after the April 1971 municipal elections, and won, he would have been able to accomplish much of his program without recourse to maneuvers of dubious legality; had his plebiscite lost, he might have charted a less ambitious course and avoided the polarization that gripped the country by 1972. Controlling the UP left and the MIR might have enabled Allende to restore order and finish his term, although this would have slowed the momentum of his movement toward socialism.

Throughout Allende's presidency, the UP and PDC periodically conducted negotiations designed to surmount specific crises and generally to arrest the erosion of political stability. Each time, narrow partisan interests and inflexibility on the UP left and PDC right prevented agreements that might have saved Chile's political institutions from destruction. A different outcome of the last PDC-UP dialogue, held at the end of July 1973, might well have dissuaded the military from acting. Allende's resignation would certainly have prevented the coup, but that was a step that he was unwilling to take. However, Altamirano's September 9 speech, in addition to infuriating him, convinced Allende to stake his continuance in office on a plebiscite, which he planned to announce via radio on the afternoon of September 11. Unfortunately, the beleaguered president arrived too late at the decision that most likely would have prevented the coup and years of harsh military dictatorship.

The overthrow of Allende was a severe blow to the hopes of Latin America's left. Many were quick to proclaim that the *vía electoral* had been an illusion all along, that there is no peaceful road to socialism. Those who had believed that its unique tradition and the strength of its political institutions made Chile an exception were forced to recognize that, beneath its trappings of constitutional stability and military noninter-vention, Chile was after all part of Latin America. For a large portion of the many Chileans who welcomed the coup as their salvation, joy quickly turned to misery as the military showed its true face. The millions of poor Chileans who feared the worst from the military regime that replaced their "comrade President" were not to be disappointed.

NOTES

1. U. S. Congress, Senate Select Committee on Intelligence Activities, *Alleged Assassination Plots Involving Foreign Leaders: Interim Report* (1975), 229, quoted in Paul E. Sigmund, *The Overthrow of Allende and the Politics of Chile, 1964–1976* (Pittsburgh: University of Pittsburgh Press, 1977), 113.

2. These figures are percentages of the total vote and do not account for blank or invalid votes (in this election, 0.9 percent). The term "valid vote" refers to a percentage of the total vote with blank and invalid ballots subtracted.

3. The author viewed the telecast, 5 September 1970.

4. Seymour M. Hersh, "The Price of Power: Kissinger, Nixon, and Chile," *The Atlantic Monthly* 250, no. 6 (December 1982), 40.

5. Quoted in Sigmund, *The Overthrow of Allende*, 131.

154 / LATIN AMERICA AND THE CUBAN REVOLUTION

6. David J. Morris, *We Must Make Haste — Slowly: The Process of Revolution in Chile* (New York: Vintage Books, 1973), 119.

7. Armand Mattelart, "La bourgeoisie à l'école de Lénine: Le 'gremialisme' et la ligne de masse de la bourgeoisie chilienne" (*Politique Aujourd'hui* [Paris], 1–2 [January-February 1974]), 23–46.

9

The Antirevolutionary
Military Regimes

Following the overthrow of the Goulart government in 1964, the Brazilian armed forces pioneered the development of a new type of regime tailored to the era of the Cuban Revolution. The primary purpose of the new military government was to make Brazil immune to revolution, and its main instruments were economic development and political purification. In 1966 the Argentine military established a forerunner of a state with the same mission, which would appear in definitive form in 1976. In Chile and Uruguay, the countries with Latin America's strongest constitutionalist traditions, the armed forces seized power in 1973 to erect states similar to the Brazilian. With the 1976 coup in Argentina, over two-thirds of South America's population found itself living under extremely repressive military regimes just 15 years after John Kennedy's prediction of the demise of the "strong man" in Latin America.[1]

Underlying the rise of the new South American military regimes, and common among Latin American military institutions in the 1960s, was the new doctrine of national security derived from the Cold War and the Cuban Revolution. With the shift of emphasis in the Inter-American Military System from external to internal threats, Latin American officers began to study social and economic conditions in their own countries as a supplement to the traditional curriculum geared to external defense. Armed with this new knowledge gained in schools such as Brazil's Superior War College (Escola Superior de Guerra) and Peru's CAEM (Centro de Altos Estudios Militares), the armed forces set out to insulate their countries against the threat of revolution. For all, national security required rapid economic development to eliminate the poverty upon which revolutionaries preyed. With the primary exception of Peru's officers, who pursued their own course, the armed forces embraced the notion that national security also required the political reeducation of the populace to root out all ideas of Marxism, class conflict, and in some cases even the concepts of liberal democracy that permitted Marxism to flourish. The patriotic mission of the armed forces would be completed only when the country had been thoroughly immunized against revolution.

The Brazilian, Uruguayan, Chilean, and Argentine military regimes of the 1960s through the 1980s varied according to national circumstances, and all had antecedents that linked them to the traditional military regimes common throughout the history of republican Latin America. However, the Brazilian, Argentine, Uruguayan, and Chilean regimes shared several important characteristics that set them apart from the standard military government and defined a discrete regime prototype. The four governments originated in major political crises that appeared to presage Marxist revolution, rather than in the more narrow political crisis of a particular civilian government. All were governments of the armed forces as an institution rather than military-supported personal or clique dictatorships — although the long-lived Pinochet regime in Chile developed distinct personalist traits. The four regimes implemented versions of liberal economic orthodoxy and sought foreign capital as the means of fostering development. All employed civilian technocrats, who supposedly operated independently of political pressures, to direct their economies. All were stridently anticommunist and, of course, anti-Castro. With hesitation in some cases, these regimes ultimately rejected all constraints on their powers of repression, becoming terrorist states. Finally, all these regimes were committed, like the Peruvian armed forces, to remaining in office as long as it took to make their countries revolution-resistant.

These military governments presented dilemmas for the United States. From a public relations standpoint, support for regimes that denied human rights as a matter of policy was a liability; it also blunted the human rights charges that Washington routinely directed at communist regimes. Relations with the hard-line military governments were especially difficult for President Jimmy Carter, who made the protection of human rights the centerpiece of his foreign policy. U.S. presidents from Johnson through Reagan scolded their military counterparts from time to time and occasionally slapped their wrists by temporarily withholding aid. Carter was certainly the most forceful in speaking out against the generals and admirals and cutting aid; his stance against Pinochet embittered U.S.-Chilean relations for several years. Yet no U.S. president gave serious consideration to applying the standard measures used against reformist governments that displeased the United States — long-term cancellation of critical aid, economic boycotts, collective diplomatic pressure, or the incitement of coups or rebellions — to effect changes in those military regimes.

The new-style military regimes spawned many descriptive terms. Scholars have attempted to apply old labels, including fascism and corporatism, and have invented terms such as the new authoritarianism, bureaucratic-authoritarianism, the national security state, and the anti-political regime. The term "antirevolutionary" seems to fit as well, in that all four military regimes were established to combat forces unleashed or movements accelerated by the Cuban Revolution — Goulart and the mobilized lower classes in Brazil, urban guerrilla forces in Uruguay and Argentina, and a Marxist-dominated government in Chile.

THE BRAZILIAN MILITARY IN POWER, 1964–85

When the Brazilian armed forces overthrew President João Goulart in March 1984, it was not immediately evident that a new model of military governance was in the making. The government of Marshal Humberto Castelo Branco (1964–67) set out to correct what it considered Goulart's mistaken economic policies and to cleanse the political system of dangerous elements. But within a short time the government was using a new term, "manipulated democracy," to describe and defend its increasingly profound reshaping of the political system and the economy. By 1969, with the accession of the third of Brazil's five military presidents, the government had become an undisguised dictatorship using terror against its citizens as a means of retaining power — the model for the new antirevolutionary state.

The first five years of military rule were dominated by the moderate faction of the armed forces that sought to govern within the framework of civilian institutions, but on the military's terms. The pattern from 1964 through 1968, however, was one of progressive stripping away of the substance of popular participation in the face of continuing civilian resistance to the military's policies. Institutional Act no. 1 of April 1964 reaffirmed the validity of the 1946 constitution, then modified the document by calling for congressional election of the president, enhancing presidential powers vis-à-vis congress and the states, and empowering the president to suspend citizens' political rights for ten years and to remove office holders for subversion or corruption. Under this act the military's candidate, Castelo Branco, was elected, hundreds of leftist and moderate politicians lost political rights and office, and the government took over labor unions and outlawed the peasant leagues.

This manipulation of the political system might have secured the desired compliance were it not for the government's economic policies. These featured austerity measures to fight inflation and the reopening of Brazil to virtually unrestricted foreign investment, underpinned by a guarantee against expropriation of U.S. investments. With strikes banned, wages controlled, and government spending on social services sharply reduced, real wages fell precipitously, unemployment increased, and the subsistence poor experienced a shrinking margin of survival. These economic measures, combined with a normal dislike for military rule, fueled a resistance that drove the military hard liners to demand firmer measures and eventually to take control themselves.

Institutional Act no. 2 of October 1965, the next step toward military absolutism, was a response to state elections held earlier in that month. Having issued a new electoral code, regulated parties, and extended the purge of politicians, the government expected its candidates to win without difficulty. Their defeat, a failure for "manipulated democracy," elicited further tightening under the October act, which enabled the president to dissolve congress and rule by decree, banned existing political parties, exempted some government actions from judicial review, packed the supreme court, and remanded those charged with subversion to military courts. Institutional Act no. 3 of February 1966 ended popular election of governors and mayors of state capitals.

Reflecting the struggle between moderates and hard-liners, Castelo Branco still tried to salvage a semblance of democracy by reviving parties, creating a two-party system consisting of a pro-government party (the "yes sir" party) with a majority in congress and a minority opposition party (the "yes" party) whose members were inoffensive enough to have survived the purges. Most changes contained in the institutional acts and presidential decrees were incorporated in the new 1967 constitution, along with press restrictions and a sweeping internal security law that stripped away individual liberties. Marshal Artur da Costa e Silva, who succeeded Castelo Branco in March 1967, thus entered office armed with what appeared to be sufficient legal authority to rule absolutely behind a facade of constitutionalism and civilian participation. However, 1968 brought Brazilian participation in the international year of student rebellion and a wave of illegal strikes protesting the continuing decline in real income. The final victory of the hard-liners over the advocates of manipulation came in December 1968 when, despite severe government pressure, the normally pliant congress refused to waive the immunity of an opposition deputy who had offended the armed forces. This display of independence and intractability led to Institutional Act no. 5 of December

1968, which suspended the 1967 constitution, dissolved congress and the state legislatures, banned habeus corpus, tightened censorship, and cancelled the political rights of thousands more Brazilians.

When he took over as president in November 1969, after Costa e Silva had suffered a disabling stroke, General Emílio Garrastazú Médici (1969–74) inherited a state apparatus with powers unprecedented in republican Brazil, even under Getúlio Vargas's fascist-inspired Estado Nôvo. With the beginning of urban guerrilla warfare in 1969, in response to the incremental closing off of legal means of opposition, Médici found ample opportunity to use the tools of repression at his disposal. In addition to attacking the guerrillas, the government followed the strategy — later developed into a fine and deadly art in Chile and Argentina — of focusing repression on actual and potential supporters of the guerrillas to dissuade them from active involvement and thus isolate the guerrillas. Arbitrary arrest and detention, indeterminate jail sentences, torture, and assassination became standard instruments of government policy in the fight against subversion; in addition to its own police and military agents, government-sanctioned or -condoned private death squads carried out the same work. Under cover of press censorship, dissolution of legislatures and parties, suspension of habeas corpus, and unlimited use of states of siege, the government could operate with no limitations on its use of repression except persistent but largely ineffectual pressure from the church. Because the guerrillas were defeated relatively easily, the Brazilian military government did not employ its repressive powers to the full extent possible. Yet in their quest for national security, the successive governments since 1964 had created the first fully developed antirevolutionary terrorist state.

Accompanying the rise of a naked military dictatorship and, to the outside world, partially masking the repressive nature of the regime, was the Brazilian economic "miracle." Beginning in 1967, the technocratic economists charged with promoting rapid development had replaced the initial anti-inflation austerity plan with an aggressive policy of state-stimulated growth. While based on private foreign and domestic capital and a contraction of state investment, the policy directed by economist Antônio Delfim Neto was managed by state controls over prices, wages, credit, and inputs — a contrast to the shock treatment advocated by the International Monetary Fund (IMF) and used by other antirevolutionary regimes. The result of the initial dampening of inflation followed by rapid expansion of production was a period of spectacular economic growth, culminating in 1969–74 with an average annual increase of over 10 percent in the gross domestic product.

The Brazilian miracle, highly touted by the government and widely admired abroad, had its dark side. A disproportionate amount of the growth took place in the industrial and coffee-exporting southeast, already the country's wealthiest area, while the impoverished northeast continued to stagnate. A major share of growth took place among the transnational corporations that flooded post-1964 Brazil. With growth concentrated in capital-intensive industries, unemployment rose significantly during the miracle. Most telling was the redistribution of income: Between 1960 and 1976, the wealthiest 5 percent of Brazilians increased their share of total national income from 28 to 39 percent while the poorest 50 percent saw their share fall from 18 to 12 percent at a time when social services were evaporating.

The administration of General Ernesto Geisel (1974–79) was essentially a continuation of the antirevolutionary state with a few modifications. Having promised a *distensão*, or gradual opening toward broader participation, Geisel reined in the use of repression and tolerated some public discussion and criticism but did not hesitate to use the full range of authoritarian power when necessary. During his presidency the miracle began to fall apart. Oil-importing Brazil was hurt by OPEC's pricing policies after 1973, recession in the industrial countries hindered exports, and the easy credit of the early 1970s began to take its toll as Brazil faced a huge foreign debt with dwindling resources. For the first time, opponents of the regime found a powerful if inconsistent ally in the Carter administration, whose emphasis on human rights put Washington and Brasília on a collision course. Students, workers, and even businessmen began to show signs of unrest late in the Geisel presidency, and in the climate of greater tolerance Geisel allowed an opposition presidential candidate to run against the man he had chosen to conclude the political opening.

When he took office in March 1979, General João Baptista Figueiredo publicly expressed the armed forces' desire to return to the barracks. One of his first acts was to offer an amnesty to all those who had lost political rights or received arbitrary punishment under the military. The subsequent gradual dismantling of the antirevolutionary state under Figueiredo reflected several factors. The military had failed in its goal of lifting the country out of poverty, and prospects for rekindling the brief miracle were dim. Despite some impressive economic growth, Brazil's basic problems of poverty, social injustice, illiteracy, poor health, and regional disparities had grown worse under military rule. The regime had also failed to develop public support beyond some of the privileged groups; hence it could govern only through the use or threat of repression. Yet, at a point 20 years after the Cuban Revolution and 15 years after the overthrow of Goulart, the armed forces could take comfort in what appeared to be the reduced threat of revolution in Brazil and in Latin America outside of Central America and the Caribbean.

Assessing its future, the officer corps, like a politician reading the polls, opted to rid itself of the increasingly unpopular and unrewarding task of governance. Added to this calculation, some military leaders undoubtedly continued to embrace the older view that the military's political role should be limited to its traditional moderating power — the removal of offending or ineffectual governments, not the right to govern. The return to civilian rule was a phased-in process lasting almost a decade, beginning with the restoration of party rights and elections for state governors in 1982, won by opposition groups. The 1985 presidential election would install the first nonmilitary president in 21 years, but fearing the consequences of a free and direct popular election, the administration prescribed an indirect election procedure to ensure acceptable results. With the election of opposition candidate Tancredo Neves, who was incapacitated before taking office, and the accession of his vice-president, José Sarney, Brazil was ready for the final steps: a new constitution, approved in 1988, and the first direct presidential election in three decades. With the inauguration of President Fernando Collor de Mello in March 1990, Brazil returned to civilian constitutional government after 26 years of direct or indirect military rule.

THE URUGUAYAN MILITARY REGIME, 1973–84

The Uruguayan military regime that took power in the aftermath of the struggle against the Tupamaros had much in common with its Brazilian counterpart. Its mission was to institute major changes in political life and in the economy in order to make the country resistant to revolution, but it proved unwilling to alter the economy and use the degree of repression necessary to make a clean break with the past. After only seven years in power, the armed forces began searching for the means of extricating themselves from the government, and the transition to civilian rule was complete by 1984.

The militarization of Uruguay was a gradual process, beginning with the decision of President Pacheco Areco in September 1971 to place the armed forces directly in charge of repressing the Tupamaros. After a year of intense counterinsurgency actions under a state of internal war, the Tupamaros were essentially defeated, but the military, apparently convinced of the need to sanitize Uruguay's liberal political system to prevent a recurrence of destabilization and insurrection, increased its demands for power. Thus a national security council, chaired by the country's ranking military officer, was created as a new governmental entity in February 1973. In June President Bordaberry, siding with the armed forces against the politicians, dissolved congress and replaced it with an appointed civilian council of state. The appointment of military men to administer state enterprises, ministries, and other bureaucracies furthered the militarization of the state. In 1976 the military replaced Bordaberry with another civilian figurehead, Aparicio Méndez.

The "institutionalization of the revolutionary process" continued.[2] It drew from the Brazilian model progressively to strip the hybrid military-civilian government of all substance of citizen participation by curtailing parties, taking over trade unions, and establishing strict censorship. "Institutional Acts" gave a legal patina to policies directly contradicting the constitution, whose integrity the military claimed to be preserving through its stewardship. The institutional acts provided the armed forces a formal role in government, infringed the independence of the courts, and suspended the political rights of some 15,000 mainline as well as left politicians for 15 years. Education came under military control, prompting a university dean to remark that "we must abolish research since it is harmful to education."[3] With this groundwork laid, the military routinized arbitrary arrest and sentencing, torture, and murder of dissidents and suspects. Although the Uruguayan military's record of human rights abuse was less dramatic that those of its Chilean and Argentine counterparts, the government developed the essential apparatus of a terrorist state.

In economic policy the Uruguayan military followed an approach similar to that of its Brazilian counterpart. The basic plan to reverse a two-decade economic decline was to force the economy to become competitive internationally through the standard IMF formula of tariff reductions, privatization of the huge state sector, wage reductions, and a decrease in government spending and direction of the economy. Yet despite possessing the power to do so, the government was unwilling to administer a "shock" to the economy, keeping instead a broad range of price controls until 1979 and lowering tariffs incrementally and selectively to ease the transition to a market economy. While modest improvements occurred in various economic indicators, Uruguay experienced no "miracle" of the Brazilian or even the Chilean type, and a 1982 crisis reversed the positive trend. Meanwhile, social costs were high: Real wages fell significantly, unemployment doubled, and social services contracted.

Just as the beginnings of the Uruguayan military regime were gradual and unspectacular, so was its end. Unable to rid itself of all of the country's traditional political values and perhaps badly miscalculating public sentiment, the military called a referendum on institutionalizing the political system it had devised. In that November 1980 election, 58 percent of the voters pronounced against the new regime, launching a four year process of military withdrawal. The traditional political parties were reauthorized in 1982 and elections were scheduled for 1984. General strikes and a broad popular mobilization in 1984 even convinced the military to legalize the left and allow its candidates to run for office. The elections returned Uruguay to civilian rule after 11 years under the leadership of President Julio Sanguinetti of the Colorado Party.

THE CHILEAN ANTIREVOLUTIONARY STATE, 1973–90

By most measures, Chile's was the most extreme of South America's antirevolutionary states. Its use of repression and state terror may have claimed more orfewer victims than did the Argentine military's "dirty war," but whatever the elusive body count may have been, the Chilean armed forces did not have the justification of facing the kind of guerrilla warfare found across the Andes. The economic policies of the Chilean regime were more orthodox and far more extreme in their consequences than were the policies pursued by the Brazilian, Uruguayan, or Argentine militaries. Finally, the Chilean armed forces were more ambitious in their goal of purifying the nation of the taint of Marxism and liberalism, to the point that they set out explicitly to create a new Chilean mentality based on patriotism, religion, family, and class solidarity.

Prior to 1973 the Chilean military had rarely overthrown governments or even expressed institutional preferences for particular candidates or policies; the last of its infrequent coups had been in 1932, when the turmoil set off by the Depression sparked military takeovers throughout the hemisphere. In 1970, the pressing question had been whether the election of Allende would strain the armed forces' long-established political neutrality. By late 1972, as the country became polarized and Allende's support dwindled, the question became how long the military would wait before removing the government.

Given the extreme deterioration of political and economic conditions by mid-1973, the coup surprised few people. What was shocking, however, was the extreme brutality with which it was carried out. Under cover of an around-the-clock curfew, troops and police set out on an orgy of killings, beatings, arrests, interrogation, and torture whose victims quickly overwhelmed the capacities of hospitals, jails, and morgues. Soldiers burned books, conducted mass executions in the National Stadium, and ransacked the home of Chile's dying Nobel laureate, poet Pablo Neruda. The brunt of the coup's fury was directed at members of the government and the UP coalition parties and at workers in factories where it was suspected that arms were being manufactured or distributed. The death toll of the coup and its immediate aftermath will never be established; the figure of 10,000 may be conservative.

A large share of the population, probably a majority, had welcomed a coup, anticipating that the armed forces would follow the traditional Latin American pattern of arresting and exiling government officials, holding power a year or so, and overseeing new elections. Their illusions about the treatment of government officials were shattered during the coup in which President Allende died — by suicide, the new government claimed, but many observers attributed the president's death to murder by a military that could not afford the liability of a jailed or exiled Allende to serve as a rallying point against it. Within weeks, the notion of a brief interruption of constitutional rule also evaporated as the military moved to consolidate its control. In contrast to Brazil and Uruguay, the Chilean military cared nothing about pretenses of civilian participation in government. The junta banned the UP parties, recessed the other parties, dissolved congress, outlawed the national trade union confederation, and appointed administrators for individual unions and the universities. A curfew, a state of siege, and censorship continued in place while the government moved to complete the destruction of the left in the following months. Under pretext of searching for arms, many of which were found, military units had carte blanche to interrogate, hold, and torture individuals suspected even of sympathy with the deposed government.

After establishing uncontested control over the country, the military began to reveal its ideology and goals. A March 1974 "Declaration of Principles of the Government of Chile" announced that the armed forces "do not set timetables for their management of the government, because the task of rebuilding the country morally, institutionally, and economically requires prolonged and profound actions." Among the military's obligations was that of "changing the mentality of Chileans."[4] The moral rebuilding involved the "extirpation of Marxism" and its doctrine of class struggle and their replacement with the values of conservative Catholicism, class harmony, and above all Chilean nationalism: "The fatherland, with its traditions and historical-cultural identity, cannot be the patrimony of any given generation, for it also belongs to those who built it in the past, and those who have a right to its future inheritance."[5] This moral reconstruction would involve complete revision of school curricula, strict control of the media, strategic placement of symbols such as that of the authoritarian "founder of the nation," Diego Portales, and of course the eradication of all Marxist concepts. It would be a job comparable in scope to the communists' task of creating the "new Soviet (or Cuban) man" and requiring a degree of control approaching totalitarianism.

The rebuilding of institutions would involve not only the proscription of Marxism but the creation of a political system that would guarantee the permanent exclusion of that noxious poison. In a 1975 speech, junta leader General Augusto Pinochet made a ringing denunciation of the permissiveness of the liberal state that had allowed Marxism to flourish: "Nothing can be of greater use to communism than the declaration of ideological neutrality by states which are not yet under its control."[6] His minister of the interior added that "all political parties . . . act only to divide citizens . . . and thus cause the soul of the nation to deteriorate."[7] The practices of liberal democracy were such an anathema to the regime that it prohibited elections in all types of formal organizations, including professional associations, mothers' centers, schools, and sports clubs.

After much internal debate the military decided to legitimize its rule by holding a plebiscite in 1980 on a new constitution it had drafted. This document did not reveal the final shape of the Chilean state; rather, it essentially codified the status quo or what it called the "transition" period and sanctioned the continuation of existing dictatorial institutions until at least 1989, with a provision for an extension of eight more years. The ongoing transition was described as a "protected democracy," based on the continued exclusion of political parties and activity and the "guardianship" of the military.[8] Ratified by an announced 68 percent of the vote after a campaign in which opposition was proscribed, the 1980 constitution legalized not only military control but also the personal power that General Pinochet had been building over the years. This made the Chilean dictatorship the most personalist of the antirevolutionary states.

The economic reconstruction of the country was based on the neoliberal model of the Chicago school and Milton Friedman, approved by the IMF, and largely financed by foreign private banks. The so-called "Chicago boys," Catholic University economists trained at the University of Chicago, were the technocrats in charge of a complete revamping of the economic rules. Their mission was to strip away nearly half a century's accretion of government regulation and ownership — to reverse a process that had begun with the Arturo Alessandri administration in the

1920s, moved ahead with the establishment of the Chilean Development Corporation in 1939, and accelerated under Frei and especially Allende. Their targets ranged from tariffs to exchange controls to government-owned manufacturing plants and eventually extended to the governmental health services and social security, which were partially privatized.

The Chicago boys' initial steps involved reducing tariffs, lifting price controls, devaluing the currency, selling off state industries, cutting government spending, opening Chile to foreign investment, and establishing good relations with U.S. lenders who had boycotted the Allende government. By 1975 the technocrats had decided to intensify the "shock" by the further lifting of controls, more privatizations, and reduction of government programs. By the end of the decade, the Chilean economy had been thoroughly transformed and integrated into the world market. The state share of total investment, which had been 77 percent in 1970 and had risen under Allende, fell to under 30 percent by 1979.

After nurturing industry for half a century, Chile deindustrialized after 1973 as protective tariffs tumbled. In 1980, no tariff exceeded 10 percent except that on automobiles; by 1981, the number of industrial enterprises had fallen by 13 percent relative to 1967 and industrial employment by 26 percent. Chile increasingly became a raw material exporter, supplementing its traditional export of copper with out-of-season fruits for Northern Hemisphere markets. After an initial contraction, the neoliberal model seemed to be working and the economy experienced what was called a "miracle" of rapid growth between 1977 and 1981. Then in 1982 a deep recession set in, leading to wage cuts, bank failures, and government intervention in financial institutions. Despite these reverses, the Chicago School model with some modifications remained in place until the end of the military government and the economy recovered some from the nadir of the early 1980s.

As in Brazil, the poor and middle classes paid the price of the Chicago boys' radical experiment. With no union or political representation, they were at the mercy of a military determined to administer strong medicine to a sick patient. While prices were freed, wages remained controlled, and at very low levels. Unemployment at least tripled over the 1970 rate, forcing the government to violate its principles and set up emergency make-work programs paying subminimum wages. By 1975 real wages had fallen by over a third from 1970 levels, with some reports claiming up to a 60 percent reduction in workers' purchasing power since the coup. Cuts in social welfare programs ensured that the needy would receive little or no government help. In the country-side the government by 1979 had returned 30 percent of the expropriated land in its possession to former owners and had assigned some 35 percent of what it held to 40,000 peasant families. However, the benefit of ownership for many proved illusory: Owing to low prices, high credit costs, and a lack of technical assistance, at least 40 percent of the new landowners had sold or leased their plots to larger operators within a few years. Thus with the government's blessing, market forces inexorably reversed one of Latin America's most far-reaching agrarian reforms.

To sustain the economic restructuring, the Pinochet government further refined the apparatus of state terror that it had used so effectively to destroy the left. The National Intelligence Directorate (Dirección Nacional de Inteligencia, DINA) was the backbone of the regime's repressive forces and the most notorious of the secret police organizations. It operated several torture centers, detained and interrogated at will, and so thoroughly intimidated the population that even good friends spoke only in guarded terms. Army and police sweeps of slum settlements became routine practices. Slum dwellers and residents of worker neighborhoods were arrested and sent to detention centers where they functioned as hostages to the good behavior of family and friends made ever more desperate by government economic policies. Under pressure from President Carter's human rights policies, DINA was dissolved in 1977 and rechristened with the more benign title of National Information Center (Central Nacional de Informaciones); this bit of image-polishing, along with periodic releases of a few prominent prisoners, did not alter the reality of the terrorist state.

The economic decline that followed the 1977–81 miracle brought forth for the first time an incipient civil opposition movement. The financial crisis led to several bankruptcies, motivating sectors of the business community, long battered by the impact of free trade, to press for changes in the Chicago School model. More important, the hobbled labor movement, reacting to growing unemployment, wage cuts, and new labor laws that further eroded worker benefits and security, called for a national strike. This stirred the outlawed parties, the Church, and some labor leaders into action to head off the strike, which in the face of an all-powerful state they considered suicidal. In the exchange, more moderate forms of protest were agreed upon; the more conservative opposition parties issued a "Democratic Manifesto" in March 1983 and established a new, extralegal national labor organization, the National Workers' Command (Comando Nacional de Trabajadores). The emboldened opposition called for monthly "national days of protest" beginning in May 1983, which featured public rallies, sick-outs, boycotting of stores and public transit, and the banging of empty pots — the hallmark of the gremios' opposition to Allende — in poor neighborhoods at night. Reacting to the first serious wave of opposition in a decade, the regime made a slight opening, lifting the state of siege, permitting some meetings, and allowing selective returns of exiles.

This modest relaxation of control, the first since 1973, encouraged the parties to greater activity, and by 1985 a "national dialogue" had begun. The return to civilian government in Argentina, Uruguay, and Brazil between 1983 and 1985 fueled the debate on Chile's future. Pinochet's 1980 constitution stipulated a plebiscite in September 1988 on the extension of military rule — whether by Pinochet himself, another officer, or a puppet civilian — to 1997. The upcoming plebiscite forced Pinochet for the first time to act like a politician and cultivate public support. Accordingly, in early 1987 he authorized the return of most remaining political exiles, legalized the non-Marxist parties, and allowed the publication of two opposition newspapers. After an intense campaign featuring television ads advocating "yes" or "no," the government lost the plebiscite, opening the way for the first presidential election in 19 years. Christian Democrat Patricio Aylwin won the presidency in December 1989, with 55 percent of the vote, over conservative candidate Hernán Buchi.

ARGENTINA'S MILITARY IN POWER, 1976–83

Argentina received a preview of the antirevolutionary state during the years of military government under Generals Juan Carlos Onganía (1966–70), Roberto Levingston (1970–71), and Alejandro Lanusse (1971–73). After 11 years of unsuccessful efforts to achieve political stability by marginalizing the Peronists and extensive internal debate about the correct institutional position, the armed forces in 1966 were ready to take on the task of national reconstruction that their Brazilian colleagues had assumed two years earlier. General Onganía spelled out the purpose of the "Argentine Revolution": "Argentina has completed a historic cycle. Our political and institutional resources have been exhausted. The time has come to live to our fullest capacity and to create a new nation for ourselves and for our posterity."[9]

Despite staking out for itself such a far-reaching task, Onganía's government instituted changes that appeared mild in comparison with those carried out in Pinochet's Chile or in Argentina after 1976. Economically, the regime applied standard monetarist remedies including devaluation, wage controls, reduction in government spending, and some trade liberalization. Politically, the Onganía government dissolved congress and the parties, employed states of siege, and generally used repression to enforce its will. Nonetheless, in both spheres the government was willing to compromise, failing to apply a full shock treatment to the economy and engaging in negotiations with the powerful Peronist unions to obtain their cooperation in the regime's economic goals.

As a result of the unforeseen tenacity of the working class, the mobilization of broad opposition, and the appearance of urban guerrillas, the Argentine Revolution never really took root. The "Cordobazo" of May 1969, a student and worker insurrection that succeeded in capturing much of the industrial city of Córdoba, was a shock to the authorities and a stimulus to further protest and resistance. Rather than a progressive tightening of the regime, as occurred in Brazil, the Onganía government fired its economic team and changed direction. Growing disagreement within the armed forces over the military's role led to coups against Onganía and his successor, Levingston, until the Lanusse government attempted to reach out for popular support by proposing a broad consensus ("Gran Acuerdo Nacional"). Sensing the softening military stance, the Peronist-led political and guerrilla resistance pressed on until the military decided to allow elections with Peronist participation. Still fearing Perón's return, Lanusse established a residency requirement that prohibited Perón's candidacy; thus his return to power required the intermediate step of electing a stand-in, Héctor Cámpora, whose prompt resignation allowed Perón's election in September 1973.

The second, more extreme period of military authoritarianism came about in response to the abject failure of Peronism in power. General Perón died in July 1974, leaving the reins of government to his widow and vice-president, Isabel Perón. An odd mix of populist and monetarist policies brought the economy near collapse, with inflation reaching an annual rate of 17,000 percent in March 1976. Labor mobilization accompanied a resumption of full-scale urban guerrilla warfare, which had declined with Perón's return. Confronted with what was arguably the worst political and economic crisis in a country known for its crises, the armed forces seized power in March 1976. The service chiefs paraphrased Onganía's 1966 statement in explaining their coup's significance: "The events which took place on March 24, 1976, represent more than the mere overthrow of a government. On the contrary, they signify the final closing of a historic cycle and the opening of a new one whose fundamental characteristics will be manifested by the reorganization of the nation."[10]

This time the military put sharp teeth behind its pledge. The "Process of National Reconstruction," inspired by the policies of the Pinochet regime, featured a severe dose of Chicago School medicine combined with all-out repression of the left and of Peronists. As in Chile, the new government headed by General Jorge Videla set out to redistribute power relationships in Argentine society so as to make a return to the past impossible. To reinforce the hoped-for irreversibility of socioeconomic change, a political and ideological purge was necessary, requiring government control and reshaping of the media and the educational curricula so as to forge a new national mentality. Also as in Chile, state terror was applied in the name of human dignity and liberty: "It is precisely to ensure the just protection of the natural rights of man that we assume the full exercise of authority: not to infringe upon liberty but to reaffirm it; not to twist justice but to impose it."[11]

Economic policy, directed by Chicago School technocrat José Martínez de Hoz, consisted of the progressive application of liberalization measures designed to control inflation, recreate a market economy, and fully reintegrate Argentina into the world market after nearly half a century of growing state control and import-substitution industrialization behind high tariff walls. The authorities applied the full-blown Chilean version of Chicago School strategy by reducing real wages, lowering tariffs, eliminating export taxes and subsidies, loosening exchange controls, and cutting social welfare expenditures. The working and middle classes paid the usual price in the form of lowered living standards and increased unemployment, coinciding with reduced government help for the greatly expanded pool of needy persons. The Argentine industrial base also began to crack under the weight of increased imports.

A powerful repressive apparatus was required to enforce such a Draconian version of neoliberal economics against the labor unions. Adding to Videla's problems of governance was the surge in urban guerrilla warfare, led by the powerful Montoneros, which had escalated under the military regime. Thus the military moved quickly, dissolving or controlling all bodies, including congress, parties, unions, and courts, that could challenge it, and imposing a state of siege. Unfettered by restrictions on its power, the military instituted a reign of terror designed to break the guerrillas by attacking them and their sympathizers: As one general put it, "First, we will kill the guerrillas. Then, we will kill the guerrillas' families. Then we will kill the friends of their families, and the friends of their friends, so that there will be no one left to remember who the guerrillas were."[12] In conducting the "dirty war" the Argentine armed forces contributed a new semantic form to the lexicon: They added a transitive dimension to the verb "disappear," as in "we must disappear the subversives." For some five years, security forces in civilian attire cruised in unmarked gray Ford Falcons, apprehending their victims and taking them to some 340 secret detention centers where they were interrogated and often tortured; many never returned. Since there were no records of arrests, those individuals simply disappeared without a trace. This use of state terror succeeded in defeating the guerrillas by late 1979.

The mothers of the Plaza de Mayo, who congregated in front of the presidential palace to seek information on their disappeared sons and daughters, came to symbolize the resistance to an unusually brutal government — one comparable to Pinochet's. Newspaper editor Jacobo Timerman, whose *Prisoner Without a Name, Cell Without a Number* dramatized the military's terrorist activities, was another symbol of resistance.[13] A formal inquiry after the return of civilian government found that nearly 9,000 individuals who had disappeared were still not accounted for by 1984; other informed estimates reach 30,000, in addition to thousands of documented assassinations. The introduction to the inquiry committee's report underscores the continuing sense of shock among Argentines:

> Many of the events described in this report will be hard to believe. This is because the men and women of our nation have only heard of such horror from distant places. The enormity of what took place in Argentina . . . is sure, still, to produce that disbelief which some used at the time to defend themselves from pain and horror.[14]

By the end of Videla's five-year administration, economic failures had begun to weaken the regime. The persistence of inflation led Martínez de Hoz to exchange manipulations, which prompted massive capital flight, bankruptcies, and a dramatic growth of foreign debt. One factor underlying the economic problems was the military's resistance to the application of Chicago School doctrine to the large military-controlled sector, which included some of the less efficient enterprises targeted for reform or extinction under the free market economy.

When he left office in March 1982, Videla left his successor, General Roberto Viola, a virtually untenable situation. The Argentine gross national product declined 11.4 percent in the last quarter of 1981 and the foreign debt mushroomed to the point that debt service costs would exceed total export earnings in 1982. Viola was sacked in December 1981 and replaced by General Leopoldo Galtieri, under whose leadership Argentina invaded the Malvinas or Falklands Islands in April 1982. The attempt to make good on Argentina's claim to sovereignty over the

British-occupied islands generated instant patriotic support for the regime, but the quick and unglorious defeat brought the Galtieri government down. His successor, General Reynaldo Bignone, had no option but to call free elections. Raúl Alfonsín of the center-right Radical Party took office in December 1983, pronouncing once again a new day for Argentina.

THE ANTIREVOLUTIONARY
STATE IN PERSPECTIVE

The retreat of the generals in all four countries was a retreat under pressure. In each case, the promise of rapid development through a partial or complete imposition of the Chicago School model proved illusory: Brazil, Uruguay, and Argentina emerged from military rule with staggering foreign debts that would hamper development for years to come; in Argentina, the economic policies of the military were particularly disastrous. Economic failure was coupled with an inability to develop popular support or even tolerance for military rule. The Brazilian attempt to build support through manipulation of civilian institutions fell short of the armed forces' hopes. In Chile and Argentina, expected citizen gratitude for saving the countries from Marxist revolution either did not materialize or largely evaporated in the climate of political excess and economic problems; support thus was limited to the few privileged sectors. For comparison, the Peruvian military's attempt to build support for a progressive, relatively unrepressive government through the elaborate mechanism of SINAMOS also failed. Having failed economically and politically, the armed forces in all four countries returned to the barracks before they were ready to do so, with the full knowledge that they had not completed their missions.

The closing of the cycle of antirevolutionary states in 1990 is an important point in Latin America's contemporary political history. The military, even with highly qualified technocrats and unlimited power to override special interests, proved no better at managing national economies than civilian governments that are subjected to the constant give and take of politics. The military governments faced seemingly insurmountable obstacles to developing broad civilian support that could sustain them in lieu of repression. The liquidation of communist party rule in Eastern Europe evokes the observation that the armed forces' mission of creating what we might call the "new antirevolutionary man" is no less demanding, in time, effort, and degree of control, than is the communist mission of creating the "new socialist man." If 40 years of communist rule — or over 70 if we count the Soviet Union — did not work, it would be naive to expect that a similar transformation of societal norms and individual mentalities could have been accomplished under regimes lasting between 7 and 21 years.

The antirevolutionary state, then, can be counted a failure in the above concrete ways. Yet despite the victory of revolution in Nicaragua, these regimes contributed significantly to dampening the momentum of revolution that swept Latin America in the 1960s in the wake of the Cuban Revolution. The antirevolutionary regimes stopped the threat of revolution at home; given the size, wealth, and influence of their countries, in conjunction with the United States under Nixon and especially under Reagan, they formed a kind of antirevolutionary alliance reminiscent of the Holy Alliance established after the French Revolution to suppress any recurrence of revolution in Europe. The effects of attempts to immunize their countries against revolution may not be permanent, but they may be more effective than the generals' undignified retreat might suggest. The use of unlimited repression — of state terror against the revolutionaries, their sympathizers, innocent civilians, and mainline politicians deemed responsible for opening the way for Marxists — is an experience likely to remain etched in the minds of the populace for a long time to come. Thus despite the evident failure to make the irreversible changes sought, the deterrent effect of the antirevolutionary state may be lasting.

NOTES

1. I do not include the hard-line Bolivian government of General Hugo Banzer (1971–78) among the regimes studied in this chapter because, despite some similarities with the military governments of the neighboring countries, the Bolivian case differs significantly in important ways.

2. Alain Rouquié, *The Military and the State in Latin America*, tr. by Paul Sigmund (Berkeley: University of California Press, 1987), 252.

3. Quoted in ibid., 256.

4. Genaro Arriagada Herrera, "The Legal and Institutional Framework of the Armed Forces in Chile," in J. Samuel Valenzuela and Arturo Valenzuela, eds., *Military Rule in Chile: Dictatorship and Oppositions* (Baltimore, Md.: Johns Hopkins University Press, 1986), 119–20.

5. General Augusto Pinochet, 11 September 1975 speech, in Brian Loveman and Thomas M. Davies, Jr., *The Politics of Antipolitics: The Military in Latin America* (Lincoln: University of Nebraska Press, 1978), 205.

6. Ibid.

7. Quoted in Alain Rouquié, "Demilitarization and the Institutionalization of Military-Dominated Politics in Latin America," in Abraham F. Lowenthal and

J. Samuel Fitch, eds., *Armies and Politics in Latin America*, rev. ed. (New York: Holmes and Meier, 1986), 449.

8. Manuel Antonio Garretón, "Political Processes in an Authoritarian Regime: The Dynamics of Institutionalization and Opposition in Chile, 1973–1980," in Valenzuela and Valenzuela, eds., *Military Rule in Chile*, 144–83.

9. Onganía, July 1966 speech, quoted in Loveman and Davies, eds., *Politics of Antipolitics*, 174.

10. 25 March 1976 announcement, quoted in Loveman and Davies, eds., *Politics of Antipolitics*, 178.

11. General Jorge Videla, April 1976 speech, quoted in Loveman and Davies, eds., *Politics of Antipolitics*, 180.

12. General Ramon Camps, quoted in Judith Laikin Elkin, "Recoleta: Civilization and Barbarism in Argentina," *Michigan Quarterly Review* 27, no. 2 (Spring 1988), 235.

13. Jacobo Timerman, *Prisoner Without a Name, Cell Without a Number*, tr. by Tony Talbot (New York: Random House, 1980).

14. *Nunca Más: The Report of the Argentine National Commission on the Disappeared*, intro. by Ronald Dworkin (New York: Farrar Straus Giroux, 1986), 9.

10

The Nicaraguan Revolution

Twenty years after Fidel Castro seized power in Cuba, his dream of a Latin American revolution appeared dead. Efforts to replicate the Cuban Revolution through rural guerrilla warfare had failed, most of them dismally. The urban variant of guerrilla warfare, while meeting with initial success in Uruguay and Argentina, ultimately succumbed to counterinsurgency measures and to its own limitations. Revolution from above, especially through the actions of the Peruvian military and the elected government of Salvador Allende, held out new hope for a few years before both experiments came to abrupt ends. By 1979 the most tangible results of two decades of attempted revolution and reform were the antirevolutionary regimes that ruled over much of Latin America's population, including its most advanced countries, and projected a reactionary influence over the rest of the hemisphere.

The praetorian peace of Latin America was interrupted in 1979 by the victory of the Frente Sandinista de Liberación Nacional (FSLN) and its allies over the Nicaraguan government of Anastasio Somoza Debayle. Originating as a fidelista political group in 1961, the FSLN launched a rural foco that met the standard fate of the naive guerrilla movements of the early 1960s. Despite military reversals and the loss of key personnel over the years, the FSLN persisted and gradually built effective rural and urban support networks. Taking advantage of changing conditions in Nicaragua and learning from the lessons of the South American urban guerrillas, the FSLN by the mid-1970s emerged as a potent force and clearly the leading armed opposition to Somoza. Aided by the regime's increasingly repressive character, the guerrillas were able to achieve a broad political-military front that combined strikes, street demonstrations, and political pressures with veteran guerrilla fighters and hundreds of new recruits. The dictatorship fell on July 19, 1979.

Although the Sandinista Revolution had important repercussions within the hemisphere, it did not have an impact of the magnitude of the Cuban Revolution 20 years earlier. This was due in part to the prevailing climate of reaction in the late 1970s and early 1980s, which limited the possibility of popular response in many countries. But it reflected primarily the nature of the Nicaraguan Revolution itself. The Sandinista leadership was collective, and hence no charismatic Fidel Castro appeared to ignite the passions of the Latin American masses. Nor was there a Che Guevara to propagate a heroic version of victory capable of inciting widespread emulation. The policies of the revolutionary government were moderate in both the foreign and domestic spheres, in contrast to the radical measures and rapid pace of the Cuban Revolution. Under Ronald Reagan, the United States applied severe economic, diplomatic, and military pressures to the Sandinista regime, demonstrating to other countries the price to be paid for straying from the fold and forcing the Nicaraguans to focus their energies on the home front. If the FSLN leadership were inclined to export revolution as Castro had attempted 20 years earlier, it did not enjoy the conditions for doing so beyond limited involvement in the immediate Central American region.

Nonetheless, the Nicaraguan Revolution clearly set the agenda for the politics of Central America for over a decade and prompted a U.S.-sponsored war and President Reagan's Caribbean Basin Initiative — a mini-Alliance for Progress emphasizing economic development through strengthening the private sector and devoid of the social reformism of President Kennedy's plan for the prevention of revolution in Latin America. As the first successful revolutionary insurrection since Castro's 20 years earlier, the FSLN victory also had major effects on the left throughout the hemisphere; in countries as remote and different from Nicaragua as Argentina and Chile, revolutionaries analyzed FSLN strategies and tactics in detail to learn from the Sandinistas' success and apply the lessons to their own struggles. Although more limited in its impact, the Sandinista Revolution became virtually as much of a preoccupation for Washington in the 1980s as the Cuban Revolution had been two decades earlier.

BACKGROUND TO REVOLUTION

Nicaragua's *ancien régime*, the Somoza dynasty, came to power in 1936 after more than two decades during which Nicaragua had been an unofficial U.S. protectorate. From its first occupation in 1912 to final withdrawal in 1933, the United States maintained troops in Nicaragua for all but one year; most of the time a small detachment of marines sufficed to guarantee political stability and U.S. interests, but from 1927 to 1933 up to 5,500 marines took the field against General Augusto C. Sandino, an ardent nationalist and reformer who broke with the elite-military consensus that tolerated U.S. control. The marines left the country after establishing the National Guard to replace the Nicaraguan army, which because of its politicization was seen as the main source of the country's endemic instability; by balancing members of the rival Conservative and Liberal parties on its general staff, the National Guard would remain politically neutral. U.S. personnel chose Anastasio Somoza García, an affable, English speaking young officer to head the National Guard. Within four years of U.S. withdrawal, Somoza had assassinated Sandino, purged the Guard's officer corps of Conservatives, packed it with Liberals of his choosing, and assumed the presidency. With the Guard as his base, Somoza quickly subverted U.S. intentions and used the "apolitical" new force as the springboard for establishing Latin America's most durable family dynasty.

Three Somozas served as president during the family's 43-year reign: Anastasio Somoza García between 1937 and 1956; son Luis Somoza Debayle from 1956 to 1963; and son Anastasio "Tachito" Somoza Debayle between 1967 and 1979. Trusted lieutenants wore the presidential sash during brief interludes, but no one other than a Somoza ever served as commander of the National Guard. The Guard had an official monopoly on armed force, serving as army, air force, police, customs agency, and fulfilling numerous other government functions. The original Somoza molded the Guard into an instrument of family power by personally selecting officers, giving them ample opportunity for enrichment, treating the troops generously and paternalistically, and segregating them from social contacts with the populace so as to create an elite institution never lacking in volunteers.

Unswerving U.S. support was a second pillar of the Somoza dynasty. With the advent of the Cold War, the Somozas' value to Washington increased: They were aggressively anticommunist at home and reliably pro-American in the United Nations and in hemispheric matters. Nicaragua provided the embarkation points for the U.S.-sponsored invasions of Guatemala in 1954 and Cuba in 1961 and was one of four Latin American countries to send troops to the Dominican Republic in 1965. It also offered troops for the Korean and Vietnam Wars. In return, Washington provided generous military and economic aid, a succession of very friendly and unquestioning ambassadors, and the stamp of approval that dissuaded most Somoza adversaries from action. The dynasty rested also on a branch of the historic Liberal Party that Somoza renamed the Nationalist Liberal Party, the support or tolerance of the country's elites, the marginality of the masses, and the direct economic power of the Somoza clan.

When the impact of the Cuban Revolution swept over the hemisphere, Central America was relatively unaffected with the exception of Guatemala, where the recent Arbenz reforms had weakened the foundations of traditional elite rule. With its backward, predominantly agrarian economy and its entrenched dictatorial rule, Nicaragua lacked the social differentiation and political institutions to respond effectively to the stimuli from Cuba. The middle class and urban proletariat were small and weak and, in contrast to those hemispheric countries with constitutional governments, unions, student organizations, left parties, and opposition press were proscribed or tightly controlled, leaving few organized means of mobilizing support for reform or revolution. When such movements did materialize, the National Guard proved effective in repressing them. An increase in exile invasions, establishment of a few fidelista groups, and the appearance of several small guerrilla focos marked the early 1960s, but the powerful Somoza dynasty felt merely a ripple from the tidal wave sweeping Latin America.

In its quest to immunize Latin America against revolution, the Alliance for Progress inadvertently helped to create conditions that would make Nicaragua vulnerable to radical change by the late 1970s. As everywhere, new institutions and bureaucracies sprang up to administer agrarian reform, peasant welfare, and worker housing programs; the presence of such purportedly reform-mongering bodies in Somoza's Nicaragua provided a greater-than-usual paradox. More significant was the Central American Common Market, founded in 1958 and implemented with Alliance funding, which broke down tariff barriers among its five members and for the first time created markets of sufficient size to support import-substitution industrialization. The economic impact on Nicaragua was immediate and substantial: Expansion of manufacturing, processing, and intraregional trade was primarily responsible for a 250 percent growth in the gross domestic product between 1960 and 1975 and for a boom atmosphere that engendered a period of optimism and rising expectations.

The boom of the 1960s had important social and economic consequences. The expansion of business and manufacturing significantly increased the country's middle class and industrial labor force, but with controls on unions, a large labor pool of former smallholders and squatters displaced by the cotton expansion of the 1950s, and the installation of capital-intensive plants, labor's share of national income fell while unemployment increased. For the middle class, educational opportunities lagged and effective political participation was denied. The beneficiaries were foreign investors and the Nicaraguan bourgeoisie, which coalesced increasingly around the Somoza regime as economic opportunities expanded. In the early 1970s, boom turned to a series of economic cycles while inflation and unemployment both increased. The result was that the expectations kindled and real gains made in the 1960s gave way to frustration and economic reversal for large segments of the population.

A 1972 earthquake that killed some 10,000 people and leveled much of Managua is generally credited with beginning the unraveling of the Somoza regime. Developments during and after the disaster brought the corruption and venality of the National Guard and Tachito Somoza himself into the national and international spotlights. Charged with security during the emergency and direction of the subsequent relief effort, the Guard virtually disbanded in Managua in a frenzy of self-interested behavior — abandoning posts to look after their own families and property, looting stores, and openly selling donated relief supplies. Internationally published photographs of National Guard jeeps bulging with looted appliances captured the essence of the breakdown of discipline in the pillar of the regime. Somoza himself moved to profit from the disaster, granting his companies lucrative demolition and construction contracts and decreeing the rebuilding of Managua on nearby land that he and close associates owned. One of his maneuvers, illustrative of the unseemly greed of a man already worth tens if not hundreds of millions, was to buy a plot of land after the earthquake at $30,000 and sell it three weeks later to the National Housing Institute for $3 million in U.S. relief funds; the land remained devoid of housing.

Somoza's avarice, his near-monopolization of the lucrative post-earthquake construction and land business, and the diminishing growth opportunities in the 1970s created a split in the bourgeoisie between the Somocistas and the increasingly marginalized groups who were not part of the inner circle. The economic wedge that Somoza had driven between himself and his fellow elites soon manifested itself in a political realignment and a growing upper and middle class opposition movement. Some of this opposition involved an intensification of historic party rivalries between Conservatives and Liberals, with some smaller parties also involved. The most significant new twist, however, was the creation in 1974 of the nonpartisan Democratic Liberation Union (Unión

Democrática de Liberación, UDEL) led by the Conservative publisher of *La Prensa,* Pedro Joaquín Chamorro.

THE FSLN

When it made international headlines in December 1974 by capturing a group of regime dignitaries and diplomats at a soiree honoring U.S. Ambassador Turner Shelton, the FSLN had been in the field for 13 years. After a visit to Cuba, Carlos Fonseca Amador, a student leader and communist from the northern town of Matagalpa, grew disillusioned with the communists' reluctance to pursue the armed struggle. He broke away and, with his friends Tomás Borge and Silvio Mayorga, formed a small revolutionary group inspired by Marxism, fidelismo, and an intense nationalism. The FSLN's beginnings typified the fate of focos during the early, naive phase of guerrilla warfare. Operating from a base in Honduras, the group attempted unsuccessfully in 1961 and 1963 to establish itself in Nicaragua. Their second defeat at the hands of Somoza's National Guard led the guerrillas to reassess the validity of a purely foco approach, and for the next four years they concentrated on building peasant support and establishing an urban network for recruitment and fund raising.

The FSLN's return to military action in 1967 was no more auspicious than its earlier armed forays. In an encounter near Pancasán in the north, the Guard killed several guerrillas, including Silvio Mayorga, and destroyed their peasant network. Despite the defeat, the slowly growing opposition to Somoza kept new recruits coming and the Sandinistas patiently rebuilt their rural structure — an endeavor that they referred to in borrowed Maoist terms as "gathering forces in silence." The key to developing rural support, they learned, was to break down peasant distrust of city people by living and working with the rural folk and using their strong family and co-godparenthood ties to establish relationships across wide areas. This work was so successful that when they returned to the offensive in 1970 the Guard was unable to engage them in frontal combat and the guerrilla column for the first time survived and grew. Systematic National Guard repression of peasants in the north now backfired, creating additional support for the Sandinistas. Omar Cabezas' colorful memoir of the struggle, *Fire from the Mountain,* clearly reveals the guerrillas' approach to winning peasant support — a crucial ingredient lacking in most of the Latin American guerrilla actions of the 1960s: "We took hold of the campesinos' hands, broad, powerful, roughened hands. 'These callouses,' we asked, 'how did you get them?'

And they would tell us how they came from machetes, from working the land. If they got those callouses from working the land, we asked, why did that land belong to the boss and not to them? We were trying to awaken the campesino to his own dream."[1]

Despite the growth of guerrilla strength to some 150 fighters and the support of an expanding and active urban network, the raid on the Somocista party in December 1974 was a bold and risky move. Given the elite credentials of those captured — Ambassador Shelton not included, for he had left just prior to the attack — Somoza acceded to most of the FSLN demands in exchange for the freeing of the hostages. He released 18 Sandinistas from jail and flew them to Cuba along with the guerrillas, paid a $5 million ransom, and ordered Nicaraguan newspapers and radio stations to disseminate two FSLN communiqués. By revealing the guerrillas' strength and the regime's weakness, the party operation thrust the heretofore obscure FSLN into the limelight.

The following three years brought mixed fortunes to the FSLN while moving Nicaragua closer to revolution. Under a state of siege declared during the party raid, Somoza formed Special Antiterrorist Activity Brigades within the Guard to spearhead the fight against the guerrillas. During the next 32 months, with civil liberties suspended, curfews imposed, and censorship tightened, the government severely repressed peasants, workers, and slum dwellers — all potential collaborators — as well as FSLN cadres and active supporters. The intensification of state repression in a country long accustomed to institutionalized but inconsistent brutality had the effect of broadening and stiffening the opposition to Somoza.

The FSLN suffered numerous casualties and arrests during the 1975–77 period but was still able to augment its ranks as disaffection spread. Still, by early 1978 the Sandinistas had less than 500 armed fighters against the Guard's 7,000 troops. Moreover, the repression contributed to a split in FSLN ranks over strategy and, to a lesser extent, over ideology. While the break among the three "tendencies" was never formalized, each group tended to go its own way militarily and organizationally until late 1978. The Proletarians (Proletarios), influenced by Jaime Wheelock, focused on the cities, organizing in factories and slums to broaden the movement's base and carrying out some urban guerrilla actions. The Prolonged People's War (Guerra Popular Prolongada) faction, led by Tomás Borge and Henry Ruíz, opted to continue and strengthen the Maoist strategy adopted in the late 1960s of gradual accumulation of forces in the countryside for an eventual peasant army capable of defeating the Guard. In contrast to the first two, the Third Way

(Terceristas), led by Daniel and Humberto Ortega and Víctor Tirado López, believed in pressing the insurrection wherever and by whatever means possible, even at the risk of being overly bold. This group was the most flexible ideologically as well. To take advantage of the broadening of opposition forces, it admitted non-Marxists of various stripes so long as they were ready to fight; the strong strain of liberation theology that influenced Sandinista ideology resulted in part from this expansion of membership. While watering down the Marxist purity of the movement, the Terceristas in their innovative way remained closest to the FSLN's original foco strategy.

The election of Jimmy Carter had serious repercussions for Somoza's fight to preserve the dynasty. State Department pressure to improve the human rights climate in Nicaragua led to a lifting of the state of siege in September 1977, which reduced the repression and allowed a freer manifestation of the generalized antiregime sentiment. The FSLN factions pressed their advantage with stepped-up military activity in late October, but the Guard, having been reinforced with new equipment and recruits, turned back the guerrilla offensive without major difficulty.

THE OVERTHROW OF SOMOZA,
JANUARY 1978–JULY 1979

While the three years since the FSLN party operation had weakened the Somoza regime, the government's demise was far from certain as 1978 dawned. A critical turning point came on January 10, 1978, when assassins gunned down Pedro Joaquín Chamorro, founder of UDEL, publisher of *La Prensa,* and a long-time and widely respected critic of the regime. Chamorro's death was ordered by owners of a blood plasma company, who included relatives and close collaborators of the dictator, in retribution for a *La Prensa* article exposing the company's exportation of plasma while Nicaragua was chronically undersupplied with the vital element. Within hours of the killing, over 50,000 people had gathered at Chamorro's house to mourn and protest his death. Disturbances followed in cities throughout the country.

The Chamorro assassination unleashed the forces that, building upon the events of the past five years, brought Somoza down within a year and a half. The first of these was the full mobilization of political opposition dominated by upper class interests. UDEL began by calling a general business strike for January 24. This strike, which shut down some 80 percent of national economic activity, launched an effective drive to cripple the regime. Resembling the Chilean gremio movement that had played a major role in the overthrow of Allende, the nationwide movement gained the adherence of trade and production associations, parties, labor unions, and the mushrooming opposition groups that sprang up to stake out a share of the emerging political turf. The effectiveness of the business shutdowns, combined with tax boycotts and other economic actions, was a significant factor in the economic collapse of Somoza's last year.

As the active opposition grew a new umbrella organization, the Broad Opposition Front (Frente Amplio Opositor, FAO) was established to coordinate the efforts of bourgeois and middle-class organizations, political parties, and some labor unions. Aggregating moderate to conservative antiregime opinion, the FAO pushed for reform, not revolution: It called for Somoza's immediate resignation, political democracy, an end to corruption, a vague agrarian reform, and improved social services. Leaders of the FAO and component groups suffered arrest and persecution as Somoza took an increasingly hard line with the political opposition.

Encouraged by the United States and the OAS, the FAO conducted negotiations with Somoza for some four months beginning in September 1978. Determined to serve out his current presidential term through 1981 and to leave the National Guard and his Nationalist Liberal Party intact thereafter, Somoza proved recalcitrant, leading the FAO to offer more concessions than many of its constituents condoned. As the negotiations proceeded toward impasse, important groups left the FAO, weakening the moderate political opposition and strengthening the groups, especially the FSLN, that advocated armed struggle to the end in order to prevent the dictator's replacement with a "Somocismo sin Somoza" (Somozaism without Somoza).

In addition to setting off a strident political opposition, the Chamorro assassination precipitated a series of spontaneous uprisings that revealed the depth of popular opposition to the regime and the Guard. The first of these occurred in February 1978 in Monimbó, the Indian neighborhood of the colonial town of Masaya. Residents celebrating the renaming of a small plaza for the late Chamorro were attacked by the Guard and, in a response without precedent, defended themselves with rocks and makeshift weapons and drove out the troops. In an action that set the model for the Guard's counteroffensive against the mounting wave of popular insurrection throughout the country, troops cordoned off Monimbó, then shelled it, bombed it, and finally attacked house to house with armor, killing 200 people in the process. Two similar insurrections took place in February and March, and the method of retaking the areas was the same. By this time, Somoza was literally at war with his people.

The unexpected ferocity of popular insurrection took both the FSLN and the political opposition by surprise. For the Tercerista tendency, the uprisings provided an opportunity to test their thesis that revolution could be provoked in the short run by heightened activity. Accordingly, in August 1978 they staged an operation reminiscent of but far bolder than the 1974 party raid. A command of 25 Sandinistas disguised as a National Guard patrol occupied the National Palace while the chamber of deputies was meeting and captured over 2,000 hostages, including most of the deputies, several high officials, 20 journalists, and hundreds of bureaucrats and citizens doing business in the building. After two days, the guerrillas won the release of important Sandinistas from prison, a large ransom, and safe passage. Thousands of sympathizers turned out to cheer the convoy of guerrillas, released Sandinistas, and hostages on its way to the airport for the flight out of the country.

The capture of the National Palace soon had the desired effect of stimulating mobilization against the regime. September 1978 was marked by uprisings in at least eight cities, including Managua, León, Matagalpa, and Estelí, which resulted in the capture of important sectors of each city. Under a new state of siege, the Guard retook the cities one by one using the same tactics unveiled in Monimbó, destroying extensive business and residential areas and killing between 1,500 and 2,000 people, mostly civilians. During follow-up operations in October the Guard took its revenge by committing atrocities, including murder and rape, on the cities' inhabitants. Youth, who had participated massively in the insurrections, were special targets for execution. Over a decade later, the mass of rubble and the many bullet holes still marking the walls of these cities testify to the intensity of the September insurrection.

Rather than cowing the populace, the terror unleashed to defend the dynasty only strengthened the will to resist. And despite internal censorship, the international media disseminated news of the brutality of Somoza's response to rebellion. The result was growing international pressure on Somoza to seek a negotiated settlement, and his inflexibility in dealing with the FAO furthered his diplomatic isolation. In late 1978 and early 1979 the United States and the OAS as well as individual member states urged his resignation, a few countries broke diplomatic relations, and some provided aid to the rebels. The U.S. position was ambivalent, shifting between condemnation of human rights abuses and congratulations on cosmetic improvements such as freeing a few prisoners; but overall, the loss of unequivocal U.S. support was a crippling blow. Somoza's status as an international pariah slowed the normal flow of aid and loans to his regime.

Events following the Chamorro assassination also had a galvanizing effect on the FSLN. The awesome demonstration of popular will to fight and willingness to die, from Monimbó through the September insurrection, convinced the Sandinistas of the need for decisive action to reestablish themselves as the vanguard in the anti-Somoza struggle. Concurrently, the determination and strength of the bourgeois-led political opposition, combined with international pressures for negotiations, raised the spectre of a political settlement that would bring the UDEL and its allies to power and exclude the FSLN. Facing both unexpected opportunities and problems, the FSLN factions set aside their differences in late 1978 and reunited under a single directorate by early 1979.

Thus strengthened and no longer competing for recruits, finances, and support, the FSLN was able to expand its regular guerrilla force to some 1,200 by May and over 2,000 by July 1979, supplemented at the end by some 3,000 irregular militia and last-minute volunteers. Meanwhile the establishment of Radio Sandino inside Nicaragua in 1978 gave the FSLN a powerful tool for recruitment and for circumventing news censorship. The Sandinistas worked assiduously to channel the manifest hostility to Somoza by organizing support groups in popular barrios throughout the country. On the political front, they fostered the establishment of two broad coalitions to compete with UDEL and FAO — Moisés Hassan's People United Movement (Movimiento Pueblo Unido) in late 1978 and their own National Patriotic Front (Frente Patriótico Nacional) in early 1979. These pro-Sandinista umbrella organizations made quick progress as the climate radicalized and the FAO lost ground by conceding too much in its negotiations with the dictator.

Despite some success in strengthening the Guard with recruits and materiel, the regime weakened under growing military, political, economic, and diplomatic pressure during the early months of 1979. Then on May 30 came the FSLN announcement of the "final offensive" to topple the government. With their swollen ranks of fighters and thousands of volunteer collaborators, the Sandinistas launched simultaneous urban insurrections and military operations north, east, and south of Managua. The north, where the FSLN had concentrated its efforts over the years, fell quickly. The Guard made its best stand in the south, where fierce fighting lasted several weeks between the Costa Rican border and the city of Rivas. After the fall of Rivas and Masaya, the only important regime-held territory was part of the capital. Fighting now for its institutional survival and the lives of its members, the Guard in a final effort drove the FSLN out of the popular neighborhoods of Managua and back to Masaya on June 24.

Washington's response to the looming Sandinista victory was the revival of its earlier attempt to fashion a settlement that would exclude the FSLN. Thus the Carter administration proposed sending a multinational peacekeeping force to Nicaragua to stop the fighting so that a political solution could be found; the OAS firmly rejected the proposal on June 21. The FSLN leadership then agreed to talk with U.S. representatives, but with victory in sight they were unmoved by Washington's plea for a new bourgeois-led government. Finally recognizing the hopelessness of his situation, Somoza agreed on July 6 to resign upon receiving the signal from Washington. When the FSLN mounted its final drive on the capital, Somoza abandoned the country on July 17 for exile in Asunción, Paraguay, at the invitation of long-term dictator General Alfredo Stroessner.[2] Congress then named a provisional government that collapsed within 48 hours. It and the last remnants of the dynasty fled Nicaragua in Guatemalan air force planes as the new government flew in from San José, Costa Rica in the Mexican presidential jet. The cost in human life and injury and in material damage was staggering: Some 15,000 were killed during the final offensive, and between 40,000 and 50,000 of Nicaragua's 2.9 million people had been killed between 1977 and the final victory. Yet Nicaragua's war was just beginning.

AT WAR WITH THE UNITED STATES

From the moment of victory, the FSLN's Marxist orientation, the glorification of "revolution," and the government's early moves to establish an independent foreign policy — which included relations with Cuba and the Soviet Union — elicited reactions in Washington that ranged from skepticism to hostility. Congress expressed its concern by attaching numerous conditions, such as the holding of elections and prohibition of U.S. funding of any projects having Cuban involvement, to a Carter aid bill for Nicaragua. President Carter himself covertly authorized $1 million for anti-Sandinista activities and denied the new government's requests for military assistance.

With the election of Ronald Reagan, suspicion in the White House was replaced by the firm conviction that the Sandinistas were tools of Moscow and Havana. Citing alleged Nicaraguan aid to the rebels in El Salvador, Reagan immediately cut all economic aid, pressured international agencies to cut off loans, and began financing the counterrevolutionaries or "Contras" — a loose grouping of Somoza adherents, National Guardsmen, and former Somoza opponents who lost out in the power struggle with the FSLN. Authorizing the expenditure of $19 million in 1981 alone, Reagan replaced the Argentine military government as the chief patron of the Contras. Congress authorized $43 million in Contra aid for the 1983 and 1984 fiscal years. In his first year in office, Reagan also pressured the Honduran government to grant the use of its territory and bases for U.S. military exercises, some 40 of which had been held by 1985. These exercises served the dual purposes of intimidating the Nicaraguan government and bringing into Honduras massive amounts of weapons and supplies, which departing troops left behind for the Contras.

By early 1982, the Contras began attacking from their refuge in Honduras, penetrating deeply into Nicaragua by the end of 1983. In 1984 the United States stepped up its military pressure by mining Nicaragua's three major harbors, blowing up oil storage tanks, and increasing the scope of its Honduran-based exercises. Reacting to the administration's blatant violations of international law, which the World Court condemned, the U.S. Congress placed restrictions on aid to the Contras and, in 1985, banned military assistance altogether while authorizing $27 million in "humanitarian" aid. President Reagan nonetheless managed to continue financing the Contras by various extralegal means, including those involved in the bizarre "Iran-Contra" affair. Meanwhile, in 1985 Reagan, citing "policies and actions of the Government of Nicaragua [which] constitute an unusual and extraordinary threat to the national security and foreign policy of the United States," banned all trade with Nicaragua.[3] The president also kept pressure on Congress, publicly referring to the Nicaraguan government as "a Communist totalitarian state" and eulogizing the Contras as "freedom fighters" and "the moral equivalent of our Founding Fathers," until it authorized $100 million for the war in June 1986.[4]

In 1987, the high water mark of the war, the Contras had approximately 15,000 troops in the field against the Ortega government — a government with which the United States maintained correct if somewhat chilly diplomatic relations. To meet the growing threat, the government built its regular army to some 60,000 troops and set up a reserve system of 200,000, including 40,000 active, and a militia approaching 100,000. It instituted conscription in 1983, and by 1986 the military effort was consuming over half the national budget. The development of an offensive plan that combined the tactics of guerrilla warfare with the material and logistical capabilities of a regular army had driven the Contras out of most parts of the country by 1988. Reacting to the ineffectiveness of the Contras and scandals in the handling of U.S. funds, Congress retreated from support other than humanitarian aid after 1987.

U.S. aggression against Nicaragua was not well received in Latin America, especially after the antirevolutionary military regimes began to fall in the early 1980s. Beginning in 1983, the "Contadora Group" of Venezuela, Colombia, Panama, and Mexico sought in vain to bring Washington and Managua together to negotiate a settlement. With the escalation of war in Nicaragua and El Salvador, a resurgence of violence in Guatemala, and the beginnings of political unrest in Honduras, Central American leaders themselves took the initiative in seeking a region-wide settlement. Under the leadership of Costa Rican President Oscar Arias, who received the Nobel Peace Prize for his efforts, the Central American Peace Accord signed on August 7, 1987, at Esquipulas, Guatemala, laid the basis for the eventual end of Nicaragua's surrogate war with the United States.

INSTITUTIONALIZING THE REVOLUTION, 1979–87

The seven and a half years between the fall of Somoza and the adoption of a new constitution were marked by intense political competition and unrelenting military, economic, and diplomatic pressure by the Reagan administration. Yet the entire process of institutionalizing the revolution involved a high degree of consistency in the balance of forces and in the composition and functioning of the government. By virtue of its military victory and subsequent control of the armed forces, the moral authority derived from its 18-year struggle against the dynasty, and the support it had developed among the rural and urban masses, the FSLN was clearly the dominant political entity from the outset. At the same time, the Sandinistas' own heterogeneity and their commitment to two political principles — pluralism and participatory democracy — moderated the power that they were capable of wielding and resulted in considerable flexibility.

The FSLN consisted of a number of mass organizations, the party itself, and a nine-member National Directorate that set party policy. Most of the mass organizations dated from the later years of the war against Somoza as the FSLN turned increasingly to the building of broad support. The most powerful of the mass organizations was the armed forces, which replaced the hated National Guard. The new military was built on the foundation of the FSLN's guerrilla force and greatly expanded as the Contra war intensified. The partisan character of the armed forces was undisguised: Their official title was the Ejército Popular Sandinista (Sandinista People's Army), and the minister of defense from the beginning was Humberto Ortega, brother of Daniel and a member of the FSLN National Directorate.

The FSLN's voluntary mass organizations included the Luisa Amanda Espinosa Nicaraguan Women's Association, the July 19th Sandinista Youth, and an extensive network of rural and urban unions grouped under the Sandinista Workers' Central. The largest union was the Association of Agricultural Workers; in 1981, smallholders split off into a separate National Union of Farmers and Cattlemen (Unión Nacional de Agricultores y Ganaderos, UNAG). While non-Sandinista unions of both left and right orientation remained a significant minority within the labor movement, there was no important competition to the Sandinistas' control over youth, women, and rural workers and smallholders.

The Sandinista Defense Committees (Comités de Defensa Sandinista, CDSs) were the FSLN's primary mass organization among the urban poor. Set up along neighborhood lines, these groups, reminiscent of Castro's CDRs, were formed during the insurrection against Somoza to support FSLN fighters; at their height in the two years after the victory, the CDSs enrolled an estimated 500,000 people, or a third of Nicaragua's adult population. The CDSs were given specific public functions, including the maintenance of order and distribution of basic commodities and rationing cards. Their security functions diminished as the revolutionary state apparatus took shape, but the CDSs continued to exercise a sort of revolutionary vigilance and to mobilize neighborhood residents for political rallies as well as clean-up campaigns and other collective projects. By the late 1980s the CDSs had declined greatly in membership and vigor, reflecting the cooling of the post-victory enthusiasm and the rigors of a shattered economy that cut into individuals' time for voluntary action.

The National Directorate, the FSLN's governing body, consisted of nine long-term FSLN members and combat veterans, all of whom held the highest military rank of *comandante*. The Directorate was the organism that balanced the differing views from within the heterogeneous movement, assessed input from the mass organizations, and articulated policy positions on a day-to-day basis. Most members of the Directorate held key government positions: Daniel Ortega as chairman of the original junta and after 1984 as president; Humberto Ortega as minister of defense; Directorate chairman Tomás Borge as minister of interior charged with internal security; Bayardo Arce as president of the Council of State to 1984; Carlos Núñez as president of the national assembly after 1984; and Jaime Wheelock as minister of agriculture. This overlap between the National Directorate and the government, which continued with little change from the victory until the electoral defeat of 1990, ensured the preeminence of the FSLN in policy making and implementation and provided consistency in the general direction of the revolution.

The FSLN exercised its political supremacy within a setting of political pluralism that featured numerous parties and economic interest groups that enjoyed broad rights of political organization and expression. The composition of the first post-Somoza government, the Governing Junta of National Reconstruction, reflected the breadth of the struggle against the dynasty: two representatives of the bourgeois opposition, including Violeta Barrios de Chamorro, widow of the slain *La Prensa* editor; two representatives of the pro-Sandinista political opposition; and Daniel Ortega of the FSLN's National Directorate. The 51-member Council of State, the appointed, corporately-structured legislative and advisory body that proposed policy to the Governing Junta, also reflected the breadth of the anti-Somoza movement. Its establishment in May 1980 also reflected the preeminence of the FSLN and the dilemmas facing the opposition over how best to defend their interests against the Sandinistas. The anti-Somoza factions had agreed upon the composition of the Council of State prior to the victory; however, in April 1980 the FSLN demanded additional seats to accommodate the new or enlarged mass organizations that it had created. The FSLN claimed that the new seats were necessary to foster participatory democracy; the opposition claimed the FSLN was packing the council with its own people. The FSLN prevailed, and the two bourgeois Junta members resigned but were replaced by members of generally similar views.

Despite this FSLN victory, political opposition to Sandinista dominance continued to be vigorous and relatively free. The parties to the right of the FSLN and the private economic interest associations vacillated and often split over strategy and tactics. The frustration of being a minority led some of the groups to boycott meetings of the Council of State and several refused to participate in the 1984 national election as a means of portraying the government as illegitimate and antidemocratic. Such tactics were encouraged by the U.S. government, played up in the U.S. media, and used to justify the surrogate war against Nicaragua. However, most of the opposition groups participated most of the time because their presence in policy-making bodies gave them the ability to modify much of the FSLN's legislative program. As examples, some 30 percent of the law regulating political parties resulted from amendments to the FSLN-sponsored bill, and the 1987 constitution was the product of extensive give and take between the Sandinista majority and the six opposition parties in the National Assembly.

By the end of the 1980s there were at least 21 political parties registered in Nicaragua, a range of economic interest associations headed by the Superior Council of Private Enterprise (Consejo Superior de la Empresa Privada, COSEP), and several opposition newspapers, magazines, and radio stations. While it would be incorrect to suggest that the FSLN had a perfect record in safeguarding all rights of the opposition, the pluralist political system was clearly at odds with President Reagan's repeated characterization of Nicaragua as a "totalitarian" state. A comparison with Mexico, another pluralist system with one-party dominance, would suggest that pluralism in Nicaragua was quite effective. The constant pressure from opposition groups combined with the FSLN's insistence on hearing and incorporating input from the mass organizations resulted in policies that were more pragmatic and flexible than dogmatic.

Policy toward the Atlantic Coast region offers an example of governmental flexibility and willingness to rectify mistakes. After the victory, FSLN cadres set out to carry the benefits of revolution as well as the controlling hand of government to the historically but informally autonomous remote Atlantic Coast peopled by English-speaking blacks and several indigenous groups, the largest of which are the Miskitos. Reacting to the imposition of new regulations and new rulers who disrupted traditional patterns of living and power relationships, many Miskitos turned to the Contras to defend their way of life and drive out an activist but unwelcome government. Learning from this bitter experience, the government changed course and gradually won over large numbers of Atlantic Coast dwellers by a guarantee of regional autonomy embodied in the new constitution combined with more sensitivity in the treatment of the populace.

The post-Somoza political system that began to take shape within a year of the victory was further institutionalized but little altered by the November 1984 election and the 1987 constitution. The election, demanded by the right-wing opposition and the United States, took place under intense U.S. pressure and international scrutiny. The Reagan administration declared the election fraudulent far in advance and pressured the right opposition to boycott as a means of denying legitimacy to the government elected. The FSLN undoubtedly used the advantages of incumbency during the campaign and instituted some security measures in response to the escalation of war that the opposition claimed restricted its ability to campaign. Despite the boycott by several right parties and interest groups, 75 percent of registered voters participated in what international observers certified as a fair election. Daniel Ortega won the presidency with 63 percent of the total vote or 67 percent of the valid vote and the FSLN obtained 61 of 96 National Assembly seats. Three parties to the right of the FSLN won a total of 29 seats and three Marxist parties on the FSLN's left, including the communists, received a total of 6 seats.

The final step in institutionalizing the revolution was the adoption of a new constitution, which took effect in January 1987. Before writing a draft, the government held open community meetings (*cabildos abiertos*) throughout the country to obtain a maximum of citizen participation in the process. The document that emerged from nearly two years of deliberation and debate defined Nicaragua as a social democracy based on an elected government, inviolable individual liberties, and enumerated social, economic, and cultural rights. The document guaranteed political pluralism, a mixed economy, and nonalignment in foreign affairs. Insofar as the 1987 constitution embodied the goals of the Nicaraguan Revolution, it is apparent that Nicaragua had chosen a new path to the future, but a far more moderate one than the path that Fidel Castro selected for Cuba.

IMPLEMENTING THE REVOLUTION

The Sandinistas' decade in power was characterized by caution and moderation in carrying out structural change in Nicaragua's economy and society. The moderation of the revolutionary government surprised many observers who expected a predominantly Marxist regime to follow Cuba's example and move quickly toward socialism. Several factors explain the relatively slow pace of change. First, the FSLN compromised its ideological purity during the final years of the anti-Somoza struggle when it broadened beyond its original Marxist core. Second, the Nicaraguan Revolution coincided with a growing skepticism among Marxists about Soviet-style economics, the beginning of *perestroika* in the Soviet Union and similar reforms in China, and strong trends toward privatization in the Third World. Fidel Castro himself reportedly advised the Sandinistas to preserve a substantial private sector. Finally, unrelenting U.S. pressure may have influenced the government toward moderation in order to avoid provoking intervention by U.S. troops. The debate persists on whether the FSLN's commitment to political and economic pluralism was transitory or permanent; considering the embodiment of those principles in the 1987 constitution and the world trends away from state ownership and single party states, it appears that the Sandinistas were simply up-to-date in their economic and political ideas.

From the outset, the new government offered assurances that it would not socialize all the economy and that the private sector would play a major role in economic reconstruction. In broad terms, the state sector of the national economy increased from an extremely low 15 percent under Somoza to approximately 45 percent in 1984 and remained at that general level — a normal one for Latin America — through 1989. Growth of the state sector began with the nationalization of Somoza- and Somocista-owned properties, which included extensive agricultural holdings, the national airline, processing and manufacturing plants, construction firms, real estate, and other investments. Overall, some 20 to 25 percent of the national economy, accounting for approximately half of the expanded state sector, came from the exiles of the old regime. Nationalization of banking, insurance, foreign trade, mining, forestry, transportation, and some manufacturing furthered the growth of the state sector. The overall tendency in nationalization was to take over the largest holdings in land, manufacturing, finance, and commerce and to fortify small and medium private property.

A closer look at changes in agriculture, which employed approximately half of Nicaragua's economically active population in 1980, illustrates the evolution of property after the revolution. The only action in the first two years was the expropriation of Somoza-owned holdings, which included about 20 percent of the country's productive land, most of which were retained as large state-owned units. The 1981 agrarian reform law was quite conservative: It targeted large inefficient and abandoned holdings and those whose land was leased or sharecropped and guaranteed the integrity of efficient holdings of any size. With these limitations, the 1981 law failed to provide sufficient land to satisfy peasant demands. Moreover, many peasants resisted governmental pressure to form production cooperatives on reformed land, preferring instead to farm individually.

The 1984 election reflected peasant dissatisfaction with the pace and direction of agrarian reform, while the escalating Contra war underscored to the Sandinistas the importance of peasant support. Therefore, agrarian reform accelerated in 1985 with an easing of the restrictions on expropriation and a deemphasis on state farms and production cooperatives. By 1988, the state sector had shrunk from 20 to 13 percent of total agricultural surface, large private owners held 12 percent, cooperatives 15 percent, and small and medium producers controlled 60 percent. The size and power of UNAG, the small and medium owners' organization with 125,000 members in 1986, combined with the shrinkage of the state farm sector, reflected the dominant position of peasants and small entrepreneurs in a capitalist agricultural economy.

While property relations changed significantly in agriculture and throughout the economy, preservation of the mixed economy meant that a majority of the population continued to be employees and wage laborers in the private sector, self-employed petty merchants or artisans, or unemployed and underemployed. The government's commitment to revolution involved improving the standard of living of the poor by redistributing income, goods, and services to them. The Sandinistas' policies for benefitting these lower social sectors were two-fold. One deeply rooted approach was to empower these citizens to improve their conditions through membership in the mass organizations — labor unions, CDSs, youth, and women's organizations. Effective unions would fight for members' bread-and-butter issues, while in the Sandinista concept of participatory democracy the other organizations would provide input into policy formulation in their members' interests. CDSs in addition often functioned as neighborhood improvement committees that could enhance members' living conditions.

The more direct approach to spreading the benefits of revolution was through government spending on social services and subsidies for essential goods. In the first five years after the victory, the government made an impressive beginning in redistributing welfare through food subsidies, rent controls, increased expenditure on education, housing, and public health, and reestablishment and reform of the collapsed social security system. A national literacy crusade in 1980 took 100,000 volunteers into every corner of the country to teach basic literacy to the illiterate 40 percent of adult Nicaraguans; the result was a reported reduction of the illiteracy rate to around 13 percent. University admission policies were standardized and tuition virtually eliminated, allowing the poor to attend the formerly elite private institutions. Establishment of basic rural clinics, vaccination campaigns, and other public health measures produced good results in lowering rates of infant mortality and crippling diseases.

The pronounced initial thrust toward indirect and direct redistribution of income and services slowed markedly under the weight of the drastic economic decline caused by war, the trade and credit boycotts, falling prices for Nicaragua's exports, and disruptions in production accompanying the partial socialization of production. Moreover, the government's commitment to preserving the private sector required it periodically to crack down on the working class by prohibiting strikes, controlling wages, and taking other measures that contradicted its program of redistribution. While the Contras never threatened to defeat the Nicaraguan government, the expense of fighting the war, in addition to the cost in lives, devastated the Sandinistas' efforts to improve the material conditions of the majority and inevitably wore down the initially high levels of popular enthusiasm for the FSLN. This inability to deliver, combined with the economic policies favoring the private sector, led to the development of a left critique aptly expressed by a representative of the Marxist-Leninist Popular Action Movement (Movimiento de Acción Popular Marxista-Leninista) in the National Assembly; in an interview with the author, he charged that "the Contra-Sandinista war is nothing but a smoke screen to allow both sides to screw the proletariat."[5]

After a decade, the Nicaraguan Revolution had assumed an identity of its own. Led by Marxists, it was an anti-imperialist but capitalist revolution anchored in the support of the lower and middle classes. At the tenth anniversary of the Sandinista victory, Nicaragua appeared to be evolving toward the model of Mexico after its 1910 revolution rather than toward the Cuban model. In contrast to the Mexican case, however, the FSLN leadership submitted its accomplishments and its continuance in power to the test of fair and open elections. The 1990 election was a referendum on the decade of Sandinista control.

THE END OF THE SANDINISTA REVOLUTION

The election, scheduled for November 1990, took place instead in February. The Central American Peace Accord of 1987 had bound all signatories to seek national reconciliation by ceasing hostilities, ending aid to guerrillas fighting other governments, and holding free elections. Constantly pressured by the Reagan administration, which continued by all possible means to sabotage any peace agreement that would leave the Sandinistas in power, the Ortega government moved much faster than any other to meet the conditions of the accord so as to end the long, debilitating war and begin rebuilding. Thus it agreed to hold elections, in which repatriated Contras would participate, nine months ahead of the date stipulated in the new constitution.

The election took place under the cloud of massive U.S. intervention. Unconcerned about the glaring electoral fraud and irregularities common to many Latin American countries, recently demonstrated in the 1988

Mexican elections, the United States held Nicaragua to a standard of electoral purity — as guaranteed by thousands of international observers — that few U.S. cities could claim. In addition, Washington openly financed the opposition's campaign with $7.7 million from the congressionally-funded National Endowment for Democracy and covertly spent an estimated $5 million more for a total investment of approximately $8.50 per voter.[6] Following a pattern set during the Reagan administration, President George Bush announced shortly before the election that a Sandinista victory, even though certified as fair, would not be enough to relax U.S. sanctions. In sum, nothing short of a change of government would satisfy Washington.

Nicaraguan voters proved most polls wrong, and by a large margin. Violeta Barrios de Chamorro, widow of slain publisher Pedro Joaquín Chamorro and a member of the first post-Somoza government, was the presidential candidate of the National Opposition Union (Unión Nacional Opositora, UNO) — a broad coalition of 14 parties ranging from conservative to communist. She received 54.7 percent of the valid vote to 40.8 for the FSLN candidate, President Daniel Ortega. UNO won 51 seats in congress, the FSLN 39, and independents captured 2 seats.

The election results revealed the success of Ronald Reagan's policy of wearing Nicaragua down through war and economic blockade. The impoverishment of an already poor country, the death toll of some 31,000 in the Contra war — a ratio of dead to total population approximately 50 times greater than U.S. losses in Vietnam — and the unpopularity of the military draft necessitated by the war eventually proved more compelling to the population than did their loyalty to a group that had played the leading role in ridding them of Somoza. Just as surely as if the U.S. Marines had invaded or the CIA had orchestrated a coup, the Reagan policy brought down the FSLN government. As Fidel Castro observed, Daniel Ortega had allowed himself to be maneuvered into playing by Washington's rules — a fatal error born of desperation. Ortega explained the FSLN defeat by saying that "the Nicaraguan people went to vote with a pistol pointed at their heads."[7]

Chamorro's victory threatened the changes wrought in Nicaraguan society during the Sandinista decade. Conservative elements within the UNO favored the privatization of state enterprises and a redistribution of income and services in favor of the upper and middle classes. Possessing legal titles to their land, Nicaragua's new small farmers would be hard to dislodge. However, the disarming of peasant militias as part of the peace process reduced the farmers' ability to defend their land, and a government oriented toward marketplace policies could follow the Chilean military's approach of starving the peasants of credit and price supports until they sell out.

Nonetheless, efforts to dismantle the transformed rural society and the new political system faced powerful obstacles. Despite its decline, the FSLN remained Nicaragua's largest and best organized political party. Sandinista influence in the military and control over most of the labor unions gave the FSLN the potential to "govern from below," as Ortega described the strategy of opposing the Chamorro government. The UNO coalition was so heterogeneous that it could not be expected to stay together after the election; if it fell apart, the FSLN could fashion a congressional majority with only eight deputies from the left or center UNO parties or six with the independents. Furthermore, although conservative elements of the UNO desired to strip the 1987 constitution of its more progressive elements, the coalition, even with the two independents, lacked the 60 percent required for congressional amendment of the constitution. Thus while the 1990 election clearly rejected another six years of Sandinista government, it did not settle the question of Nicaragua's future.

NOTES

1. Omar Cabezas, *Fire from the Mountain: The Making of a Sandinista* (New York: Crown, 1985), 210.

2. Argentine urban guerrillas assassinated Somoza in Asunción in September 1980 by blowing up his automobile with a bazooka.

3. Quoted in E. Bradford Burns, *At War in Nicaragua: The Reagan Doctrine and the Politics of Nostalgia* (New York: Harper & Row, 1987), 32.

4. Ibid., 35.

5. Interview with Deputy Carlos Cuadras, Managua, 22 June 1988.

6. Part of the U.S. funding went to ostensibly independent but clearly UNO-affiliated groups, while according to Nicaraguan law, half of the amount donated directly to candidates or parties was deducted to underwrite the costs of conducting the election. Foreign funding of political campaigns in the United States is prohibited by law.

7. *El País* (Madrid), 25 April 1990, 15.

Epilogue

At the dawn of the 1990s Fidel Castro still held power in Cuba. Approaching his mid-sixties, Fidel was vigorous, charismatic, even electrifying in his speeches which, 31 years after the triumph of the barbudos, still warned of Yankee aggression and called on the Cuban people to sacrifice more for the revolution. Yet all was not well for Fidel and his revolution. The fall of the communist regimes in Eastern Europe in late 1989 and early 1990 and the reformism of Soviet leader Gorbachev made Fidel feel isolated. The loss of his only ally in Latin America, the Sandinista government of Daniel Ortega, was a major blow to Castro. Yet apparently convinced of the correctness of Cuba's model of economy and government and undoubtedly fearful that, as in Eastern Europe, minor reforms would unleash unstoppable currents of change, Fidel dug in his heels against reform, proclaiming that Cuba had no need for *perestroika* or *glasnost*. Thus as the 1990s commenced, an aura of anachronism began to settle over the Castro regime.

With communism in retreat globally, the period of preeminent Cuban influence in Latin America was moribund or dead. That "something new, exciting, dangerous, and infectious" that Herbert Matthews had detected at the beginning of the 1960s was gone.[1] But the end of the era of the Cuban Revolution was not a sudden development nor was it linked exclusively or even predominantly to the collapse or reform of Europe's communist regimes. Rather, the eclipse of the Cuban Revolution as the prevailing political influence in Latin America was a long and gradual process resulting primarily from factors intrinsic to the Western Hemisphere and the interplay of the forces of revolution and reaction.

The decline of Cuban influence resulted in part from the secular tarnishing of the lustre of the revolution. As the limitations of the revolution itself became manifest over the years, the Cuban model appealed to an ever-shrinking pool of Latin Americans who desired a

Cuban-style revolution in their own countries. Inevitably, the honeymoon period of Fidel's first few months, when he was a popular hero to most Latin Americans, could not last. The great accomplishments — the social revolution and the escape from U.S. dominance — ended sympathy for Fidel among some moderates. His embrace of communism alienated another bloc of supporters who, favorably impressed by the revolution's achievements, rejected the Soviet model being established on the island. The failure of the touted economic miracle of overnight industrialization and development, followed by the relative austerity and drabness of Cuba in the 1970s and 1980s, was another factor in the gradual loss of appeal.

Cuba's increasing dependence upon the Soviet Union further eroded the revolution's standing among Latin American nationalists. Fidel's endorsement of the 1968 Soviet invasion of Czechoslovakia, the dispatch of 50,000 Cuban troops to Africa in the 1970s, and the growing dependence of the Cuban economy on massive Soviet aid were taken as signs that Cuba had not achieved national sovereignty but merely changed masters. Finally, the worldwide rise of concern for human rights — more precisely, for Western-style individual liberties — prompted largely by President Carter's foreign policy, placed some aspects of the Cuban Revolution, such as its thousands of political prisoners and its continuing denial of personal freedoms, in an increasingly unfavorable light.

More fundamentally, the influence of the Cuban Revolution waned because of the abject failure of revolution in Latin America. Even the few qualified victories proved to be ephemeral, validating the skeptics' thesis that the Cuban Revolution was an exception, an aberration that could not be replicated. The results of three decades of attempted revolution were grim. A generation of revolutionaries and hundreds of thousands of sympathizers, innocent victims, government troops, and police were killed, jailed, tortured, and exiled. The popular classes of Latin America paid the price of unprecedented political repression and socially retrograde economic policies that exacerbated their poverty and shattered their illusions of betterment. By 1990 the spirit of revolution, which had swept strongly over Latin America in the 1960s, had been brutally extinguished.

The apparent ease of Castro's victory in Cuba undoubtedly led to a serious underestimation of the resilience of Latin America's elites and of the United States' resolve to prevent other revolutions. Fidel and Che themselves bore major responsibility for this fatal misperception by fostering the idea that others could repeat the Cuban experience with reasonable certainty, by establishing focos and following Che's guidelines. Despite the launching of scores of guerrilla focos based on the embellished Cuban model, the "heroic guerrilla" formula for insurrection yielded no victories. Nicaragua's Sandinistas, the one successful rural guerrilla group, initially embraced foquismo but only achieved victory following a protracted campaign and the assiduous cultivation of mass support. One is led to wonder whether an accurate recounting of the Cuban insurrection might have inspired some successes during the height of the revolutionary impulse of the 1960s, where the presentation of the official version as a model led to failure.

Despite the unprecedented pan-Latin American mobilization and the political effervescence ignited by the Cuban Revolution, the habits and the mechanisms of domination that underpinned Latin America's established societies did not suddenly crumble. While some peasants shook off their traditional lethargy and joined the ranks of the mobilized, it was quite another thing to join a guerrilla band or even to offer aid to city-bred guerrillas operating in their areas. Shantytown dwellers might join the clamor for material improvements, but few could set aside their transplanted rural attitudes and values to join revolutionary movements.

Reinforcing these obstacles to revolution was the determination of Latin America's elites and much of its middle classes to fight to preserve their way of life. The widespread recourse to military solutions, including in several cases the institutionalization of state terror when political systems collapsed in the face of revolutionary threats, reflected this resolve. The willingness of the elites, most notably in Chile and Nicaragua, to stay and fight the revolutionaries rather than, as in Cuba, abandon the battlefield to the class enemy further illustrated the deeply rooted resistance to change. The heroic guerrilla model, as broadcast from Cuba, simply did not take into account the inherent conservatism of the Latin American lower classes and the resolve and superior resources of the establishment.

Revolution also ran squarely into the historic, unswerving resistance of the United States to radical change in the hemisphere. From its first challenge, the Mexican Revolution of 1910, the United States consistently opposed revolution and was normally hostile even to committed reformist governments. During the era of the Cuban Revolution, all presidents from Eisenhower to Bush, with some vacillation on the part of Carter, repeatedly demonstrated their willingness to use U.S. power to thwart revolution and preserve U.S. hegemony and economic interests, casting aside all but the pretenses of principled behavior and adherence to international law. U.S. training and arming of the Latin American militaries and police for counterinsurgency and the numerous instances of overt and covert U.S. military and CIA intervention generally proved effective in keeping revolutionaries and suspect reformers from power.

U.S. support of the antirevolutionary military regimes was an effective means of dampening the momentum of revolution not only in the countries where they were established but also throughout the hemisphere. And things were not easier for the few progressives who, despite the odds, attained power: While Velasco, being head of a military government, was harder to handle, U.S. treatment of Allende's Chile and Sandinista Nicaragua demonstrated an iron will to use war, subversion, and economic strangulation to bring down those offending governments.

Concomitant to the defeat of the revolutionaries and the tarnishing of his own revolution, Castro saw his influence in Latin America decline over the years. It was a slow and uneven process — one that eludes the neat periodization that historians seek — but a decade-by-decade overview reveals the gradual eclipse of the era of the Cuban Revolution. The decade of the 1960s was clearly the crest of the wave. The Cuban model was broadly appealing throughout Latin America, revolutionary forces were active virtually everywhere, and the U.S. and Latin American elites reacted defensively. The death of Che Guevara in 1967 dampened the revolutionary momentum, but within a short time urban guerrilla warfare began to yield promising results, while the Peruvian military created hope for revolution from above. The rise of the urban guerrillas and the Peruvian experiment in the late 1960s marked a maturing of the revolutionary trend in Latin America. Inspired by the Cuban Revolution, both represented important innovations that went beyond the sterile "heroic guerrilla" model and broadened the currents of change, both in the form of seizing power and, in the Peruvian case, in the model for a new society.

The 1970s brought mixed signals about the continuing influence of the Cuban Revolution. On one hand, several moderate to conservative governments normalized relations with Cuba during the decade, and at the insistence of a majority of the Latin American countries, over Washington's objections, the OAS in 1975 lifted its economic and diplomatic sanctions against Cuba. This move demonstrated a renewed confidence in those countries' ability to cope with revolutionary movements. Few important insurrectionary movements took the field during the 1970s, yet the decade began and ended with major victories for the forces of revolution. Allende's election in September 1970 and the Sandinista victory in July 1979 bracketed the decade, and the Velasco regime in Peru became increasingly radical until its removal in 1975. Meanwhile the return of Perón in 1973, the nationalist Panamanian government of Omar Torrijos that spanned the decade, the Echeverría administration in Mexico, and the "peruanista" Rodríguez Lara regime in Ecuador manifested the continuing impulse toward revolution or reform, even though these governments produced few lasting results.

Most revealing of the continuing influence of the Cuban Revolution was the establishment of the antirevolutionary military regimes in the 1970s or, in the case of the existing Brazilian government, its evolution into a more fully repressive state after 1968. These governments were clearly responses to threats of revolution, and their ambitious goals and extreme methods were testimony to the profound effects of the revolutionary current still flowing strong in Latin America. Meanwhile the replacement of civilian government with more traditional military regimes, a trend begun during the unstable 1960s, continued in the 1970s until only a handful of countries — Mexico, Costa Rica, Venezuela, and Colombia — retained civilian institutions. On balance, despite some signs of relaxation of tensions, the Cuban Revolution continued as a major influence in Latin American politics during the decade of the 1970s.

During the 1980s there was unmistakable evidence of the waning of the era of the Cuban Revolution, the most convincing of which was the return to civilian rule throughout most of Latin America. From a low point in the late 1970s, civilian governments had returned through the 1980s until only Cuba, Haiti, and Chile ended the decade under governments that had not been elected in a minimally competitive process. The phasing out of the South American antirevolutionary regimes was the most significant development. Their termination in Argentina, Uruguay, and Brazil between 1983 and 1985 indicated the officers' perception that the immediate danger of revolution in their countries was over. Even so, upon relinquishing direct control the armed forces continued to exercise close vigilance through either institutionalized or extralegal means to prevent a reversion to the status quo ante.

The 1980s also brought a marked decline of ideological politics. Saddled with massive foreign debts and reeling from over a decade of severe recession, Latin America turned from redistributive issues to the pragmatic matter of inducing economic growth. By the late 1980s, governments everywhere were submitting themselves to the IMF formula while stalwart statists such as the Mexican PRI and Argentina's Peronists were busily privatizing their countries' economies and proclaiming that development must precede reform. Also by the mid-1980s, both the extreme left and the extreme right had failed; the revolutionaries had failed to seize power, with a few exceptions, while the counterrevolutionaries had withdrawn from power without completing their missions. Neither side could offer many heroes and no models for emulation, and thus the appeal of both left and right declined. Shorn of its extremes, the political spectrum contracted toward the center. This development, in concert with the ascendancy of economic development issues, gave rise to a new politics of pragmatism.

Yet the revival of civilian government and the rise of pragmatic politics in the 1980s did not close out the era of the Cuban Revolution in all of Latin America. Two of the bloodiest guerrilla wars, those of the FMLN in El Salvador and the Sendero Luminoso abetted by the MRTA in Peru, began or escalated in 1980 and continued through the decade. The destabilization of Central America in the 1980s resulted to a large extent from the Sandinista victory in Nicaragua, which grew from seeds planted in the heady early days of the Cuban Revolution. The extremism of the U.S. reaction to the FSLN government, the massive aid to El Salvador, and the launching of the Caribbean Basin Initiative all revealed Washington's preoccupation with Nicaragua and Cuba while the 1983 invasion of Grenada was a direct blow at Cuban influence in the Caribbean. In general terms, the revolutionary impulse unleashed by Fidel's revolution reached its high point in Central America only in the 1980s, even while South America showed signs of returning to a more calm and orderly political life after long years of revolutionary and antirevolutionary violence.

The arrival of the decade of the 1990s finally appeared to mark the extinction of significant Cuban influence in Latin America. The fall of the Sandinistas by ballot in February 1990 confirmed the difficulties of making revolution in the United States' backyard. The inauguration of Patricio Aylwin as president of Chile in March 1990 completed the return to civilian government in continental Latin America. One of the main Colombian guerrilla groups, M-19, laid down its arms in February 1990 after 17 years to participate in politics as a party. Meanwhile negotiations began in Oslo in March to end the war in Guatemala, Central America's longest, and peace talks began soon thereafter between the Salvadoran government and guerrillas.

The general situation at the beginning of the 1990s was exactly the reverse of that at the onset of the 1960s: Having placed the United States and the elites and governments of Latin America on the defensive in the early years of his revolution, Fidel himself was on the defensive 31 years later. On one hand, he was rallying support by invoking the time-honored Yankee threat, made newly credible by the opening of Televisión Martí in March 1990 to beam anti-Castro propaganda from Florida to Cuba. On the other hand, he was acting as a normal member of the Latin American community as he fraternized with heads of state and government at the inauguration of conservative Brazilian President Collor de Mello in March

1990. Fidel was under increasing pressure from sources as diverse as Mikhael Gorbachev, Spanish Prime Minister Felipe González, and half the members of the Brazilian congress, who during his visit to Brasília petitioned him to institute democratic reforms in Cuba. By the beginning of the new decade, the prospect of Cuban-inspired revolution in Latin America had become remote indeed. The issue now was the survival of Castro's revolution itself.

NOTE

1. Herbert Matthews, *The Cuban Story* (New York: George Braziller, 1961), 185.

Selected Bibliography

These suggestions for further reading are limited to books in English.

CHAPTER 1

Aguilar, Luis E. *Cuba 1933 — Prologue to Revolution*. Ithaca, N.Y.: Cornell University Press, 1972.

Benjamin, Jules R. *The United States and Cuba: Hegemony and Dependent Development, 1880–1934*. Pittsburgh: University of Pittsburgh Press, 1977.

Bonachea, Rolando, and Marta San Martín. *The Cuban Insurrection, 1952–1958*. New Brunswick, N.J.: Transaction Books, 1974.

Bonachea, Rolando, and Nelson P. Valdés, eds. *Revolutionary Struggle 1947–1958: Volume I of the Selected Works of Fidel Castro*. Cambridge, Mass.: MIT Press, 1972.

Castro, Fidel. *History Will Absolve Me*. Bungay, U.K.: Richard Clay (The Chaucer Press), Ltd., 1968.

The Cuban Economic Research Project (José R. Alvarez Díaz, chairman). *A Study on Cuba*. Coral Gables, Fla.: University of Miami Press, 1965.

Farber, Samuel. *Revolution and Reaction in Cuba, 1933–1960: A Political Sociology from Machado to Castro*. Middletown, Conn.: Wesleyan University Press, 1976.

Franqui, Carlos. *Diary of the Cuban Revolution*. Tr. by Georgette Felix et al. New York: Viking, 1980.

Guevara, Che. *Reminiscences of the Cuban Revolutionary War*. Tr. by Victoria Ortiz. New York: Grove Press, 1968.

Liss, Sheldon B. *Roots of Revolution: Radical Thought in Cuba*. Lincoln: University of Nebraska Press, 1987.

MacGaffey, Wyatt, and Clifford R. Barnett. *Twentieth Century Cuba: The Background of the Castro Revolution*. Garden City, N.Y.: Anchor Books, 1965.

Matthews, Herbert L. *The Cuban Story*. New York: George Braziller, 1961.

Nelson, Lowry. *Rural Cuba*. Minneapolis: University of Minnesota Press, 1950.

Pérez, Louis A., Jr. *Cuba: Between Reform and Revolution*. New York: Oxford University Press, 1988.

____. *Cuba Under the Platt Amendment, 1902–1934*. Pittsburgh: University of Pittsburgh Press, 1986.

____. *Intervention, Revolution, and Politics in Cuba, 1913–1921.* Pittsburgh: University of Pittsburgh Press, 1978.

Ruíz, Ramón Eduardo. *Cuba: The Making of a Revolution.* New York: W. W. Norton, 1970.

Smith, Earl E. T. *The Fourth Floor: An Account of the Castro Communist Revolution.* New York: Random House, 1962.

Smith, Robert Freeman, ed. *Background to Revolution: The Development of Modern Cuba.* New York: Alfred A. Knopf, 1966.

____. *The United States and Cuba: Business and Diplomacy, 1917–1960.* New York: Bookman Associates, 1960.

____. *What Happened in Cuba? A Documentary History.* New York: Twayne Publishers, 1963.

Suchlicki, Jaime. *Cuba from Columbus to Castro.* New York: Charles Scribner's Sons, 1974.

____. *University Students and Revolution in Cuba, 1920–1968.* Coral Gables, Fla.: University of Miami Press, 1969.

Szulc, Tad. *Fidel: A Critical Portrait.* New York: William Morrow, 1986.

Thomas, Hugh. *Cuba: The Pursuit of Freedom.* New York: Harper and Row, 1971.

CHAPTER 2

Abel, Elie. *The Missile Crisis.* New York: J. B. Lippincott, 1965.

Bernardo, Robert M. *The Theory of Moral Incentives in Cuba.* Tuscaloosa: University of Alabama Press, 1971.

Blasier, Cole, and Carmelo Mesa-Lago, eds. *Cuba in the World.* Pittsburgh: University of Pittsburgh Press, 1979.

Bonachea, Rolando E., and Nelson P. Valdés, eds. *Cuba in Revolution.* Garden City, N.Y.: Anchor Books, 1972.

Bonsal, Philip W. *Cuba, Castro, and the United States.* Pittsburgh: University of Pittsburgh Press, 1972.

Boorstein, Edward. *The Economic Transformation of Cuba.* New York: Monthly Review Press, 1968.

Brundenius, Claes. *Revolutionary Cuba: The Challenge of Economic Growth with Equity.* Boulder, Colo.: Westview Press, 1984.

del Aguila, Juan M. *Cuba: Dilemmas of a Revolution.* Boulder, Colo.: Westview Press, 1985.

Divine, Robert A., ed. *The Cuban Missile Crisis.* Chicago: Quadrangle Books, 1971.

Domínguez, Jorge I., ed. *Cuba: Internal and International Affairs.* Beverly Hills, Calif.: Sage Publications, 1982.

____. *Cuba: Order and Revolution.* Cambridge, Mass.: Harvard University Press, 1978.

Draper, Theodore. *Castroism: Theory and Practice.* New York: Praeger, 1965.

____. *Castro's Revolution: Myths and Realities.* New York: Praeger, 1970.

Duncan, W. Raymond. *The Soviet Union and Cuba: Interests and Influence.* New York: Praeger, 1985.

Ellison, Graham T. *Essence of Decision: Explaining the Cuban Missile Crisis.* Boston: Little, Brown, 1971.

Erisman, H. Michael. *Cuba's International Relations: The Anatomy of a Nationalistic Foreign Policy*. Boulder, Colo.: Westview Press, 1985.

Fagen, Richard R. *The Transformation of Political Culture in Cuba*. Stanford, Calif.: Stanford University Press, 1969.

Falk, Pamela S. *Cuban Foreign Policy*. Lexington, Mass.: Lexington Books, 1986.

Franqui, Carlos. *Family Portrait with Fidel: A Memoir*. Tr. by Alfred MacAdam. New York: Random House, 1984.

Geyer, Georgie Anne. *Guerrilla Prince: The Untold Story of Fidel Castro*. Boston: Little, Brown, 1991.

González, Edward. *Cuba Under Castro: The Limits of Charisma*. Boston: Houghton Mifflin, 1974.

Halperin, Maurice. *The Rise and Decline of Fidel Castro*. Berkeley: University of California Press, 1972.

____. *The Taming of Fidel Castro*. Berkeley: University of California Press, 1981.

Horowitz, Irving Louis, ed. *Cuban Communism*. 2d ed. New Brunswick, N.J.: Transaction Books, 1972.

Johnson, Haynes. *The Bay of Pigs*. New York: W. W. Norton, 1964.

Judson, C. Fred. *Cuba and the Revolutionary Myth: The Political Education of the Cuban Rebel Army, 1953–1963*. Boulder, Colo.: Westview Press, 1984.

Karol, K. S. *Guerrillas in Power*. Tr. by Arnold Pomerans. New York: Hill and Wang, 1970.

Kenner, Martin, and James Petras, eds. *Fidel Castro Speaks*. New York: Grove Press, 1969.

LeoGrande, William M. *Cuba's Policy in Africa, 1959–1980*. Berkeley: University of California, Institute of International Studies, 1980.

Lockwood, Lee. *Castro's Cuba, Cuba's Fidel*. New York: Vintage Books, 1969.

Matthews, Herbert L. *Fidel Castro*. New York: Simon and Schuster, 1969.

____. *Revolution in Cuba: A Lesson in Understanding*. New York: Charles Scribner's Sons, 1975.

Mazaar, Michael J. *Semper Fidel: America and Cuba, 1776–1988*. Baltimore, Md.: The Nautical and Aviation Publishing Company of America, 1988.

Mesa-Lago, Carmelo. *Cuba in the 1970s: Pragmatism and Institutionalization. Rev. ed.* Albuquerque: University of New Mexico Press, 1978.

____. *The Economy of Socialist Cuba: A Two-Decade Appraisal*. Albuquerque: University of New Mexico Press, 1981.

____, ed. *Revolutionary Change in Cuba*. Pittsburgh: University of Pittsburgh Press, 1974.

Mesa-Lago, Carmelo, and June S. Belkin, eds. *Cuba in Africa*. Pittsburgh: University of Pittsburgh, Center for Latin American Studies, 1982.

Montaner, Carlos Alberto. *Secret Report on the Cuban Revolution*. Tr. by Eduardo Zayas-Bazán. New Brunswick, N.J.: Transaction Books, 1981.

Nelson, Lowry. *Cuba: The Measure of a Revolution*. Minneapolis: University of Minnesota Press, 1979.

O'Connor, James. *The Origins of Socialism in Cuba*. Ithaca, N.Y.: Cornell University Press, 1970.

Ritter, Archibald R. M. *The Economic Development of Revolutionary Cuba*. New York: Praeger, 1974.

Seers, Dudley, et al. *Cuba: The Economic and Social Revolution*. Chapel Hill: University of North Carolina Press, 1964.

Smith, Wayne S. *The Closest of Enemies: A Personal and Diplomatic Account of U.S.-Cuban Relations Since 1952*. New York: W. W. Norton, 1987.

Suárez, Andrés. *Cuba: Castroism and Communism, 1959–1966*. Cambridge, Mass.: MIT Press, 1967.

Suchlicki, Jaime, ed. *Cuba, Castro, and Revolution*. Coral Gables, Fla.: University of Miami Press, 1972.

Wyden, Peter. *Bay of Pigs*. New York: Simon and Schuster, 1979.

Zeitlin, Maurice. *Revolutionary Politics and the Cuban Working Class*. Princeton, N.J.: Princeton University Press, 1967.

CHAPTER 3

Aguilar, Luis E. *Marxism in Latin America*. New York: Alfred A. Knopf, 1968.

Alexander, Robert J. *Communism in Latin America*. New Brunswick, N.J.: Rutgers University Press, 1957.

Bernard, Jean-Pierre, et al. *Guide to the Political Parties of South America*. Tr. by Michael Perl. Harmondsworth, England: Penguin Books, 1973.

Blanco, Hugo. *Land or Death: The Peasant Struggle in Peru*. New York: Pathfinder Press, 1972.

Feder, Ernest. *The Rape of the Peasantry: Latin America's Landholding System*. Garden City, N.Y.: Doubleday, 1971.

Frank, Andre Gunder. *Latin America: Underdevelopment or Revolution*. New York: Monthly Review Press, 1969.

Goldenberg, Boris. *The Cuban Revolution and Latin America*. New York: Praeger, 1966.

Halperin, Ernst. *Nationalism and Communism in Chile*. Cambridge, Mass.: MIT Press, 1965.

Hodges, Donald C. *The Latin American Revolution: Politics and Strategy from Apro-Marxism to Guevarism*. New York: William Morrow, 1974.

Horowitz, Irving Louis, Josué de Castro, and John Gerassi, eds. *Latin American Radicalism*. New York: Vintage Books, 1969.

Jackson, Bruce D. *Castro, the Kremlin, and Communism in Latin America*. Baltimore, Md.: Johns Hopkins University Press, 1969.

Johnson, John J. *Political Change in Latin America: The Emergence of the Middle Sectors*. Palo Alto, Calif.: Stanford University Press, 1958.

Landsberger, Henry A., ed. *Latin American Peasant Movements*. Ithaca, N.Y.: Cornell University Press, 1969.

Levinson, Jerome, and Juan de Onís. *The Alliance That Lost Its Way*. Chicago: Quadrangle Books, 1970.

Lieuwen, Edwin. *Generals vs. Presidents: Neo-Militarism in Latin America*. New York: Praeger, 1966.

Mercier Vega, Luis. *Roads to Power in Latin America*. Tr. by Robert Rowland. New York: Praeger, 1969.

Parker, Phyllis R. *Brazil and the Quiet Intervention, 1964*. Austin: University of Texas Press, 1979.

Petras, James, and Maurice Zeitlin, eds. *Latin America: Reform or Revolution?* New York: Fawcett, 1968.

Porter, Charles O., and Robert J. Alexander. *The Struggle for Democracy in Latin America.* New York: Macmillan, 1961.

Ratliff, William E. *Castroism and Communism in Latin America, 1959–1976: The Varieties of Marxist-Leninist Experience.* Washington, D.C.: American Enterprise Institute for Public Policy Research, 1976.

Sigmund, Paul E., ed. *Models of Political Change in Latin America.* New York: Praeger, 1970.

Silvert, Kalman. *The Conflict Society: Reaction and Revolution in Latin America.* New Orleans: The Hauser Press, 1961.

Skidmore, Thomas E. *Politics in Brazil, 1930–1964: An Experiment in Democracy.* New York: Oxford University Press, 1967.

Stavenhagen, Rodolfo, ed. *Agrarian Problems and Peasant Movements in Latin America.* Garden City, N.Y.: Doubleday, 1970.

Szulc, Tad. *Twilight of the Tyrants.* New York: Henry Holt and Co., 1959.

Véliz, Claudio, ed. *Obstacles to Change in Latin America.* London: Oxford University Press, 1965.

____, ed. *The Politics of Conformity in Latin America.* London: Oxford University Press, 1967.

Whitaker, Arthur P., and David C. Jordan. *Nationalism in Contemporary Latin America.* New York: Free Press, 1966.

CHAPTER 4

Alexander, Robert J. *Rómulo Betancourt and the Transformation of Venezuela.* New Brunswick, N.J.: Transaction Books, 1982.

____. *The Venezuelan Democratic Revolution.* New Brunswick, N.J.: Rutgers University Press, 1964.

Ayers, Bradley E. *The War That Never Was: An Insider's Account of CIA Covert Operations Against Cuba.* Indianapolis: Bobbs-Merrill, 1976.

Ball, M. Margaret. *The OAS in Transition.* Durham, N.C.: Duke University Press, 1969.

Barber, Willard F., and C. Neale Ronning. *Internal Security and Military Power: Counterinsurgency and Civic Action in Latin America.* Columbus: Ohio State University Press, 1966.

Bender, Lynn Darrell. *The Politics of Hostility: Castro's Revolution and United States Policy.* Hato Rey, Puerto Rico: Inter American University Press, 1975.

Berle, Adolf A. *Latin America: Diplomacy and Reality.* New York: Harper & Row (published for the Council on Foreign Relations), 1962.

Blasier, Cole. *The Hovering Giant: U. S. Responses to Revolutionary Change in Latin America, 1910–1985.* Rev. ed. Pittsburgh: University of Pittsburgh Press, 1985.

Child, John. *Unequal Alliance: The Inter-American Military System, 1938–1978.* Boulder, Colo.: Westview Press, 1980.

Dreier, John C. *The Organization of American States and the Hemispheric Crisis.* New York: Harper and Row (published for the Council on Foreign Relations), 1962.

Gleijeses, Piero. *The Dominican Crisis: The 1965 Constitutionalist Revolt and American Intervention*. Baltimore, Md.: The Johns Hopkins Press, 1978.

Hanson, Simon C. *Five Years of the Alliance for Progress*. Washington, D. C.: Inter American Affairs Press, 1967.

Immerman, Richard H. *The CIA in Guatemala: The Foreign Policy of Intervention*. Austin: University of Texas Press, 1982.

Klare, Michael T. *War Without End: American Planning for the Next Vietnams*. New York: Vintage Books, 1972.

Klare, Michael T., and Cynthia Arnson. *Supplying Repression: U. S. Support for Authoritarian Regimes Abroad*. Washington, D. C.: Institute for Policy Studies, 1981.

LaFeber, Walter. *Inevitable Revolutions: The United States in Central America*. Expanded ed. New York: W. W. Norton, 1984.

Levine, Daniel H. *Conflict and Political Change in Venezuela*. Princeton, N.J.: Princeton University Press, 1973.

Levinson, Jerome, and Juan de Onís. *The Alliance That Lost Its Way*. Chicago: Quadrangle Books, 1970.

Lieuwen, Edwin. *U. S. Policy in Latin America*. New York: Praeger, 1965.

Lowenthal, Abraham F. *The Dominican Intervention*. Cambridge, Mass.: Harvard University Press, 1972.

Martz, John D. *Acción Democrática: Evolution of a Modern Political Party in Venezuela*. Princeton, N.J.: Princeton University Press, 1966.

Martz, John D., ed. *United States Policy in Latin America: A Quarter Century of Crisis and Challenge, 1961–1986*. Lincoln: University of Nebraska Press, 1988.

Martz, John D., and Lars Schoultz, eds. *Latin America, the United States, and the Inter-American System*. Boulder, Colo.: Westview Press, 1980.

Morley, Morris T. *Imperial State and Revolution: The United States and Cuba, 1952–1986*. London: Cambridge University Press, 1987.

Musicant, Ivan. *The Banana Wars: A History of United States Military Intervention in Latin America from the Spanish-American War to the Invasion of Panama*. New York: Macmillan, 1990.

Needler, Martin C. *The United States and the Latin American Revolution*. Rev. ed. Los Angeles: UCLA Latin American Center Publications, 1977.

Nystrom, J. Warren, and Nathan A. Haverstock. *The Alliance for Progress: Key to Latin America's Development*. Princeton, N. J.: D. Van Nostrand, 1966.

Parkinson, F. *Latin America, the Cold War, and the World Powers, 1945–1973*. Beverly Hills, Calif.: Sage Publications, 1974.

Perloff, Harvey S. *Alliance for Progress: A Social Invention in the Making*. Baltimore, Md.: Johns Hopkins University Press, 1969.

Petras, James F., and Robert LaPorte, Jr. *Cultivating Revolution: The United States and Agrarian Reform in Latin America*. New York: Random House, 1971.

Plank, John, ed. *Cuba and the United States: Long-Range Perspectives*. Washington, D. C.: The Brookings Institution, 1967.

Rodríguez, Felix I., and John Weisman. *Shadow Warrior*. New York: Simon and Schuster, 1989.

Schlesinger, Arthur M., Jr. *A Thousand Days*. Boston: Houghton Mifflin, 1966.

Schlesinger, Stephen, and Stephen Kinzer. *Bitter Fruit: The Untold Story of the American Coup in Guatemala*. Garden City, N.Y.: Doubleday & Co., 1982.

Schoultz, Lars. *Human Rights and United States Policy Toward Latin America*. Princeton, N.J.: Princeton University Press, 1981.

Stuart, Graham H. and James L. Tigner. *Latin America and the United States*. 6th ed. Englewood Cliffs, N.J.: Prentice-Hall, 1975.

Welch, Richard E., Jr. *Response to Revolution: The United States and the Cuban Revolution, 1959–1961*. Chapel Hill: University of North Carolina Press, 1985.

CHAPTER 5

Alexander, Robert J. *The Bolivian National Revolution*. New Brunswick, N.J.: Rutgers University Press, 1958.

Armstrong, Robert, and Janet Shenk. *El Salvador: The Face of Revolution*. Boston: South End Press, 1982.

Béjar, Héctor. *Peru 1965: Notes on a Guerrilla Experience*. Tr. by William Rose. New York: Monthly Review Press, 1970.

Blackburn, Robin, ed. *Strategy for Revolution: Essays on Latin America by Régis Debray*. New York: Monthly Review Press, 1970.

Bonachea, Rolando, and Nelson P. Valdés. *Che: Selected Works of Ernesto Guevara*. Cambridge, Mass.: MIT Press, 1969.

Bravo, Douglas. *Douglas Bravo Speaks: Interview with Venezuelan Leader*. New York: Merit, 1970.

Camejo, Peter. *Guevara's Guerrilla Strategy: A Critique and Some Proposals*. New York: Pathfinder Press, 1972.

Debray, Régis. *Che's Guerrilla War*. Tr. by Rosemary Sheed. Harmondsworth, England: Penguin Books, 1975.

____. *Revolution in the Revolution? Armed Struggle and Political Struggle in Latin America*. Tr. by Bobbye Ortiz. New York: Grove Press, 1967.

Dunkerley, James. *The Long War: Dictatorship and Revolution in El Salvador*. London: Junction Books, 1982.

Durham, William H. *Scarcity and Survival in Central America: Ecological Origins of the Soccer War*. Stanford, Calif.: Stanford University Press, 1979.

Fals Borda, Orlando. *Subversion and Social Change in Colombia*. New York: Columbia University Press, 1969.

Fauriol, Georges, ed. *Latin American Insurgencies*. Washington, D. C.: National Defense University Press, 1985.

Fogelquist, Alan F. *Revolutionary Theory and Practice in Colombia*. Buffalo: Council on International Studies, State University of New York at Buffalo, 1981.

Fried, J. L., et al., eds. *Guatemala in Rebellion: Unfinished Revolution*. New York: Grove Press, 1982.

Gadea, Hilda. *Ernesto: A Memoir of Che Guevara*. Garden City, N.Y.: Doubleday, 1972.

Galeano, Eduardo. *Guatemala: Occupied Country*. Tr. by Cedric Belfrage. New York: Monthly Review Press, 1969.

Gerassi, John, ed. *Revolutionary Priest: The Complete Writings and Messages of Camilo Torres*. New York: Random House, 1972.

____, ed. *Venceremos! The Speeches and Writings of Che Guevara.* New York: Macmillan, 1968.

González, Luis J., and Gustavo A. Sánchez Salazar. *The Great Rebel: Che Guevara in Bolivia.* Tr. by Helen R. Lane. New York: Grove Press, 1969.

Gott, Richard. *Guerrilla Movements in Latin America.* Garden City, N.Y.: Anchor Books, 1972.

Guevara, Che. *Guerrilla Warfare.* Introduction and case studies by Brian Loveman and Thomas M. Davies, Jr. Lincoln: University of Nebraska Press, 1985.

Hodges, Donald C., ed. *The Legacy of Che Guevara: A Documentary Study.* London: Thomas and Hudson, 1977.

Huberman, Leo, and Paul Sweezy, eds. *Régis Debray and the Latin American Revolution.* New York: Monthly Review Press, 1968.

James, Daniel. *Che Guevara: A Biography.* New York: Stein and Day, 1969.

James Daniel, ed. *The Complete Bolivian Diaries of Che Guevara and Other Captured Documents.* New York: Stein and Day, 1968.

Lartéguy, Jean. *The Guerrrillas.* Tr. by Stanley Hochman. New York: New American Library, 1972.

Lavan, George, ed. *Che Guevara Speaks: Selected Speeches and Writings.* New York: Grove Press, 1968.

Lowy, Michael. *The Marxism of Che Guevara.* New York: Monthly Review Press, 1973.

Mallin, Jay, ed. *"Che" Guevara on Revolution.* Coral Gables, Fla.: University of Miami Press, 1969.

Malloy, James M. *Bolivia: The Uncompleted Revolution.* Pittsburgh: University of Pittsburgh Press, 1970.

Maullin, Robert. *Soldiers, Guerrillas, and Politics in Colombia.* Lexington, Mass.: Lexington Books, 1973.

Mercier Vega, Luis, ed. *Guerrillas in Latin America.* Tr. by Daniel Weissbert. New York: Praeger, 1969.

Montgomery, Tommie Sue. *Revolution in El Salvador: Origins and Evolution.* 2d ed. Boulder, Colo.: Westview Press, 1989.

Pomeroy, William J. *Guerrilla Warfare and Marxism.* New York: International Publishers, 1968.

Rojo, Ricardo. *My Friend Che.* Tr. by Julian Casart. New York: Dial Press, 1968.

Sauvage, Léo. *Che Guevera: The Failure of a Revolutionary.* Tr. by Raoul Frémont. Englewood Cliffs, N.J.: Prentice-Hall, 1973.

Sinclair, Andrew. *Che Guevara.* New York: Viking Press, 1970.

CHAPTER 6

Gilio, María Esther. *The Tupamaro Guerrillas.* Tr. by Anne Edmondson. New York: Ballantine Books, 1973.

Gillespie, Richard. *Soldiers of Perón: Argentina's Montoneros.* New York: Oxford University Press, 1983.

Halperin, Ernst. *Terrorism in Latin America.* Vol. 4 of *The Washington Papers.* Beverly Hills, Calif.: Sage Publications, 1976.

Hodges, Donald C. *Argentina, 1943–1987: The National Revolution and Resistance.* Rev. ed. Albuquerque: University of New Mexico Press, 1988.

Hodges, Donald C., ed. and tr. *Philosophy of the Urban Guerrilla: The Revolutionary Writings of Abraham Guillén*. New York: William Morrow, 1973.

Jackson, Sir Geoffrey. *Surviving the Long Night*. New York: Vanguard, 1974.

Kohl, James, and John Litt, eds. *Urban Guerrilla Warfare in Latin America*. Cambridge, Mass.: MIT Press, 1974.

Marighela, Carlos. *For the Liberation of Brazil*. Tr. by John Butt and Rosemary Sheed. Harmondsworth, Eng.: Penguin Books, 1971.

___. *The Terrorist Classic: Manual of the Urban Guerrilla*. Tr. by Gene Hanrahan. Chapel Hill, N.C.: Documentary Publications, 1985.

Moreira Alves, Marcio. *A Grain of Mustard Seed: The Awakening of the Brazilian Revolution*. Garden City, N.Y.: Doubleday, 1973.

Moss, Robert. *Urban Guerrillas in Latin America*. London: Institute for the Study of Conflict, 1970.

Núñez, Carlos. *The Tupamaros: Urban Guerrillas of Uruguay*. New York: Times Change Press, 1970.

Porzecanski, Arturo C. *Uruguay's Tupamaros: The Urban Guerrillas*. New York: Praeger, 1973.

Quartim, João. *Dictatorship and Armed Struggle in Brazil*. Tr. by David Fernbach. London: New Left Books, 1971.

Weinstein, Martin. *Uruguay: The Politics of Failure*. Westport, Conn.: Greenwood Press, 1975.

Wilson, Major Carlos. *The Tupamaros: The Unmentionables*. Boston: Branden Publishers, 1974.

CHAPTER 7

Alberts, Tom. *Agrarian Reform and Rural Poverty: A Case Study of Peru*. Boulder, Colo.: Westview Press, 1983.

Alexander, Robert J., ed. *Aprismo: The Ideas and Doctrines of Víctor Raúl Haya de la Torre*. Kent, Ohio: Kent State University Press, 1973.

Astiz, Carlos A. *Pressure Groups and Power Elites in Peruvian Politics*. Ithaca, N.Y.: Cornell University Press, 1969.

Baines, John M. *Revolution in Peru: Mariátegui and the Myth*. University, Ala.: University of Alabama Press, 1972.

Becker, David G. *The New Bourgeoisie and the Limits of Dependency: Mining, Class, and Power in "Revolutionary" Peru*. Princeton, N.J.: Princeton University Press, 1983.

Bourricaud, François. *Power and Society in Peru*. New York: Praeger, 1970.

Chaplin, David, ed. *Peruvian Nationalism: A Corporatist Revolution*. New Brunswick, N.J.: Transaction Books, 1976.

Chavarría, Jesús. *José Carlos Mariátegui and the Rise of Modern Peru, 1890–1930*. Albuquerque: University of New Mexico Press, 1979.

Einaudi, Luigi R., and Alfred C. Stepan. *Latin American Institutional Development: Changing Military Perspectives in Peru and Brazil*. Santa Monica, Calif.: The Rand Corporation, 1971.

Goodsell, Charles T. *American Corporations and Peruvian Politics*. Cambridge, Mass.: Harvard University Press, 1974.

Gorman, Stephen M. *Post-Revolutionary Peru: The Politics of Transformation.* Boulder, Colo.: Westview Press, 1982.

Jacquette, Jane S. *The Politics of Development in Peru.* Ithaca, N.Y.: Cornell University Dissertation Series, 1971.

Kantor, Harry. *The Ideology and Politics of the Peruvian Aprista Movement.* New York: Octagon Books, 1966.

Lowenthal, Abraham F., ed. *The Peruvian Experiment: Continuity and Change Under Military Rule.* Princeton, N.J.: Princeton University Press, 1975.

Mariátegui, José Carlos. *Seven Interpretive Essays on Peruvian Reality.* Tr. by Marjory Urquidi. Austin: University of Texas Press, 1971.

McClintock, Cynthia. *Peasant Cooperatives and Political Change in Peru.* Princeton, N.J.: Princeton University Press, 1982.

McClintock, Cynthia, and Abraham F. Lowenthal, eds. *The Peruvian Experiment Reconsidered.* Princeton, N.J.: Princeton University Press, 1983.

Middlebrook, Kevin J., and David Scott Palmer. *The Military and Political Development: Lessons from Peru.* Beverly Hills, Calif.: Sage Publications, 1975.

North, Liisa, and Tanya Korovkin. *The Peruvian Revolution and the Officers in Power, 1967–1976.* Montreal: McGill University Center for Developing-Area Studies, 1981.

Palmer, David Scott, ed. *Peru: The Authoritarian Tradition.* New York: Praeger, 1980.

Philip, George D. E. *The Rise and Fall of the Peruvian Military Radicals, 1968–1976.* London: The Athlone Press, 1978.

Pike, Frederick B. *The Modern History of Peru.* New York: Praeger, 1967.

Rose, Stanley F. *The Peruvian Revolution's Approach: Investment Policy and Climate, 1968–1980.* Buffalo, N.Y.: William S. Hein, 1981.

Saba, Raúl. *Political Development and Democracy in Peru: Continuity and Change in Crisis.* Boulder, Colo.: Westview Press, 1987.

Saulniers, Alfred H. *Public Enterprise in Peru: Public Sector Growth and Reform.* Boulder, Colo.: Westview Press, 1988.

Stepan, Alfred. *The State and Society: Peru in Comparative Perspective.* Princeton, N.J.: Princeton University Press, 1978.

Stephens, Evelyne Huber. *The Politics of Workers' Participation: The Peruvian Approach in Comparative Perspective.* New York: Academic Press, 1980.

Vanden, Harry E. *National Marxism in Latin America: José Carlos Mariátegui's Thought and Politics.* Boulder, Colo.: Lynne Rienner, 1986.

Webb, Richard Charles. *Government Policy and the Distribution of Income in Peru, 1963–1973.* Cambridge, Mass.: Harvard University Press, 1977.

Wils, Frits. *Industrialization, Industrialists, and the Nation-State in Peru: A Comparative/Sociological Analysis.* Berkeley: University of California, Institute of International Studies, 1979.

CHAPTER 8

Alexander, Robert J. *The Tragedy of Chile.* Westport, Conn.: Greenwood Press, 1978.

Allende, Salvador. *Chile's Road to Socialism.* Ed. by Joan E. Garcés, tr. by J. Darling. Harmondsworth, England: Penguin Books, 1973.

Birns, Laurence. *The End of Chilean Democracy: An IDOC Dossier on the Coup and Its Aftermath*. New York: Seabury Press, 1974.

Bitar, Sergio. *Chile: Experiment in Democracy*. Tr. by Sam Sherman. Philadelphia: Institute for the Study of Human Issues, 1986.

Castro, Fidel. *Fidel Castro on Chile*. New York: Pathfinder Press, 1982.

Cusack, David F. *Revolution and Reaction: The Internal Dynamics of Conflict and Confrontation in Chile*. Denver: University of Denver, Graduate School of International Studies, 1977.

Davis, Nathaniel. *The Last Two Years of Salvador Allende*. Ithaca, N.Y.: Cornell University Press, 1985.

Debray, Régis. *The Chilean Revolution: Conversations with Allende*. New York: Pantheon, 1971.

de Vylder, Stefan. *Allende's Chile: The Political Economy of the Rise and Fall of the Unidad Popular*. Cambridge: Cambridge University Press, 1976.

Evans, Les, ed. *Disaster in Chile: Allende's Strategy and Why It Failed*. New York: Pathfinder Press, 1974.

Falcoff, Mark. *Modern Chile, 1970-1989: A Critical History*. New Brunswick, N.J.: Transaction Publishers, 1989.

Faúndez, Julio. *Marxism and Democracy in Chile: From 1932 to the Fall of Allende*. New Haven, Conn.: Yale University Press, 1988.

Feinberg, Richard E. *The Triumph of Allende: Chile's Legal Revolution*. New York: New American Library, 1972.

Fleet, Michael. *The Rise and Fall of Chilean Christian Democracy*. Princeton, N.J.: Princeton University Press, 1985.

Gil, Federico, Ricardo Lagos E., and Henry A. Landsberger, eds. *Chile at the Turning Point: Lessons of the Socialist Years, 1970-1973*. Tr. by John S. Gitlitz. Philadelphia: Institute for the Study of Human Issues, 1979.

Horne, Alistair. *Small Earthquake in Chile*. Rev. ed. New York: Penguin Books, 1990.

Johnson, Dale L., ed. *The Chilean Road to Socialism*. Garden City, N.Y.: Anchor Press, 1973.

Kaufman, Edy. *Crisis in Allende's Chile: New Perspectives*. New York: Praeger, 1988.

Loveman, Brian. *Struggle in the Countryside: Politics and Rural Labor in Chile, 1919-1973*. Bloomington: Indiana University Press, 1976.

MacEoin, Gary. *No Peaceful Way: Chile's Struggle for Dignity*. New York: Sheed and Ward, 1974.

Medhurst, Kenneth, ed. *Allende's Chile*. New York: St. Martin's Press, 1972.

Morris, David J. *We Must Make Haste — Slowly: The Process of Revolution in Chile*. New York: Vintage Books, 1973.

North American Congress on Latin America (NACLA). *New Chile*. New York: NACLA, 1972.

O'Brien, Philip, ed. *Allende's Chile*. New York: Praeger, 1976.

Petras, James F., and Morris H. Morley. *The United States and Chile: Imperialism and the Overthrow of the Allende Government*. New York: Monthly Review Press, 1975.

Pollack, Benny. *Revolutionary Social Democracy: The Chilean Socialist Policy*. New York: St. Martin's Press, 1986.

Roxborough, Ian, Philip O'Brien, and Jackie Roddick. *Chile: The State and Revolution.* New York: Holmes and Meier, 1977.

Sigmund, Paul E. *The Overthrow of Allende and the Politics of Chile, 1964–1976.* Pittsburgh: University of Pittsburgh Press, 1977.

Sobel, Lester A. *Chile and Allende.* New York: Facts on File, 1974.

Stallings, Barbara. *Class Conflict and Economic Development in Chile, 1958–1973.* Stanford, Calif.: Stanford University Press, 1978.

Sweezy, Paul M., and Harry Magdoff, eds. *Revolution and Counter-Revolution in Chile.* New York: Monthly Review Press, 1974.

Valenzuela, Arturo. *The Breakdown of Democratic Regimes: Chile.* Baltimore, Md.: Johns Hopkins University Press, 1978.

Valenzuela, Arturo, and J. Samuel Valenzuela, eds. *Chile: Politics and Society.* New Brunswick, N.J.: Transaction Books, 1976.

Winn, Peter. *Weavers of Revolution: The Yarur Workers and Chile's Road to Socialism.* New York: Oxford University Press, 1986.

Wolpin, Miles D. *Cuban Foreign Policy and Chilean Politics.* Lexington, Mass.: D. C. Heath & Co., 1972.

CHAPTER 9

Arriagada, Genaro. *Pinochet: The Politics of Power.* Tr. by Nancy Morris. Winchester, Mass.: Allen and Unwin, 1988.

Black, Jan Knippers. *Sentinels of Empire: The United States and Latin American Militarism.* Westport, Conn.: Greenwood Press, 1986.

Bruneau, Thomas C., and Philippe Faucher. *Authoritarian Capitalism: Brazil's Contemporary Economic and Political Development.* Boulder, Colo.: Westview Press, 1981.

Collier, David, ed. *The New Authoritarianism in Latin America.* Princeton, N.J.: Princeton University Press, 1979.

Flynn, Peter. *Brazil: A Political Analysis.* Boulder, Colo.: Westview Press, 1978.

Handelman, Howard, and Thomas G. Sanders, eds. *Military Government and the Movement Toward Democracy: South America.* Bloomington: Indiana University Press, 1981.

Hojman, David E., ed. *Chile After 1973: Elements for the Analysis of Military Rule.* Liverpool: The University of Liverpool, 1985.

Ianni, Octavio. *Crisis in Brazil.* Tr. by Phyllis B. Eveleth. New York: Columbia University Press, 1970.

Kaufman, Edy. *Uruguay in Transition: From Civilian to Military Rule.* New Brunswick, N.J.: Transaction Books, 1979.

López, George A., and Michael Stohl, eds. *Liberalization and Redemocratization in Latin America.* Westport, Conn.: Greenwood Press, 1987.

Loveman, Brian, and Thomas M. Davies, Jr. *The Politics of Antipolitics: The Military in Latin America.* Lincoln: University of Nebraska Press, 1978.

Lowenthal, Abraham F., and J. Samuel Fitch, eds. *Armies and Politics in Latin America.* Rev. ed. New York: Holmes and Meier, 1986.

Malloy, James M., and Mitchell A. Seligson, eds. *Authoritarians and Democrats: Regime Transition in Latin America.* Pittsburgh: University of Pittsburgh Press, 1987.

McDonough, Peter. *Power and Ideology in Brazil.* Princeton, N.J.: Princeton University Press, 1981.

Moreira Alves, María Helena. *State and Opposition in Military Brazil.* Austin: University of Texas Press, 1985.

Nunca Más: The Report of the Argentine National Commission on the Disappeared. Intro. by Ronald Dworkin. New York: Farrar Straus Giroux, 1986.

O'Brien, Philip, and Paul Cammack, eds. *Generals in Retreat: The Crisis of Military Rule in Latin America.* Manchester: Manchester University Press, 1985.

O'Donnell, Guillermo. *Bureaucratic Authoritarianism: Argentina, 1966–1973.* Berkeley: University of California Press, 1988.

O'Donnell, Guillermo, Philippe C. Schmitter, and Laurence Whitehead, eds. *Transitions from Authoritarian Rule: Latin America.* Baltimore, Md.: Johns Hopkins University Press, 1986.

Peralta Ramos, Mónica, and C. H. Waisman, eds. *From Military Rule to Liberal Democracy in Argentina.* Boulder, Colo.: Westview Press, 1987.

Ramos, Joseph. *Neoconservative Economics in the Southern Cone of Latin America, 1973–1983.* Baltimore, Md.: The Johns Hopkins University Press, 1986.

Remmer, Karen. *Military Rule in Latin America.* Boston: Unwin Hyman, 1989.

Rouquié, Alain. *The Military and the State in Latin America.* Tr. by Paul Sigmund. Berkeley: University of California Press, 1987.

Schneider, Ronald. *The Political System of Brazil: Emergence of a "Modernizing" Authoritarian Regime, 1964–1970.* New York: Columbia University Press, 1971.

Selcher, Wayne A., ed. *Political Liberalization in Brazil: Dynamics, Dilemmas, and Future Prospects.* Boulder, Colo.: Westview Press, 1985.

Simpson, John, and Jana Bennett. *The Disappeared and the Mothers of the Plaza.* New York: St. Martin's Press, 1985.

Skidmore, Thomas E. *The Politics of Military Rule in Brazil, 1964–1985.* New York: Oxford University Press, 1988.

Stepan, Alfred, ed. *Democratizing Brazil: Problems of Transition and Consolidation.* New York: Oxford University Press, 1989.

___. *The Military in Politics: Changing Patterns in Brazil.* Princeton, N.J.: Princeton University Press, 1971.

Timerman, Jacobo. *Prisoner Without a Name, Cell without a Number.* Tr. by Tony Talbot. New York: Random House, 1980.

Valenzuela, J. Samuel, and Arturo Valenzuela, eds. *Military Rule in Chile: Dictatorship and Oppositions.* Baltimore, Md.: Johns Hopkins University Press, 1986.

Weinstein, Martin. *Uruguay: Democracy at the Crossroads.* Boulder, Colo.: Westview Press, 1988.

Wesson, Robert, ed. *New Military Politics in Latin America.* New York: (Hoover Institution/Stanford University) Praeger, 1982.

Wirth, John D., Edson de Oliveira Nunes, and Thomas E. Bogenschild, eds. *State and Society in Brazil: Continuity and Change.* Boulder, Colo.: Westview Press, 1987.

Wynia, Gary W. *Argentina: Illusions and Realities.* New York: Holmes and Meier, 1986.

CHAPTER 10

Arnove, Robert F. *Education and Revolution in Nicaragua.* New York: Praeger, 1986.

Black, George. *Triumph of the People: The Sandinista Revolution in Nicaragua.* London: Zed Books, 1981.

Booth, John A. *The End and the Beginning: The Nicaraguan Revolution.* 2d ed. Boulder, Colo.: Westview Press, 1985.

Burns, E. Bradford. *At War in Nicaragua: The Reagan Doctrine and the Politics of Nostalgia.* New York: Harper and Row, 1987.

Cabezas, Omar. *Fire from the Mountain: The Making of a Sandinista.* Tr. by Kathleen Weaver. New York: Crown, 1985.

Christian, Shirley. *Nicaragua: Revolution in the Family.* New York: Random House, 1985.

Close, David. *Nicaragua: Politics, Economics, and Society.* London: Pinter Publishers, 1988.

Colbourn, Forrest. *Post-Revolutionary Nicaragua: State, Class, and the Dilemmas of Agrarian Policy.* Berkeley: University of California Press, 1986.

Conroy, Michael E., ed. *Nicaragua: Profiles of the Revolutionary Public Sector.* Boulder, Colo.: Westview Press, 1987.

Coraggio, José Luis. *Nicaragua: Revolution and Democracy.* Winchester, Mass.: Allen and Unwin, 1986.

Cruz, Arturo J. *Memoirs of a Counterrevolutionary.* New York: Doubleday, 1989.

Gilbert, Dennis. *Sandinistas: The Party and the Revolution.* New York: Basil Blackwell, 1988.

Harris, Richard L., and Carlos M. Vilas, eds. *Nicaragua: A Revolution Under Siege.* London: Zed Books, 1985.

Hodges, Donald C. *Intellectual Foundations of the Nicaraguan Revolution.* Austin: University of Texas Press, 1986.

Kornbluh, Peter. *Nicaragua, the Price of Intervention: Reagan's Wars Against the Sandinistas.* Washington, D. C.: Institute for Policy Studies, 1987.

Levie, Alvin. *Nicaragua: The People Speak.* South Hadley, Mass.: Bergin and Garvey, 1985.

Macaulay, Neill. *The Sandino Affair.* Chicago: Quadrangle Books, 1971.

Millett, Richard. *Guardians of the Dynasty: A History of the U. S. Created Guardia Nacional de Nicaragua and the Somoza Family.* Maryknoll, N. Y.: Orbis Books, 1977.

Nolan, David. *FSLN, the Ideology of the Sandinistas and the Nicaraguan Revolution.* Miami: Institute of Latin American Studies, University of Miami, 1984.

O'Shaughnessy, Laura Nozzi, and Luis H. Serra. *The Church and Revolution in Nicaragua.* Athens: Ohio University, Center for International Studies, Latin American Studies Program, 1986.

Pastor, Robert A. *Condemned to Repetition: The United States and Nicaragua.* Princeton, N.J.: Princeton University Press, 1987.

Robinson, William I. *David and Goliath: The U.S. War against Nicaragua.* New York: Monthly Review Press, 1987.

Rosset, Peter, and John Vandermeer, eds. *Nicaragua: Unfinished Revolution. The New Nicaragua Reader.* New York: Grove Press, 1986.

Ruchwarger, Gary. *People in Power: Forging a Grassroots Democracy in Nicaragua.* South Hadley, Mass.: Bergin and Garvey, 1987.

Spalding, Rose J., ed. *The Political Economy of Revolutionary Nicaragua.* Winchester, Mass.: Allen and Unwin, 1986.

Valenta, Jiri, and Esperanza Durán, eds. *Conflict in Nicaragua: A Multidimensional Perspective.* Boston: Allen and Unwin, 1987.

Vilas, Carlos. *State, Class, and Ethnicity in Nicaragua: Capitalist Modernization and Revolutionary Change on the Atlantic Coast.* Tr. by Susan Norwood. Boulder, Colo.: Lynne Rienner, 1989.

Walker, Thomas W. *Nicaragua: The Land of Sandino.* 2d ed. Boulder, Colo.: Westview Press, 1986.

____, ed. *Nicaragua in Revolution.* New York: Praeger, 1982.

____, ed. *Nicaragua: The First Five Years.* New York: Praeger, 1985.

____, ed. *Reagan versus the Sandinistas: The Undeclared War on Nicaragua.* Boulder, Colo.: Westview Press, 1987.

Weber, Henri. *Nicaragua: The Sandinista Revolution.* Tr. by Patrick Camiller. London: Verso Editions, 1981.

Index

Act of Bogota, 71
Advisory Committee to the Presidency (COAP) (Peru), 122
Agency for International Development (AID), 68
agrarian reform: and Alliance for Progress, 48; in Argentina, 49, 50; in Bolivia, 49, 93; in Brazil, 49; in Chile, 48, 49, 50, 57–58, 136, 137, 139, 144, 167; in Colombia, 86; in Costa Rica, 49; in Cuba, 26–27, 45–53, 62; in Ecuador, 50; in El Salvador, 51, 95–96; in Guatemala, 48–49, 50, 82–83; in Haiti, 49; in Honduras, 49; in Mexico, 48, 49, 50; in Nicaragua, 48, 193–94; in Peru, 50, 97, 123–25, 128, 131–32; as political issue, 48–53; in Uruguay, 49, 50; in Venezuela, 84
Agricultural Production Cooperatives (Peru), 124
Agricultural Societies of Social Interest (Peru), 124
Alessandri, Arturo, 165–66
Alessandri, Jorge, 137, 140–41
Alfonsín, Raúl, 172
Allende, Salvador (Chile), 45, 52, 56, 65, 70, 106, 135, 138, 166, 175; confrontation and polarization under, 145–49; counterattack and overthrow of, 149–53; election of, 94, 140–43, 163–64, 202; reforms under, 143–45; suicide of, 164
Alliance for Progress, 70–74, 119, 138,

178; accomplishments of, 71–72; and agrarian reform, 48; end of, 74–76; and fidelismo, 73; formation of, 71; goals of, 71; reasons for failure of, 73–74; and U.S. intentions, 73
Altamirano, Carlos, 145, 148, 152, 153
Amador, Carlos Fonseca, 180
Amaru II, 105
American Popular Revolutionary Alliance (APRA) (Peru), 45, 56, 97, 119–20, 132, 135
Amodio Pérez, Héctor, 107
Andean Pact, 129
anti-Americanism, in Cuba, 2
anti-Batista movement, 2
antirevolutionary military regimes, 155–73
anti-Somoza movement, 190
Aprista Party (Peru), 120
Aramburu, Pedro, 113
Arbenz, Jacobo (Guatemala), 48, 66, 82, 121; overthrow of, 64; reforms of, 178
Arce, Bayardo, 190
Areco, Pacheco, 161
Arévalo, Juan José, 82
Argentina, 159; agrarian reform in, 49, 50; and Cuban relations, 65; fidelismo in, 46; influence of Trotskyism on, 112; Marxism influence on, 111; military government in, 122, 155, 156, 157, 172; rural guerrilla warfare in, 111; and U.S. relations, 73–74; urban

About the Author

Thomas C. Wright is Professor of History at the University of Nevada, Las Vegas. He became interested in the impact of the Cuban revolution during his junior year at the University of San Marcos in Lima, where Peruvian student politics and a national presidential election focused his attention on the pervasive influence of *fidelismo* in the early 1960s. Wright's publications include *Landowners and Reform in Chile*; *Food, Politics and Society in Latin America,* and articles and chapters in volumes such as the *Hispanic American Historical Review* and the *Journal of Latin American Studies.*